D1518598

The First Black
United States Marines

The First Black United States Marines

The Men of Montford Point, 1942–1946

Ronald K. Culp

McFarland & Company, Inc., Publishers
Jefferson, North Carolina, and London

Library of Congress Cataloguing-in-Publication Data

Culp, Ronald.
The first black United States marines: the men of Monford Point,
1942–1946 / Ronald K. Culp.
p.   cm.
Includes bibliographical references and index.

ISBN-13: 978-0-7864-3000-0
illustrated case binding : 50# alkaline paper ∞

1. United States. Marine Corps.
2. United States. Marine Corps — African Americans.
3. United States. Marine Corps — Recruiting, enlistment, etc.—
World War, 1939–1945.   4. World War, 1939–1945 — Participation,
African American.   5. Montford Point Camp (Camp Lejeune, N.C.)—
History — 20th century.   I. Title
D769.369.C85   2007   940.54'597308996073 — dc22   2007013623

British Library cataloguing data are available

On the cover: Negro volunteers in their dress uniforms, ca. May 1943,
Roger Smith, Still Picture Branch (NNSP), National Archives,
Washington, DC; United States Marine Corp Insignia

Manufactured in the United States of America

*McFarland & Company, Inc., Publishers
Box 611, Jefferson, North Carolina 28640
www.mcfarlandpub.com*

Acknowledgments

Many people have helped me in writing this book, in particular my wife and first critical reader, Judy. She went with me on research trips, proved her mettle as a determined miner of archives, pushed me to get the words down and then cleaned up my style and errors.

I wish to express my appreciation to the man who inspired my interest in Montford Point Marines, Colonel Herbert Lawrence Brewer, USMCR (ret.), one of the first to dare. I also wish to thank Sergeant Eugene Smith, USMCR, for his willingness to reach across the miles to help a man he had never met. Special thanks go to Finney Greggs, director of the Montford Point Marines Museum at Camp Lejeune, North Carolina, his wife Louise, and to the Montford Point Marines who trusted me enough to take the time to recall how they came to be in the Marine Corps and relive what they endured so long ago.

I am grateful to historian Ms. Annette Ammerman of the History Division, Historical Reference Branch, for her patience in leading me through the files on blacks in the Corps, and to my old friend Major Charles D. "Chuck" Melson, USMC (ret.), Chief Historian at the History Division, Marine Corps University, at Quantico, Virginia. My thanks to Dr. Jim Ginther, Manuscript Curator, Archives Branch at the Marine Corps University, and to Mr. Tony Magnotta, Visual Archives Specialist at the Marine Corps University, for his help in locating oral histories.

Finally, I want to acknowledge in advance that any mistakes in this book are mine alone.

Table of Contents

Section IV. 1944

Section V. 1945–1946

Preface

Early in 1942, blacks were semi-citizens of a segregated nation. To fight and win a two-ocean war America required that unprecedented numbers of men and women be enlisted and trained for military service, yet a significant source of new recruits was ignored by the U.S. Marine Corps—there were absolutely *no* black Marines. That service had enlisted "no Negro" in its 144-year existence, and the Major General Commandant, Thomas Holcomb, publicly declared his opposition to any change in policy regarding blacks. He saw the Corps as an exclusive "club" blacks had no right to join, and went on to say, "If it were a question of having a Marine Corps of 5,000 whites or 250,000 Negroes, I would rather have the whites."[1]

When ordered by President Franklin D. Roosevelt to accept blacks, the Corps complied. However, in doing so, Headquarters Marine Corps made plans that would impose the subject of race onto the Corps to the least possible degree—blacks would train in an isolated camp and then be assigned to some out-of-the-way station. Because the Corps had never had black Marines, officers admitted they did not "know how to handle them." White officers were "afraid of them."[2] Because there had never been any black Marines, there was no tradition of service in the Corps—no one joined because his father, brother, or uncle had been a Marine.

Several years ago friends introduced me to the Verger at St. Luke's Episcopal Church in San Antonio, Texas, a tall black man who, the friends told me, was one of the first black Marines in World War II. That man was Colonel Herbert L. Brewer, USMCR (ret.). During my Marine Corps career, I had heard about the first blacks in the Corps, known as Montford Point Marines for the segregated camp where they trained in the 1940s.

When I retired, I tried to learn more. I found little written about the Montford Point Marines. Curious, I set out to learn more. Who were the young men who dared become Marines? Why did they join a service reputed to be the most difficult in America? Where and how did they train? How were they treated in the U.S. and overseas? How did they treat their fellow black Marines? How did they fight? What weapons did they use? Did their service earn increased opportunity for them? Were there any blacks in the leadership roles as noncommissioned and com-

1

missioned officers? Were they then and are they now proud to have served? Those questions and more led me to libraries where I found black Marines mentioned almost as an aside in books about black servicemen. The Tuskegee Airmen and the Buffalo Soldiers of the old frontier cavalry days seemed to attract the most interest. When I asked about black Marines, the usual answer was a question: "Were there any?"

I set out to meet and interview some of the World War II Montford Point Marines at the camp where they trained (today's Camp Johnson, a part of Camp Lejeune, North Carolina), and to explore old files in the Marine Corps's History Division at Marine Corps Base, Quantico, Virginia. Several years and many miles later, this book is the result of my attempt to let the men answer my many questions by telling their stories.

By the end of World War II, 19,168 blacks proved themselves as Marines. They made up almost four percent of the Corps's enlisted strength. Even though no blacks received commissions as Marine officers while the fighting raged, four black enlisted men were recommended by their white officers and sent to Purdue University under the navy's V-12 program. All four received commissions as second lieutenants.

Most whites and many blacks do not know there were black Marines in World War II. Even fewer know that 12,738 of the black Marines served overseas where some fought and died in the intense amphibious assaults on the Marianas Islands of Saipan and Guam, on the islands of Peliliu, Iwo Jima and Okinawa. After VJ-Day, some of the black Marines took part in the occupation of China and Japan.

While black Marines trained at Montford Point Camp until 1949, I chose to end the book at the end of December 1946. My goal in writing this book is not to revise history nor to enumerate or catalog racial mistreatment directed at the first black Marines. The book is based on my personal interviews of some of the men who served and any comments they made about racial incidents are included as part of their stories. I have made every effort to tie their memories to facts reported at the time, official histories, oral histories, unpublished memoirs, and old files and orders now shelved in archives.

I ask the reader to keep in mind that recorded facts can and often do conflict with memory. As author Tony Hillerman reminds us, "an authentic memory may not represent an authentic truth."[3] What men recall today of a war fought sixty years ago, memories that may have been seared in their minds in the fiery stress of the moment, may or may not be absolutely accurate to the events because of the capricious nature of the human mind.

Today we have difficulty understanding the "Jim Crow" laws in place long ago, along with the conditions, emotions and feelings so prevalent and raw in that distant past because we interpret them through filters of our own post–Jim Crow experiences. This book brings readers back to the sharply divided racist society that was America in the 1940s.

Fewer and fewer of those with first-hand knowledge are alive to talk about the

World War II years, and many of the black men who served in the Marine Corps did not themselves write down the events as they happened. For those almost forgotten black men who answered the challenge and for the nation as well, June 1, 1942, marks a significant rite of passage. It was a door that had to be opened, one of many small gains that led to the 1950 integration of all of America's armed forces and serves as a stepping-stone to the 1964 Civil Rights Act that required employers to provide equal employment opportunities and made racial discrimination in public places, such as theaters, restaurants and hotels, illegal. Today black Americans enjoy freedoms and opportunities of choice earned in part by those Montford Point Marines.

A black Marine officer, for the first time in history, now commands Camp Johnson, the renamed Montford Point Camp where those black Marines trained beginning in 1942. He would not be in such a position if not for those young men who, sixty-four years ago, dared to become Marines.

Finally, I use the term "black" in place of "African American" not meaning to offend anyone but because it is widely accepted and most often used by the men I interviewed for this work. Where a man preferred the term African American, I used his words. Also, I sometimes used the term "logistics" with full understanding that the word only came into wide usage well after World War II; the terms "Quartermaster" and "Supply" were in common use during the World War II years.

Kerrville, Texas, 2007

SECTION I
Pre–World War II

1

"No Negro, Mulatto, or Indian to be enlisted...">[1]

Retreat? Hell, We Just Got Here

One can imagine a lanky young man spending an idle afternoon at the movies, eyes fixed on the flickering images dancing across the screen, imagining he is ... there....

Flashes rip the darkness. The mind-numbing roar of exploding artillery shells engulfs the German trenches on the low ridgeline a short three hundred yards away. The increasing morning light reveals blackened skeletons of a few shell-torn trees standing starkly in the cratered strip of no man's land that had once been a wheat field. The blasted ruins of a French farmhouse a sad reminder of a more settled time. Twisted strands of barbed wire wait to entrap the unwary.

The deep thunnk *of heavy mortars punctuates the sharp* crack *of quick-firing French 75s. A pall of smoke drifts across the trenches. Assault ladders are in place along the sandbagged parapet of the trench where nervous, scared men — boys, really — stand shoulder to shoulder.*

Suddenly, a panic-stricken French major splashes through ankle-deep water of the communications trench. He looks around and finds a grim-faced Marine captain in a muddy trench coat. "The Boche *are coming!" the Frenchman cries, "You must retreat!" With that, the man turns and splashes back the way he came.*

"Retreat? Hell," the Marine growls, glancing at his watch, "we just got here." The time is zero five fifty-nine. The captain grips a stubby pipe in his teeth. "Get ready, boys!"

"Fix bayonets!" the sergeants order.

Long bayonets rasp from their scabbards and shaking hands lock them into place on Springfield '03 rifles. The boys are ready but wide-eyed under jaunty little "tin hat" helmets with an eagle, globe and anchor device centered on the front.

In the pale morning light the hands on the captain's watch draw a vertical line on the face of the timepiece — zero six hundred. The artillery ceases, and in the sudden silence the captain's voice booms, "Over the top! Let's go Marines!"

All along the line, men scramble out of the trenches. Holding their rifles at high port, they run toward the German lines, screaming and yelling wildly. Above them roars a squadron of DeHavilland bi-planes, pilots and gunners lashing the German trenches with their machine guns. As the Marines charge across the open ground they see figures moving on the German lines. The Huns are leaving their bomb proofs and manning their guns!

"Run faster!"

"Hurry up, boys!"

Muzzle flashes light the German line. A hail of machine gun bullets slashes the running Marines. Men fall, throwing up their arms, collapsing into water-filled shell craters. It is a slaughter! Marines dive to the ground, taking cover from the murderous fire.

The captain and the sergeant huddle in a crater.

"Look!" the sergeant points.

"It's Smitty!" the captain says, "What's that fool doing?"

Far in advance, young Private Smith, the seventeen-year-old company mascot, crawls along an abandoned trench close to the German command post. The captain and the sergeant watch as Smitty tugs a grenade from the pouch at his belt, pulls the pin with his teeth and tosses the bomb with deadly accuracy.

"Wham!" The grenade explodes and German officers fall in a smoky tangle of field telephones and binoculars. Smitty heaves a second grenade to blow up a heavy Maxim gun pinning down the Marines. German soldiers, in their distinctive coal bucket shaped helmets, sprawl lifelessly beside their ruined gun.

The captain and the sergeant exchange happy grins. "Good old Smitty!"

A German soldier, sinister sneer on his face, raises the long barrel of his Mauser rifle, aims at the American "Devil Dog" and fires. Smitty drops from sight.

"They got Smitty!" the sergeant cries.

"We'll make 'em pay for that!" The captain stands, a big Colt .45 automatic pistol in his hand. Waving the gun, he calls, "Follow me, Marines!" and the renewed attack rolls over the enemy trench. Demoralized, the Germans throw down their rifles and raise their hands in surrender.

A few days later the Marines stand at attention in the streets of a small French village. The captain and the sergeant, resplendent in their dress blue uniforms, pin a medal on Smitty's chest, careful of the sling that holds Smitty's wounded left arm.

"Congratulations, Marine," the captain smiles sternly. "You saved the company."

The Reality

Music rises in the background — the stirring sounds of The Marines' Hymn, "The End," appears on the screen.

Lights come up, and all around him people stand, stretch, and step into the aisles to leave the theatre. Sixteen-year-old Herbert Lawrence Brewer makes his way down from the balcony of the Majestic Theatre on East Houston Street in San Antonio, Texas. The year is 1941 and the completely air-conditioned Majestic, built in 1929, is the largest, most modern theatre in Texas. In the bright sunlight outside, Herb soon passes the Alamo and then crosses the railroad tracks at the Southern Pacific Railroad Station, a stopping point for the famous Sunset Limited coast-to-coast train, walking the mile to his home on North Mesquite Street just east of downtown. Herb liked to go to the movies. He especially liked movies about U.S. Marines.

German soldiers respectfully called Marines "devil dogs" after the battle of Belleau Wood in World War I. Heavily armed, tough-talking Marines guarded the U.S. Mail during the 1920s. Marines were the first to fight. Trouble overseas? Send in the Marines.

Black and white movies were okay, but in the new Technicolor process, the Marines' dress blue uniforms were handsome, manly. Herb wanted to wear that uniform.[2] He wanted to be a Marine. The movies were pure Hollywood fiction but Herb's dream was real. Herb Brewer, a Marine? Not likely. Herb was black, and there had never been a black U.S. Marine. The reason why is almost as old as the nation itself.

2

The U.S. Marine Corps—
A Very Brief History

Thousands of years ago the ancient Phoenicians, Greeks, and Romans placed men aboard ships for the specific purpose of fighting rather than as crews or rowers.[1] Closer to the modern era, the British Royal Navy raised a regiment of ground troops in the last half of the seventeenth century specifically for duty with the fleet and for service ashore. When Britain's American colonies revolted, they established their own army and navy, both modeled after those of the mother country.

The First Marines

Continental Marines, at least three of whom were black men, kept order and were responsible for internal security aboard Continental Navy ships. In battle, Marines became the ship's small arms fighters: They manned the fighting tops— small rectangular platforms high on the masts of wooden sailing ships from which they tossed grenades and fired muskets at the officers and crews of enemy ships during engagements—and on deck joined boarding parties for close quarters fighting or in repelling enemy boarders. Some Continental Marines seized positions on hostile shores while others guarded naval stations. However, within a year after the Treaty of Paris ended the American Revolution in 1783, most of the Continental Army disbanded, and the Continental Marines completely disbanded, as did the Continental Navy in 1785.

Marines Re-born

The peace was short-lived. Soon corsairs of the Barbary Coast in the Mediterranean Sea began to attack and seize American merchant ships, no longer sailing under the protection of the British Royal Navy. In order to protect American maritime commerce, Congress passed in March 1794 a naval act that called for the construction of a half-dozen frigates, with Marines to be part of the ships' complements.

By 1797, when the French began preying on U.S. merchant ships at sea, taking hundreds of ships and cargoes, the U.S. Navy consisted only of the frigates *Constitution, Constellation* and *United States.* Although the naval act required that each frigate have a detachment of Marines, a Marine Corps to provide the men did not exist.[2] Officers commissioned to command Marines on each frigate were required to find and enlist the men to fill their detachments. In July 1798, Congress established the U.S. Marine Corps as a separate service within the naval establishment. The Marine Corps, 881 men commanded by a major, formed to maintain discipline aboard Navy ships, "give a military tone to men-of-war," and protect the ships' captains from mutinous crews.[3]

Origins of the All-White Marine Corps

As a condition to enlisting Marines to serve on the *Constellation,* Secretary of the Navy Benjamin Stoddert specified that "No Negro, Mulatto or Indian" could join. Major William Ward Burrows, the second commandant of the Marines (Major Samuel Nicholas was commandant of the Continental Marines and so is regarded as the first commandant of Marines), took Stoddert's policy prohibiting the enlistment of Negroes and applied it to all enlistments. Thus, the infant U.S. Navy sallied forth to engage in a two-year undeclared quasi-war with France with all-white U.S. Marine Corps detachments aboard the ships. Unchallenged, Stoddert's policy regarding Negroes continued in effect and would remain so for the next one hundred and forty-four years.

As part of their uniform, Marines of this era received a black leather stock to be worn around the neck, three and one half inches wide with buckles in the back. Legend has it that the stock protected the wearer's neck from an enemy's saber blows; whether it did or not, it earned the nickname "Leatherneck" for Marines and the name still endures.

Marines Re-invent Themselves for a New Role

Marines served in the limited capacities above until the late 19th century, when the steam-powered Navy began to recognize the need for advanced bases ashore for coaling and the need for ground forces to seize and defend them. However, when the Spanish-American War started in 1898, the navy still had not solved the advanced base problem. Marine Corps Lt. Col. R. W. Huntington led a hastily assembled expeditionary battalion, complete with its own artillery, to seize Guantanamo Bay, Cuba, for an advanced base. Marine success ashore enabled the U.S.

Fleet to operate indefinitely in Caribbean waters.[4] When the 114-day war was over, the United States had gained an island empire made up of the station at Guantanamo Bay, Cuba, and the island of Puerto Rico in the Caribbean, the Philippine Islands, the Hawaiian Islands, Guam, and Wake Island in the Pacific. Marines established a small garrison on Guam as early as 1899. Few could foresee that the actions at Guantanamo Bay were an evolutionary step culminating in the Navy-Marine Corps amphibious assault doctrines that allowed America to defeat the Japanese in the Pacific some forty years later.

Marines Re-invent Themselves (Again)— As Imperial Light Infantry

The 20th century brought for the United States a new role as a colonial power and for the Marines likewise a new role: imperial light infantry. While the U.S. Army needed a formal declaration of war to go overseas, that limitation did not apply to the Marine Corps. Beginning a long, troubled period of American involvement in overseas intervention, Marine detachments came to Guam and Wake Islands and the Philippines, and Marines went to help put down the Boxer Rebellion in China in 1900. In 1904 (an election year) President Theodore Roosevelt exercised his "big stick" form of diplomacy and sent navy ships and Marines to intervene in Morocco (the Pedicaris Affair).

To say the Marines of the time were busy is gross understatement: In addition to stations in the United States and in Marine detachments aboard battleships, other Marines occupied Santo Domingo from 1905 to 1907, served in Cuba from 1906 to 1909 and landed in Nicaragua in 1911. Under President Woodrow Wilson, Marines landed in Mexico in 1914, Cuba again in 1914, and Haiti in 1915 and then went back to Santo Domingo in 1916. Marines fought rebels from 1915 to 1934, almost twenty years, in Haiti. The withdrawal of Marines from Haiti and Nicaragua in 1934 marked the end of the so-called "Banana Wars." In truth, U.S. Marines had become the most visible symbol of American intervention around the world.

"White Man's Burden"

The Marine Corps capitalized on its success at Guantanamo Bay by forming a permanent Advanced Base Force of two regiments, about 1800 men, in 1913 but made few advances in doctrine because of the nation's heavy and continuous demand for Marines to intervene in the affairs of other nations.

The United States' responsibilities for its empire came to be called "the white man's burden," after British poet Rudyard Kipling's 1899 poem of the same name penned in response to America's takeover of the Philippines.[5] Marines, drawn into service from a segregated society, were heavily involved with bashing non-whites overseas until the middle of the 1930s. Could that have further hardened their attitudes toward blacks in America and reinforced their resolve against enlisting them as Marines?

In 1914, while the United States was preoccupied with trouble at Vera Cruz, Mexico, war erupted in Europe. Japan declared war on Germany and then quickly sent her navy to seize Germany's holdings in Micronesia, the Mariana, Caroline, Marshall, and Palau Island groups (except for the island of Guam in the Marianas, which was under U.S. control). It was a bold move with far-reaching consequences for the United States. After the war in Europe, Japan refused to relinquish control of the former German island possessions. Fortified and protected by the Japanese fleet, the islands would become a strategic threat to the free movement of the U.S. Pacific Fleet.[6]

Marines in the Protracted Land Warfare Role

Marine strength skyrocketed to almost 73,000 when Leathernecks became a part of the American Expeditionary Force fighting in the world war against the German army in France. Few recall the exploits of the "imperial" Marines, but the men who fought at Belleau Wood, Soissons, Blanc Mont and in the Argonne in France earned their place in history. James Montgomery Flagg, the artist who created the famous recruiting poster of a finger-pointing Uncle Sam captioned "I want *YOU*" for the U.S. Army, produced two similarly eye-catching posters. "Tell that to the Marines" featured a citizen, angered by newspaper headlines proclaiming Hun atrocities, doffing his jacket and ready to fight. "Want Action? Join U.S. Marines" was a question asked and answered by a grinning all–American Marine extending one welcoming hand while in the other hand he holds a rifle. Both posters fired America's patriotism and imagination on the home front, and they certainly did nothing to detract from the Marines' growing aura of toughness. In the reality of the trenches of France, the Marines' fierceness in battle earned them the respectful nickname "Devildogs" from the Germans.

Marines Change Focus

The 1915 British attempt to force passage through the Dardanelles Straits by an amphibious assault at Gallipoli and force Turkey out of World War I was a fiasco that convinced most military theorists and politicians of the day that attacking defended beaches is foolhardy in the extreme. Nevertheless, the operation at Gallipoli attracted the interest of a few Marines. In 1920, the navy published a manual for ships' landing forces, but only seven of 760 pages were devoted to discussion of an actual amphibious landing. Prevailing thought at the time was that Marines were only good for forward base defenses.

In the 1920s Louisiana-born Major General Commandant John A. Lejeune led a small, post-war Marine Corps. Under his guidance, the Corps, suffering from stingy budgeting and greatly reduced manpower, gradually shifted its interest to amphibious doctrine and technique.

Lieutenant Colonel Earl Hancock "Pete" Ellis was a brilliant planner and had been a principal staff officer to General Lejeune in World War I. For fifteen years, Ellis had studied the development of Japanese power in the Orient. He had come to certain conclusions, and he had been forceful in voicing them. In 1920, Ellis predicted the course of the war in the Pacific and wrote that Japan would strike the first blow with a great deal of success. He also described what the success would be with prophetic accuracy. Ellis wrote *Advanced Base Operations in Micronesia* in 1921 and forecast the amphibious struggle for the Pacific more than 20 years prior to World War II.

Believing war with Japan was inevitable, Ellis took a leave of absence from Headquarters Marine Corps and during the next few years, he visited Australia, the Philippine Islands, and Japan. He studied methods and formulated war plans for the Marine Corps in the event that the Japanese should strike. In the Palau Islands on May 12, 1923, he died at age 43 under mysterious circumstances when his last and greatest military-intelligence task was almost complete. Twenty-one years later, his prophecies became reality.

Redesigned, the Advanced Base Force, located at Quantico, Virginia, became known as the Expeditionary Force in 1921. Marines struggled to refine amphibious war concepts in training maneuvers at the island of Culebra off Puerto Rico until 1925 when Marine manpower shortages forced a halt. Demands of the "White Man's Burden" sent many Marines to put down a rebellion in Nicaragua and even more to protect American interests in China while details of heavily armed Marines guarded the U.S. Mail against an increasingly bold criminal element in the United States. By 1928 the Commandant reported that he had so few Marines left he could barely keep open the bases at Quantico, Virginia, and San Diego, California.

The Corps's interest in amphibious warfare paid off when, in 1927, the Joint Board of the Army and Navy (predecessors of the present day Joint Chiefs of Staff) issued a directive called *Joint Action of the Army and Navy*. That directive officially assigned the Marine Corps the mission to provide and maintain forces "for land operations in support of the fleet for the initial seizure and defense of land bases and for such limited auxiliary land operations as are essential to the prosecution of the naval campaign."[7] However, this time only five pages were devoted to discussion of an amphibious landing.

Against a backdrop of insufficient funds, rigidly conventional naval thinking, and domestic/international distractions, Government Order No. 241 of December 7, 1933, created the Fleet Marine Force (FMF), "a force of Marines ... maintained by the MGen Commandant of the Marine Corps in a state of readiness for operations with the Fleet." Thus, the Marine Corps gambled its entire existence on working with the navy to develop a capability that few believed the country needed. It was a risk because there was little historical support for such a capability. The navy, engaged in internal battles between battleship and aircraft carrier proponents, had little interest in developing amphibious capabilities.

Next, Marines wrote the "book" for amphibious operations — the *Tentative Manual for Landing Operations*, a theoretical guide for conducting a landing against opposition — an amphibious assault.[8] The advanced base/expeditionary nature of the Corps's mission continued to evolve, requiring Marines to defend existing bases while at the same time seizing and holding new bases as needed by the navy.

Defense Battalion Program

Imperial Japan pushed into China in 1931, seized large areas of land and even sank a U.S. Navy river gunboat in 1937. The United States became uneasy with the security of the island outposts protecting naval and air bases in Hawaii, the most logical staging area for any war in the Pacific. The Marine Corps considered placing battalion-size security detachments on three of the Hawaiian outposts — Wake, Midway, and Johnston Islands, for defense. Before any such moves occurred, the Corps needed to increase its strength beyond the 19,432 officers and men it had near the end of the 1930s.

The nation held firmly to a policy of isolationism that made Congress hesitant to appropriate funds for any offensive purpose. For example, the navy and the army air corps presented Congressional budget staffs with plans for new battleships and long-range heavy bombers but classified them as "defensive" weapons in hopes of securing funding. Officers at Headquarters Marine Corps studied plans for placing Marine units as garrisons on Pacific islands and conceived the idea for a new type of unit, and in keeping with the times called it a defense battalion.

The Major General Commandant of the Marine Corps, Thomas Holcomb, described his strategy for getting congressional approval for the defense battalions this way: "If you said, 'I want an offensive outfit,' the politicians would say, 'No sir, you want to fight a war.' But if you said, 'I want a defensive outfit and I want to defend this country,' you could get men."[9] Successfully convincing Congress to fund men and equipment to prepare for war demanded that the commandant have a good sense for the direction political winds blew in Washington as well as a creative approach to problem solving.

The new defense battalions consisted of about nine hundred men organized and armed according to the mission requirements of the area where each unit was to go. Most would include seacoast artillery and a variety of antiaircraft artillery and guns. Unlike units composed only of infantry or artillery, some were to be composites of both, that is, to have pack howitzers, a rifle company, and a light tank platoon as well as other components added to make it a self-sustaining unit. These units would include the word "composite" in their name.

U.S. Remains Neutral, Marines Prepare for War

When war in Europe broke out on September 1, 1939, two days later President Roosevelt, in a radio broadcast, urged Americans to remain neutral in the European conflict.[10] Declaring a national position of neutrality, Roosevelt next announced a limited national emergency on September 8. During this time, the Marine Corps succeeded in getting Congress to fund more men and pushed ahead with its defense battalion program. Beginning with an odd numbering sequence, the 3d Defense Battalion was activated in October 1939, and the 1st in November 1939.

American military planners, suddenly faced with the possibility of multinational war with Germany, Japan, and Italy, were unprepared. They rushed to combine existing war plans that called for fighting one nation at a time; the result was a series called the "Rainbow" plans (potential enemy nations were assigned a color, and Japan's color was "Orange"). Published in late 1940, the fifth plan in the series, called simply Rainbow-5, updated an earlier Orange plan.[11]

Rainbow-5 levied significant responsibilities on the Marine Corps in case of war with Japan. To meet those responsibilities, U.S. Navy and Marine officers drafted plans capitalizing on the defensive aspect of the Marine Corps's mission. These called for Marines to garrison an arc of island outposts stretching across the Pacific from Wake, Midway, Johnson, and Palmyra Islands to American Samoa. (Wake, Midway, Johnston, and Palmyra are usually referred to as islands. However, they are actually atolls, small coral islands connected by an apron of coral reefs surrounding a lagoon, usually formed on the rims of seamounts or undersea volcanoes. Most are less than fifteen feet above sea level.) Those outposts were critical for protecting both Hawaii, the staging area for any war America would fight in the Pacific, and the sea-lanes to Australia and New Zealand. In case of war with Japan, Marines had to defend them against attacks from the sea and from the air. Continuing with the defense battalion program, the 4th Defense Battalion was activated in February 1940 and the 2d in March. Twenty defense battalions took to the field until they became obsolete.

Proving a Theory

Amphibious warfare theory for attacking and seizing advanced bases had been tested and proven through a series of Fleet Landing Exercises (FLEXs) in the last half of the decade of the 1930s. To simplify the broad terms used in early amphibious warfare doctrine, any landing *opposed* by the enemy is an amphibious assault, while an *unopposed* landing is an amphibious operation. For both types of landings, it was crucial to work out the details of command relationships, naval gunfire support, air support, and the ship-to-shore movement. In short, the Marine Corps had to learn how to get people and things from ships to the shore and then to sustain the operation ashore.

Aside from a limited number of trucks and a few airplanes, the Marines had no way to move themselves anywhere. Marines depended on Navy transport ships to bring them to the objective. Before the Marines went ashore, the theory called for planes from aircraft carriers to attack the objective and battleships, cruisers, and destroyers to use their big guns to bombard known enemy strongholds. A color and a number designated the objective beaches, each assigned to a particular unit for capture. For example, 2/5 (2d Battalion 5th Marine Regiment) to seize GREEN BEACH ONE and 3/5 to seize GREEN BEACH TWO.

The theory evolved with practice. Men of the assault force climbed down cargo nets draped over the sides of the transports anchored offshore and climbed into smaller, shallow draft landing boats. When loaded, the small boats circled in a landing craft rendezvous area until all the boats carrying the assault Marines were loaded and ready. The boats turned toward the beaches and formed line abreast into a "wave." As the assault waves neared the beaches, the naval gunfire shifted to targets inland. When the boats hit the beaches, the Marines charged ashore. Follow-on waves brought additional riflemen, tanks, artillery pieces, and supplies, and the returning boats evacuated wounded men.

Confusion on the beaches as men and equipment piled ashore became a serious problem in the early FLEXs. To deal with that problem, amphibious doctrine — the book — called for the navy to establish a Beach Party. The sailors were to control the landing boats, mark hazards to navigation, evacuate casualties and unload landing force supplies from the boats onto the beach. The Marine landing force would establish a Shore Party responsible for moving the supplies and equipment off the beach to assigned storage areas, handling prisoners of war and stragglers. The Marines would assist the Navy Beach Party in unloading supplies on the beaches, almost all of which was done by hand. The Shore Party was not a permanent unit, but consisted of detachments from medical, supply, working details, engineers, and military police and communications units organized when needed.

Where were the men for the "working details"—the ones who would do the muscle work of moving things—to come from? In the absence of any guidance, an unofficial "make do" policy of using the infantry units held in reserve to provide labor details soon developed. To move supplies, Marine commanders were willing to give up the use of a portion of their infantry reserves.

Realistic testing of Shore Party doctrine, which would have exposed the flaws in methods used for moving supplies, received little emphasis when compared with the importance of working out naval gunfire support procedures and command relationships. In fact, during one brigade size landing exercise, the Shore Party consisted of "one elderly major and two small piles of ammunition boxes." During an exercise at New River, North Carolina, in August 1941, the lack of Shore Party personnel resulted in significant delays in getting troops and supplies ashore at the right time and place. The landing force commander, Major General (Maj. Gen.) Holland M. "Howlin' Mad" Smith, reported to Rear Admiral (R. Adm.) Ernest J. King, the Commander in Chief, Atlantic Fleet, that "special service troops (labor) must be provided" for moving supplies during amphibious operations.[12] The problem was noted, but the practice of using riflemen to sort and move supplies continued.

Marine Corps Headquarters took a first step in solving the labor force problem when it added a Pioneer (Shore Party) Battalion of 34 officers and 669 enlisted men to the Marine division organization table. However, the change, made in January 1942, came too late for implementation and testing during peacetime exercises. As a result, one of the most serious problems that would plague amphibious operations in the early years of the war in the Pacific was congestion on the beaches as thousands of men and tons of supplies piled ashore while intense fighting raged in narrow beachheads. Real changes in procedures and working detail assignments based on lessons learned in earlier amphibious operations would not take place until the Marshall Islands operations early in 1944. While there had never been such a thing as a black U.S. Marine, their time was coming, and many of them would play a significant role in the solving of that problem.

A Note About the Pre–World War II Corps

During the forty years leading up to World War II, a strong Southern culture influenced the Marine Corps's officer ranks. Alexander Vandegrift was a Virginian, Clifton Cates was a Tennessean, John Thomason a Texan, Holland Smith was from Alabama, Lewis Puller was a Virginian and Roy Geiger came from Florida, to name but a few. A hint of his Southern roots may be found in Major General John A. Lejeune's thoughts regarding the relations between Marine officers and their men. These should, he wrote, "partake of the nature of the relation between father and son," or teacher and scholar.[13] His words have been handed down to generation after generation of Marines in the Marine Corps Manual. These are a few of the men whose ideas and attitudes shaped the Marine Corps in the years leading up to the 1942 decision to enlist the first black men ever to wear the eagle, globe and anchor emblem of a U.S. Marine.

3

A Closer Look

What Is *a Marine?*

"At the very heart of the Corps and its relationship to each Marine is our service culture," said a recent Marine Corps commandant. "The Marine Corps is *sui generis*— [something entirely of its own sort] ... we have a nature that is distinct from all others."[1] A Marine is an anomaly — a soldier who goes to sea and a sailor who fights on land. The name applies to any man or woman who serves in the U.S. Marine Corps. To be a Marine is to be a member of "a mysterious fraternity born of the smoke and the danger of death."[2] Since the Corps formed, its watchword has been *readiness*, that is, to be the first to fight. Aggressive in battle, most Marines volunteer — they *want* to become Marines — but in wars of the twentieth century the draft meant that many men became Marines whether they wanted to or not.

Standards are high in the Corps, whether in physical fitness, personal appearance, marksmanship, or other combat skills. Training is demanding, at times it has been brutal, and a man or woman's best effort is but an acceptable *minimum*. Marines hold themselves to the highest standards of military virtue as a point of great pride. Discipline is uncompromising. The motto of the Marines, *Semper Fidelis*, is Latin for "Always faithful," faithful to oneself, to fellow Marines, to the unit, the Corps, and to the United States.

Why Join?

Some men and women seek the title "U.S. Marine" because they have something to prove. To them the Corps is a way of showing that they are as tough as the toughest; others want to share the pride in being a part of the best. Some just like the way the dress blue uniform looks. Regardless of why someone asks to join, the Corps is, always has been, very selective in deciding who can become a Marine.

An Insurmountable Obstacle

Unlike the army and the navy, from 1798 onward the Corps did not simply segregate blacks from whites — it was for whites only.[3] In 1939, there were only 19,432 Marine officers and enlisted men on active duty.[4] Every one of them was white. According to Marine tradition this was a given. Never mind what *he* wanted. Herbert Brewer, patriotic American citizen, did not have the right to join the Marines.

In Washington DC, Delaware-born Major General Commandant of the Marine Corps Thomas Holcomb spoke his mind. In keeping with Marine Corps tradition, Holcomb, commandant since 1936, took an aggressively proactive stance against enlisting blacks into the Corps. In an August 1940 letter to a civil rights group, the Northern Philadelphia Voters League, he argued that enlisting blacks was impractical because the Corps, with fewer than 28,000 officers and men, was too small to form racially separate units.[5]

The Marine Corps was expanding rapidly in men and equipment in a race to prepare for war. By December 1941, the Organized Marine Reserve stood mobilized and the active strength of the Corps had grown to almost 66,000 Marines, 30,000 of which served in the Fleet Marine Force.[6] Although the Corps needed even more men, Major General (Maj. Gen.) Holcomb called President Franklin D. Roosevelt's intention to enlist blacks in the Marine Corps "absolutely tragic." Furthermore, he added, "the Negro race has every opportunity now to satisfy its aspirations for combat in the Army — a very much larger organization than the Navy or Marine Corps — and their desire to enter the naval service is largely, I think, to break into a club that doesn't want them."[7] Holcomb referred to the fact that the navy was almost as restrictive as the Corps (with a total force of 170,000 in 1940, only 4007 sailors were black, all serving in the messmen's branch).[8]

Maj. Gen. Holcomb went on to say, "there would be a definite loss of efficiency in the Marine Corps if we have to take Negroes."[9] If anyone failed to understand how he felt, Holcomb told the General Board of the Navy, "If it were a question of having a Marine Corps of 5,000 whites or 250,000 Negroes, I would rather have the whites."[10]

Understanding the professional officer behind the comments demands a closer look. A Marine officer since 1900, Holcomb had served in a vast range of staff and command billets, in peacetime and in war. Early in his career, he was a part of the "big stick" of America's use of Marines as imperial light infantry during interventions in the Pacific and Asia. He served in the Philippine Islands from April 1904 to August 1905, and in October and November 1906.

He was on duty with the Legation Guard in Peking, China, from September 1905 to September 1906. From December 1908 to July 1910, he again served with the Legation Guard at Peking. Until May 1911, he remained in Peking as attaché on the staff of the American minister for study of the Chinese language. In December 1911 he returned to the Legation at Peking to continue his study of the Chinese language and remained there until May 1914.

During World War I he commanded the 2d Battalion 6th Marines from August 1918 and served as second in command of the 6th Marines. He took part in the Aisne Defensive (Chateau Thierry), the Aisne-Marne Offensive (Soissons), the Marbache Sector, the St. Mihiel Offensive, the Meuse-Argonne (Champagne) Offensive, the Meuse-Argonne (Argonne Forest) Offensive, and the March to the Rhine in Germany following the Armistice. In recognition of his distinguished services in France, he was awarded the Navy Cross, America's second highest award for bravery, the Silver Star with three Oak Leaf Clusters, a Meritorious Service Citation by the Commander-in-Chief, AEF, the Purple Heart for wounds suffered in combat, and was three times cited in General Orders of the Second Division, AEF. The French Government conferred on him the Cross of the Legion of Honor and three times awarded him the Croix de Guerre with Palm.

He was a Distinguished Graduate of the Command and General Staff School of the Army at Fort Leavenworth, Kansas. He went to the Naval War College as a student, Senior Course and then transferred to the Army War College in 1931, graduating a year later. On December 1, 1936, he became the Major General Commandant of the Marine Corps.[11]

Here was a man who should not be seen as a simple "racist" because of what he said. His beliefs echoed those of many, being perfectly acceptable and legal in the segregated American society of the day. Holcomb was a Marine officer, first and foremost, and he acted on what he believed was best for the Corps. During his tenure as commandant he saw the Corps increase from 16,000 to over 300,000 men. Testifying in hearings concerning the "Enlistment of Men of the Colored Race" before the General Board of the Navy in January 1942, Maj. Gen. Holcomb said, "it will take a great deal of character and technique to make the thing a success, and if it is forced upon us we must make it a success."[12] This comment, often overlooked, is not out of character. There is a tendency today to focus only on Holcomb's earlier comments against enlisting blacks in the Corps, and that is a failure to understand a military professional of his time. To explain: When the commander in chief, President Roosevelt, was considering expanding black opportunity and participation in the naval services — *before* he made his decision — he allowed the heads of each service the time to discuss, deliberate and debate the issue. Among military professionals, this is the "war council" period when a good commander hears the thoughts of his subordinates, both pros and cons, and so Holcomb stated his views publicly and clearly. Good subordinates owe it to their commanders to be honest in providing their opinions. All said, the commander then makes his decision. Ideally, once that happens, a Marine subordinate responds with "Aye aye, sir," and makes the commander's decision his own. He carries it out smartly, with all energy as if it were *his* decision from the start. This is what Holcomb did when he said about enlisting blacks, "we must make it a success." Such was not always the case, for President Roosevelt and Secretary Knox continued to have to "veto Navy reluctance" to have black sailors.[13]

Finally, there is no doubt that Holcomb had President Roosevelt's complete confidence. In August 1935, at Holcomb's retirement age, Roosevelt announced he was continuing Holcomb for a second term as commandant in recognition of his outstanding service in that capacity.

4

A Chance to Join "The Club"

A Color Line

The Corps of 1940 mirrored attitudes and conditions prevalent all across the country in the first half of the twentieth century. In most parts of America whites refused to work for a black boss — it simply was not done. Blacks were allowed to sit in the back of a bus or the balcony of a movie theatre. They drank at public water fountains marked *Colored* and used separate *Colored* restrooms if there were any. Black kids did not play in parks designated *White Only*. As bad as the few foregoing examples are, even worse restrictions were imposed under the Jim Crow laws most states passed to separate whites from blacks. America was a nation divided by race, or as W.E.B. Du Bois, the founder of the NAACP called it, a color line.

Forced Change

With the Japanese surprise attack on American military installations at Pearl Harbor, Territory of Hawaii, on December 7 and in the Philippines on December 8, all talk of neutrality ceased. President Roosevelt asked Congress to declare war on Japan on December 8. Three days later on December 11, 1941, Germany and Italy declared war on the United States. This, at least, should have come as no surprise to anyone. The Tripartite Pact between Germany, Japan, and Italy, signed on September 27, 1940, created an Axis coalition. The pact called for political, economic, and military assistance from the other two nations should any one of the three contracting parties be attacked. Therefore, on December 11 Congress in turn declared war on Germany and on Italy.

Dramatic Expansion of the Corps

When President Roosevelt had declared an unlimited national emergency in May 1941, the Marine Corps began training some 2,000 new recruits per month at

Parris Island, South Carolina, and San Diego, California. Following the declaration of war with the Axis nations, December saw over *18,000* new Marine volunteers![1] With the sudden rush of volunteers and draftees, recruit depot housing was hard pressed to keep up with the influx of men (see appendix A, Monthly Inductions into the Marine Corps, 1941–1945).

Before the national emergency of 1939, Marine recruit training lasted eight weeks. Between September 1939 and January 1940, in the rush to get more men into the service, recruits received only four weeks training. In February the training lengthened first to six, then seven weeks, where it remained until 1944, when it returned to eight weeks.[2]

In the early months of 1942, the services needed replacements for large numbers of men killed or captured by the Japanese in the opening weeks of the war. Furthermore, America needed to enlist and train the soldiers, sailors, airmen and Marines needed to wage the kind of global war that would have to be fought to defeat Germany, Italy, and Japan. However, as recruit depots were hard-pressed to contend with the plenitude of white recruits, the Commandant of the Marine Corps held to the prewar racial policy. The Corps would enlist no blacks.

Calls for Change

The nation needed military manpower to fight and win a war, and black civil rights leaders along with some congressmen kept up a steady pressure on the president to increase black opportunities to serve in the navy as something other than messmen. The Fair Employment Practices Committee (FEPC) lent its weight to the argument when it too came out in favor of change in the navy's assignment policy for blacks. (The committee was created by Roosevelt's Executive Order Number 8802 of June 1941, an order that banned racial discrimination in any defense industry receiving federal contracts.) While the committee had no legal jurisdiction over the navy, ignoring its opinion in the matter was impossible.

The Corps Prepares

On February 18, 1942, the General Board of the Navy requested the commandant of the Marine Corps prepare a list of assignments, ashore and afloat, where "men of the colored race" could take jobs other than as messmen. The General Board's intent was clear: do not "inject into the whole personnel of the Navy the race question."[3] That the Marine Corps would soon enlist blacks was equally clear.

As planning for that eventuality went forward, a staff officer at Marine Corps Headquarters made a surprising proposal. In a February 19 memo, classified SECRET, he recommended that the Corps, with two raider battalions already in existence, should organize an all-black raider battalion. He believed that black men would be "ideal for night raids as no camouflage of faces and hands would be necessary." Furthermore, the navy could assign black sailors to man APDs (high speed transports) in order to transport the black Marine raider battalion.[4] The memo shows just how awkward and uninformed Marines were when it came to blacks; it also shows that among Marines, as with their civilian counterparts, there were some very odd notions and prejudices about blacks.

The Division of Plans and Policies at Headquarters Marine Corps went to work. A February 25 memorandum to Lieutenant General Holcomb — he had advanced to that rank on January 20, 1942 — cited the "spirit of the very evident desires of higher authority" (i.e., the president and the secretary of the navy) and recommended enlisting the "minimum number" required by the General Board. In light of the restrictions of segregation, separate training facilities for the new recruits posed an immediate problem.[5]

White recruits went for basic training at either Marine Corps Recruit Depot (MCRD) Parris Island, South Carolina, or at MCRD San Diego, California. The established recruit training cycle lasted seven weeks, with "138 hours on weapons training, 62 on garrison duties, 57 on field subjects, and 14 on physical training."[6] After recruit training, Marines either attended technical schools or reported to Fleet Marine Force units for combat training.

While Parris Island met the "separate" criteria in that it was isolated, it was small in area with a sizeable portion of its useable land set aside for its own airfield. The Broad River, the Beaufort River, Port Royal Sound, salt marshes and tidal streams surrounded the island. Struggling to accommodate huge numbers of white recruits, it offered little space for the kind of expansion needed for segregated training. San Diego was not isolated but neither did it have room to expand for segregation; the camp was small and surrounded by the city, a naval training center, a commercial airfield, an aircraft manufacturing plant and San Diego Bay. Rather than attempt to shoehorn segregated facilities into the Parris Island and San Diego camps, a new training camp would be easier to find.

The Division of Plans and Policies looked south to its newest camp. Congress had authorized the construction of Marine Barracks New River in coastal North Carolina on February 15, 1941. It was remote, with no significant population center nearby. Lt. Gen. Holcomb, writing to a fellow general, said, "those who want to be near big cities will be disappointed because it is certainly out in the sticks."[7] The site, covering over 100,000 acres, was located near the small town of Jacksonville.

Organized into a composite battalion (infantry, maintenance personnel, antiaircraft batteries, shore defense guns), the blacks would ultimately be employed in the defense of "some island." Existing barracks at a "Negro CCC" (Civilian Conservation Corps) camp near buildings occupied by the Post Headquarters at Marine Barracks New River was an answer to the suggestions for a place to train the black recruits. Newspapers were predicting that the Negro CCC was soon to disband, so the Post Headquarters could easily relocate to another part of the base.[8] Finally, such uses of existing buildings would separate the blacks from the other Marines, yet both would still have all the facilities at New River for training. The February 25 memorandum concluded with the recommendation to limit black enlistments to a maximum of 1,000 until after the composite battalion had nearly completed its training.

1941–1942: The War Begins

5

The Exigencies of War

The End of an Era

The combination of a worsening military situation and increasing civil rights pressure became irresistible. President Roosevelt decided he could no longer permit a recruiting "business as usual" attitude in the naval service. In April 1942, Roosevelt directed the secretary of the navy to make a change — the naval service, including the Marine Corps and the Coast Guard, must accept black volunteers for general service. Following Secretary of the Navy Frank Knox's press conference on April 7, 1942, a press release announced the Navy Department's plan to accept blacks for general service in the navy, Marine Corps, and Coast Guard.[1]

Carry Out the Order

Accordingly, the Lieutenant General Commandant approved an April 30 memo from the Director, Plans and Policies to enlist "1,200 colored troops for duty," 900 of them prior to August 1, 1942.[2] The remaining 300 were to follow in October 1942. Staff officers in Washington had moved smartly if cautiously. The blacks would train in an isolated location and then languish on some remote, out of the way base.[3] Blacks would not be a part of the expeditionary units of the Fleet Marine Force because "the inevitable replacement and redistribution of men in combat would prevent the maintenance of necessary segregation."[4] Secretary of the Navy Frank Knox approved the plan.

An announcement went out to newspapers and radio stations:

NAVY DEPARTMENT

IMMEDIATE RELEASE
PRESS AND RADIO
MAY 20, 1942

MARINES ANNOUNCE PLANS FOR RECRUITING NEGROES IN USMC

The first battalion of Negroes, numbering about 900, will be enlisted in the U.S. Marine Corps Reserve during the months of June and July, it was announced at U.S. Marine Corps Headquarters.

Those volunteers will form a composite battalion which is a unit including all combat arms of the ground forces composed of artillery, anti-aircraft, machine guns, tanks and infantry, and including also billets for recruits who are skilled in various trades and occupations such as radio operators, electricians, accountants, carpenters, draftsmen, band musicians, riggers and blacksmiths.

Until a training center is ready for their reception recruits will be temporarily placed in an inactive duty status. The training center will be in the vicinity of New River, North Carolina where a large Marine Corps post is now located. As required, Negro recruits will be ordered directly from their homes to duty in this training area.

The black press, in particular the widely read *Pittsburgh Courier*, made sure the news reached as many blacks as possible. However, many Americans, both black and white, were not immediately aware of the new policy. Some learned of the existence of black Marines when they saw one in uniform for the first time. Others, like Turner Blount, found out about black Marines only when they arrived at an induction center expecting to go to either the army or the navy. "I didn't know anything about it [the Marine Corps] prior to that."[6]

The composite battalion recommended by the Division of Plans and Policies and mentioned in the press release referred to a defense battalion. America was on the defensive in the Pacific Ocean in April 1942, so adding a new composite defense battalion of Marines, even one manned by blacks, was a sound decision.

Mission has always dictated the numbers and skills of personnel and types of equipment found in Marine units. In fact, the organization of Marine defense battalions was different, depending on where each would serve. Therefore, choosing a composite defense battalion for the first black unit gave Marine planners, faced with many unknowns, flexibility.

"We are afraid of them."[7]

Faced with the prospect of enlisting blacks into the Corps for the first time, Colonel Ray A. Robinson, a staff officer at Marine Headquarters, went to the Selective Service office in downtown Washington DC, in April. There he met with its director, Army Brigadier General Lewis Blaine Hershey, to discuss Marine concerns. Colonel Robinson then met with Lieutenant Colonel Campbell C. Johnson, an army officer who was also a black. Robinson said to Johnson, "Eleanor [First Lady Mrs. Franklin D. Roosevelt] says we gotta take in Negroes, and we are just scared to death; we've never had any in; we don't know how to handle them; we are afraid of them." Johnson told Robinson, "I'll do my best to help you get good ones. I'll get the word around that if you want to die young, join the Marines. So anybody that joins has got to be pretty good!"[8]

Jim Crow Drives Decisions

It was a given that the Marine Corps could not mix black recruits with whites. *Where* to train blacks was already decided — New River. The next problem — *how* to form, train and assign the black unit — would be more difficult.

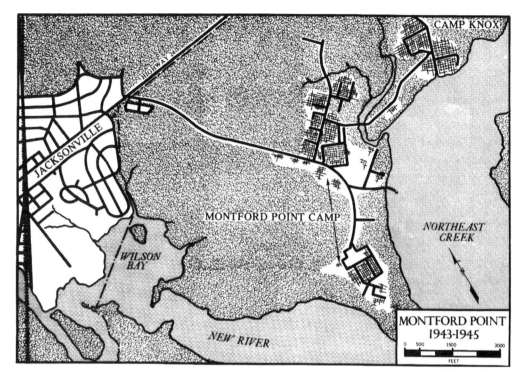

From Henry I. Shaw, Jr., and Ralph W. Donnelly. *Blacks in the Marine Corps* (Washington, D.C.: GPO, History and Museums Division, HQMC, 1975), 6.

The commandant's decisions were in keeping with the times. In 1942, *all* of the services were segregated, as was most of America. Because of the Corps's small size, segregation seemed more noticeable in the Marine Corps than it did in the army. Given that separation of the races was a fact of the day, Marine Corps planners had no choice but to create a duplicate yet separate recruit training camp, activate a small black unit and then put relatively few blacks in it. From the outset, the variety of military occupations and opportunities for black Marines was limited.

According to the base's camp engineer, April 1941 saw the establishment of the first headquarters for Marine Barracks New River. It was in a cottage on a bluff at "Sleepy Hollow" near the black CCC camp (Camp Knox). A small detail from the 1st Marine Regiment arrived soon after and set up at Paradise Point in an old hotel and some cottages there. Later that summer the expanding Marine Barracks headquarters relocated to Mumford Point in a group of farmhouses. The national colors were run up about September 20. A Tent Camp, under the command of Colonel (Col) Samuel A. Woods, Jr., was constructed at mainside for the newly created 1st Marine Division.[9]

The base, where the division would train before sailing for the Pacific, was a perfect place for training Marines. The reservation had 10 miles of Atlantic beaches for amphibious operations while for other training there were sandy forests, low-lying swamps populated by black bears, alligators, ticks, chiggers, mosquitoes, sand fleas, and four different kinds of poisonous snakes. One Marine veteran of the fighting in Nicaragua later said of the brand-new base at New River, "They had mosquitoes there with snow on the ground."[10]

On April 21, 1942, $750,000 was allotted to enlarge the camp at Mumford Point and for new construction in the camp.[11] The expanded camp would consist of six washrooms for enlisted men, a mess (dining) hall, an administration building, a medical dispensary, a recreation building, a post exchange, two warehouses, and a heating plant, all of wooden frame construction. Marines undergoing training would live in one hundred and eight portable huts made of "homosote" (described as a cross between cardboard and tarpaper), all laid out in nine rows of 12 huts. Each hut would accommodate sixteen men. The camp at Mumford Point, soon renamed as Montford Point, covered over five square miles in area.

Montford Point was located on a finger of land jutting into the New River (see map 1, Montford Point, 1943–1945). Surrounded by thick pine forests, it was bordered on the west by Wilson Bay, New River, and Jacksonville, and on the east by Scales Creek and a war dog-training center located in Camp Knox. Beyond that was Northeast Creek. New River emptied into the Atlantic a few miles to the southeast. It was the perfect place to train black Marines, and there were good reasons for this choice. First, the camp was already constructed and in use. Second, because of its isolation it satisfied segregation requirements. White Marines packed up the Marine Barracks New River headquarters and moved to the main part of the reservation into permanent buildings at Hadnot Point.

6

Blacks Accept the Challenge

Quotas Go Out

The Marine Corps in 1942 had almost 850 men assigned in four recruiting divisions around the country. In a letter, the commandant issued his instructions to the recruiters. To recruit the first 900 blacks, the Eastern and Central Divisions were to enlist 200 men each, while the Southern Division was to enlist 500.

The recruiting sergeants (called "Walking Johns" for their habit of buttonholing men on the streets to deliver their pitches) were to enlist black men between the ages of 17 and 29 years as Class III (c) Volunteer Marine Corps Reserves. The front covers of enlistees' service record books were stamped with the word COLORED.[1] More than half the black men to be enlisted had to have specific skills — typists, truck drivers, and cooks — skills needed in the black composite unit. If such men could be found, the Corps would not have to send them to specialist schools for training; the skilled men could immediately go to work. These first men had to arrive at New River by August 26 to help set up and to operate the camp for the black recruits who would follow.

Trouble Achieving Enlistment Quotas

Meanwhile, officers at Headquarters Marine Corps soon discovered that their plan to recruit blacks was in trouble. By the middle of June, only sixty-three blacks had met the Corps's enlistment standards. In a memorandum for the secretary of the navy, Lt. Gen. Holcomb noted that "physical and mental examinations quickly deleted most of the original black applicants."[2] The situation should have come as no surprise to anyone.

Long recognized for exercising an exceptional degree of selectivity in recruiting, the Marines had accepted only 38,080 out of approximately 205,000 white applications for first-time enlistment in the Corps between 1939 and 1941, roughly one of every five applicants.[3] By mid–1942, the Corps's approach to recruiting blacks, a continuation of its pre-war selectivity, was failing.

Were blacks subjected to higher standards for voluntary enlistment than whites were? Was Lt. Gen. Holcomb's exclusive club using unusually high qualification standards to admit only the best black applicants? Was that the reason the Corps was not getting the number of black recruits it needed? The answer to these questions is simply that the Corps's requirements were unrealistic considering the number of men needed.

Early Volunteers

In Boston, one of the first blacks to enlist was Obie Hall. He went to the Marine Corps recruiter to volunteer and learned that he could enlist immediately if he had the right skills. Hall declared, "I'm a truck driver," but later admitted he "no more could drive a truck than the man in the moon."[4]

In Gadsden, Alabama, twenty-two-year-old Edgar R. Huff worked in a steel mill earning $1.40 a day. Standing six feet six inches tall and weighing two hundred and two pounds, Huff *looked* like the kind of man who should be a Marine. On June 25, 1942, Huff read a newspaper article announcing that the Marine Corps was enlisting qualified black men. Huff had no way of knowing that the Corps was struggling to carry out the president's order to enlist blacks. He said later, "I heard the Marines were the toughest outfit in the world, and I knew they couldn't be any tougher than what I was going through. So, I decided to join."[5]

Arnold R. Bostic, an eighteen-year-old from New Jersey, did not want to wait for a draft notice, and the loss of choice that came with it. "I wanted to be in the toughest branch of the service and was willing to accept the challenges to succeed in that branch."[6] He enlisted in the Marine Corps in July 1942.

An Unlikely Volunteer

Physically and intellectually, Herbert Lawrence Brewer just didn't seem the type to become a Marine. Soft-spoken, serious, Herb was tall and thin and wore glasses. He was an honor graduate of San Antonio's Phillis Wheatley High School (named for the 18th Century slave poet, it was one of Texas's few black high schools) where he played the violin. He earned many merit badges as a Boy Scout, and regularly attended St. Paul Methodist Church with his parents.

Besides movies, Herb loved building and flying model airplanes. Rubber bands or gas engines powered some of the balsa wood and tissue paper airplanes he made, and the larger models had wings that spanned up to five feet. Always inquisitive, Herb liked to build things. He wanted to become an engineer.

In addition, he wanted to be a Marine.

During his busy first year of college at Tuskegee Institute in Alabama, Herb kept his grades up, earning all A's and B's. He continued with the violin, and in the school's Army Reserve Officer Training Program (ROTC) Herb discovered a real knack for things military. He earned a place on the unit's rifle team and tied for top honors as the best competition shooter. He finished the year with a letter of commendation for achieving the second highest ranking among all the first year ROTC students.[7] Militarily sharp in his army uniform, Herb never gave up on wearing Marine dress blues. The dark blue uniform coat had a high stock collar, red piping and shiny brass buttons. Sharply creased sky blue trousers set off the dark coat. People would notice.

Herbert Brewer was certain that he would be drafted into the army soon after his eighteenth birthday. Luckily, Brewer read an article in the newspaper announcing that on the first day of June the Marine Corps was to accept blacks for enlistment.

On a Saturday morning near the end of June Brewer walked the few blocks from his home to the Marine recruiting office located in downtown San Antonio on Broadway. The recruiting office was located above the store where Brewer bought many of his model airplane kits. He climbed the stairs, curious to hear what the recruiting sergeant had to say.

After questions about Brewer's background and education, the sergeant measured and weighed him. The recruiter found that Brewer met the standards set by Headquarters Marine Corps for enlistment of blacks in the Corps.[8] However, the recruiter told Brewer, "There are just two problems here. First, we're going to need your parents' consent because you're only seventeen, and the second is you don't weigh enough. I'll tell you what you do, you go home, eat a big meal, eat all you can, get your parents to come down with you, I will weigh you again, and let your parents sign, and I think you'll be okay."[9]

Brewer hurried home, eagerly discussed his plans with his parents and then ate a huge meal of Boston baked beans. Accompanied by his mother and father Brewer returned to the recruiting office. His weight was acceptable, his parents signed, and Herbert Lawrence Brewer became one of the first of his race to enlist in the Marines.

Army Lt. Col. Johnson's assurance given to Marine Col. Ray Robinson in April at the Selective Service office may have been prophetic, for some of the early volunteers were *very* good men. Two of the new recruits were veterans of service with the army's 10th Cavalry Regiment, and another was a former army lieutenant. One of the new Marines was a graduate of Morehouse College who went on to become the first black sergeant major of the Montford Point Camp. Another man was a graduate of Alcorn A & M who had taken his Masters degree at the University of Illinois and eventually became the Sergeant Major of the 51st Defense Battalion.[10] John T. Pridgen was a permanent master sergeant in the Army's 9th Cavalry and scheduled to go to Officer Candidates School when the Marines began accepting blacks, so he became a Marine. Benny C. Jones had already enlisted in the

Corps when he found out his appointment to the U.S. Military Academy at West Point had come through. He chose to remain a Marine.[11]

Separate But...

The 12th Defense Battalion activated in August 1942 at San Diego, California. Then the Corps broke the numbering sequence for activating defense battalions. The black defense battalion forming at New River, North Carolina, in the same month took the unit designation of 51st Composite Defense Battalion. The 51st was the first black combat unit in the Corps. Getting back to the normal numbering sequence for white units, in September the 13th Defense Battalion activated at Guantanamo Bay, Cuba.

The 51st Composite Defense Battalion Is Formed

On August 18, 1942, Colonel (Col.) Samuel A. Woods, Jr., activated the nucleus of the 51st Composite Defense Battalion. The battalion, such as it was, moved into the recently vacated Marine Barracks Headquarters at Montford Point Camp that was barely a year old. He would be the first Marine officer to command a black unit. Col. Woods, a South Carolinian and graduate of The Citadel, was a veteran with 25 years service as a commissioned officer. He had served in France in World War I, Cuba, the Dominican Republic, and the Philippines. One black Marine, G. H. Johnson, would remember him as a fair man who would give blacks an opportunity to prove themselves.[12] Col. Woods, like Maj. Gen. John A. Lejeune, believed that a Marine officer should relate to his subordinates the way a father relates to a son. Black Marines sometimes referred to Col. Woods as "the Great White Father of everybody." While Col. Woods accepted the separation of the races required by the times, he held his men to high standards. Woods insisted that the black Marines demonstrate the traits of self-pride and military competence expected of all Marines.[13]

The battalion executive officer (XO), a lieutenant colonel who had served as an enlisted man in World War I and as a commissioned officer since 1924, was the officer in charge of training the black recruits. The XO was also a veteran of service in the Philippines, China, and Nicaragua.

The first element of the 51st to form was the Headquarters and Service (H&S) Battery with twenty-three officers and ninety enlisted men, all white. This was the cadre, or core, on which the battalion would build. Among the officers, lieutenants recently graduated from the Base Defense Course at Quantico, Virginia, was composer/musician Second Lieutenant (2d Lt.) Robert W. Troup, Jr.[14]

Most of the enlisted men were noncommissioned officers (NCOs) who had been around, the "Old Salts," carefully screened and chosen because they did not object to blacks serving in the Marine Corps. Along with a few lower ranked enlisted men they made up the Special Enlisted Staff (known as SES men). They were about to engage in something that had never been done by Marines — accepting black men as Marine recruits.

7

American Strategy

Take Back the Pacific

In January 1942, the Japanese attacked and seized Simpson Harbor at Rabaul on New Britain Island in the Bismarck Archipelago east of New Guinea and Australia (see map 2, Solomon Islands, Santa Cruz Islands and New Caledonia, and map 3, Central and South Pacific Area). Rabaul became home to the Japanese Naval Headquarters in the South Pacific.

On July 2, 1942, the U.S. Joint Chiefs of Staff ordered Allied forces in the Pacific to mount a limited offensive to halt the Japanese advance toward the line of communications from the United States to Australia and New Zealand. Concurrently, the United States was committed to a program for building up forces in Great Britain to launch an offensive in Europe expected to take place in 1942 or 1943.

In the Pacific so few warships, transports, and cargo ships, so few trained troops, so few weapons and supplies were available that any offensive, for which the United States would have to provide most of the forces, would be limited in scale. The decision to attempt that limited offensive grew out of an earlier strategic decision made by President Roosevelt and Prime Minister Churchill at the Arcadia Conference held in Washington, DC, in January 1942: Defeat Germany first, and after Germany fell, everyone would concentrate on Japan. The United States assumed responsibility for directing the war in the Pacific, subject to decisions of the U.S.-British Combined Chiefs of Staff on global strategy.

Therefore, it was imperative to halt the Japanese who were then moving ever nearer to being in position to sever the tenuous lines of communications between the United States and Australia. The only troops then in the Pacific trained for and ready to conduct amphibious operations were the men of the 1st Marine Division. The Joint Chiefs' decision of July 2 led to the six-month-long struggle for the possession of Guadalcanal, an island in the British Solomon Islands Protectorate that, while not specifically named by the Joint Chiefs, was chosen because the Japanese were constructing an airfield there.[1]

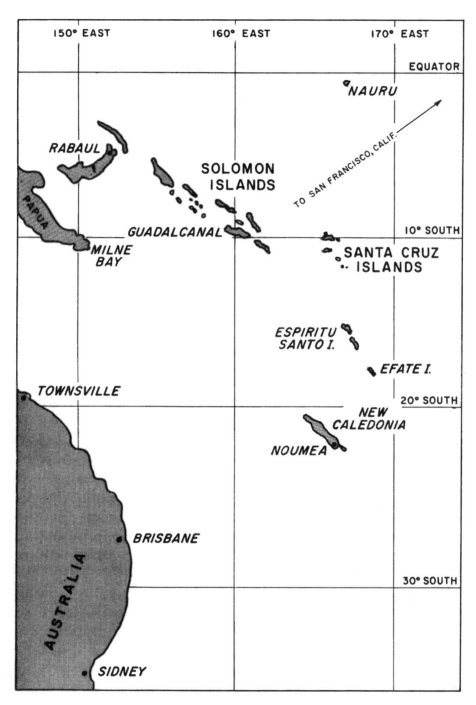

Solomon Islands, Santa Cruz Islands and New Caledonia.

Source: George Carroll Dyer, Vice Admiral, USN (Ret.). *The Amphibians Came to Conquer*, Vol I (Washington, D.C.: GPO. U.S. Department of the Navy, 1972), 236. (Hereafter Dyer, *The Amphibians*, Vol I).

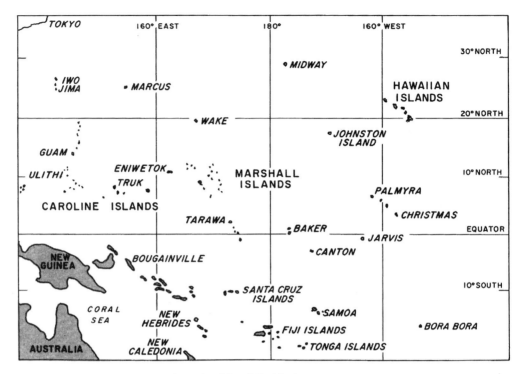

Central and South Pacific Area.

Source: George Carroll Dyer, *The Amphibians,* Vol. I, 231.

Realizing that Rabaul would have to be captured if the Allies were to accomplish the Joint Chiefs' goal, plans to ensure Allied control of the sea-lanes were drawn. These called for operations to be conducted in three stages: first, bases in the southern Solomon Islands (Guadalcanal and, fifteen miles across Sealark Channel, Tulagi) would be captured; second, capture bases in the Central Solomons (and the north coast of New Guinea); and third, the recapture of Rabaul itself and the rest of the Bismarck Archipelago.

Shore Party Problems Resurface

While preparations for training blacks at New River continued, the first stage of the JCS plan was carried out. The 1st Marine Division, commanded by Major General (Maj. Gen.) Alexander Archer Vandegrift, landed unopposed on D-Day, August 7, on the Japanese-held island of Guadalcanal in the South Pacific in Operation WATCHTOWER. It was America's first offensive amphibious operation of the war. It was also the first large-scale *wartime* application of the amphibious warfare doctrine developed by the Marine Corps in the previous ten years.

An explanation of the terms D-Day and H-Hour is in order. These indicate the day and hour on which an attack or operation is to begin. They designate the day and hour of the start of an operation when the actual day and hour have not yet been determined, or where secrecy is essential. The letters derive from the words for which they stand, "D" for the day of the invasion and "H" for the hour operations actually begin. There is but one D-Day and one H-Hour for all units participating in a given operation. It is unnecessary to state that H-Hour occurs on D-Day.

In voice radio or Morse code messages, phonetic alphabet terms such as "Dog-Day" for D-Day or "How-Hour" for H-Hour reduce the possibility of confusion. When used in combination with minus or plus signs and figures, these terms indicate the length of time preceding or following the specific action. For example, H-3 means 3 hours before H-Hour, H+75 minutes means H-Hour plus 1 hour and 15 minutes and D+3 means 3 days after D-Day.

Plans for amphibious operations are drawn up in minute detail long before specific dates are set. Thus, orders are issued for the various steps to be carried out on D-Day or H-Hour minus or plus a certain number or days, hours, or minutes. At the appropriate time, a subsequent order states the actual day and times for the operation.[2]

While a detailed analysis of the Guadalcanal operation is beyond the scope of this work, readers may wish to study separately the decisions that contributed to many problems in the execution of the plans. However, it is relevant here to look into one of those problems.

Prior to the start of Operation WATCHTOWER, some elements of the 1st Marine Division had to unload cargo ships that had been administratively loaded in the United States. Admin loading means no consideration is given to quick access to critical war fighting material; rather, it simply gets the most tonnage possible in a ship going from Point A to Point B. Arriving at Aotea Quay at Wellington, New Zealand, the Marines had just eleven days to empty and reload a large number of ships before sailing for Guadalcanal. Supplies and material had to be unloaded, sorted and then reloaded so that things needed first on the beaches would be on top in the cargo holds, easy to get to and send ashore. The process is known as "combat loading." Wellington's unionized stevedores, involved in a dispute with management, went on strike and refused to help the Americans. Troops who had been living in cramped quarters during the long trip across the Pacific were put to work in eight-hour shifts, and parties of 300 men were assigned to each ship that had to be unloaded. The work of moving supplies and equipment from the ships to the dock, sorting it, and moving it back to the ships again had hardly started when a cold rain blew in. Work continued around the clock. Cardboard carton-packed food and other supplies "deteriorated rapidly," as did the morale of the men. "On the dock, cereal, sugar, and other rations mushed together with globs of brown pulp that once had been cardboard boxes."[3] When the ships were combat loaded, there was a shortage of cargo space. Much rolling stock and equipment remained in camps at Wellington to be brought forward later when shipping was available.

When all the ships were loaded, the Marines carried 60 days' supplies, ammunition for 10 days, and less than half the authorized motor transport.[4] It was an unsatisfactory start to the operation.

In what soon was called "Operation Shoestring," problems continued. At Guadalcanal on the first day of the unopposed invasion, movement of supplies from the narrow beaches to dumps quickly broke down. The approximately 740 men of the three companies of the 1st Pioneer Battalion (added to the division's table of organization in January) constituted Marine labor resources trained for the unloading of supplies and equipment from ships' boats at the high-water mark (see appendix D: Marine Division Service and Supply Units — World War II). The Pioneer Battalion was also part of the force assigned the task of ground defense in the beachhead area. With the exception of one platoon employed in another part of the operation, the remainder of the battalion was piecemealed out to reinforce the rifle regiments. It was a recipe for supply chaos at the beachhead.

On D-Day, Japanese aircraft from their huge base at Rabaul attacked the ships unloading supplies. Fortunately, only one American destroyer was damaged. From the transport ship *USS George F. Elliott* (AP-13) the Assistant Beachmaster, in charge of getting supplies from his ship to the beach, reported "literally hundreds of Marines were sitting on the beach watching the confusion mount, while hundreds of others were roaming through the cocoanut groves." Another navy officer reported that "there were approximately fifteen or twenty men unloading boats and about fifty others in swimming ... I saw about one hundred men lounging around under the palm trees eating cocoanuts, lying down shooting cocoanuts from the trees; also playing around and paddling about in rubber boats. All of these men were Marines that should have been unloading boats."[5]

Commander (Comdr.) L.W. Perkins, U.S. Coast Guard, captain of the *USS Hunter Liggett* (AP-27) reported that on the night of August 7–8, conditions on the beach "reached a complete impasse" with "nearly one hundred boats ... gunwale to gunwale on the beach, while another fifty boats waited, some of these up to six hours for a chance to land."

By 0600 August 8, the supply situation ashore had not improved. Seeing canned rations floating on the waves about one mile off the beach, a navy officer from the transport ship *USS Barnett* (AP-11) noted that "most of the supplies which had been unloaded during the night had been dumped at the low water mark." Of course, as the tide came in, these supplies, "such as sugar, coffee, beans, cheese and lard ... were being ruined." Comdr. Perkins on the *Hunter Liggett,* observed that "despite the quiet night, the Marines had failed to clear the beach and very little cargo was worked prior to the air alarm for the second Japanese air raid on the Allied ships at 1043 on 8 August."[6] Supplies remained piled up on the beach. Fortunately, Japanese pilots again concentrated on attacking the ships instead of going after the irreplaceable supplies lying undispersed and uncamouflaged on the beach.

The situation worsened, however, when an Australian scout plane sighted a Japanese task force of five heavy and two light cruisers and one destroyer the morning of August 8. The Japanese were steaming toward Guadalcanal down "the Slot," the central passage that runs southeast to northwest through the thirteen large islands of the Solomons. The ensuing Battle of Savo Island on the night of August 8–9 was one of America's most humiliating naval defeats. Three American cruisers and one Australian cruiser were sunk, and one American cruiser and one destroyer were damaged while none of the attacking Japanese ships were lost. Since most of the Pacific Fleet's battleships remained out of action following the Japanese attack at Pearl Harbor the previous December, this represented a serious reduction in Allied naval strength in the Pacific.

As a result, American transport and cargo ships lying off Guadalcanal became dangerously vulnerable to further Japanese attack. After only two or three hours more of unloading, Marines ashore watched as the ships sailed for the safer waters of Noumea, New Caledonia, taking their remaining supplies with them. Since the ships brought only a portion of the equipment and supplies needed by the Marines in the first place, this proved to be a critical loss. With Sealark Channel devoid of ships, the Marines on Guadalcanal took stock of their situation. They had food and ammunition for about thirty days. For everything else, including barbed wire, there were severe shortages or in many cases even complete absences of critical supplies and equipment. If the Japanese pilots had targeted and set fire to the supplies heaped high on the beaches, Lt. Gen. Vandegrift said, "the consequences might well have been incalculable and ruinous."[7]

The Marines learned a harsh lesson at Guadalcanal in August 1942. They needed more men on the beach to handle supplies — division officers later reported that they needed "additional personnel in the proportion of at least 100 men for each vessel discharging cargo across the beach" — and their procedures needed to be greatly improved.[8] Lt. Gen. Vandegrift observed that pre-war FLEXs had revealed problems with the shore party.

Soon the irrepressible make-do spirit of the Marines coupled with Herculean efforts by the navy to supply the landing force by means of fast destroyer transports would see the operation through its darkest days when Vandegrift dealt with Japanese counter-landings on Guadalcanal. A regular system for resupplying Marines on Guadalcanal was finally in place by November. Fixing the procedures would prove easier than finding the men to move supplies on the beaches.

8

The First Black Marine Unit

Like No Other

When Headquarters Marine Corps ordered the activation of a composite defense battalion at Montford Point, it levied requirements that no other unit in the Corps had ever been given:

- Most of the enlisted men in the battalion would be black.
- White Drill Instructors (DIs) would conduct segregated basic, entry-level training for black recruits.
- Blacks would replace white DIs and take over basic training of other blacks as soon as possible.
- The battalion staff had to train other newly graduated black Marines in a wide range of technical and gunnery skills required to operate and maintain modern heavy caliber guns, all the supporting trucks, trailers, generators, searchlights, radar and more that made up a defense battalion.
- Since segregation prevented blacks from attending white technical schools, instructors would have to come to train them on the job at Montford Point.

The Marine Corps had grown from a pre-war 19,432 officers and enlisted men to over 143,000 by July 1942.[1] It desperately needed white NCOs to form a solid core of experience in newly activated units. Marine Corps personnel officers knew that assigning a cadre of a few of the "Old Salts" to a newly forming battalion helped the new unit quickly become combat ready. It was Standing Operating Procedure (SOP) in the Corps for activating new units.

Headquarters Marine Corps planned to transfer all of the white Montford Point drill instructors within a year. Therefore, it was imperative that some blacks from the first graduating platoons train as DIs to quickly take over all basic training duties from the whites. It would be the first time the 51st would suffer the loss of "experienced" men to form other units, but it would not be the last.

Defense Battalions

Marine planners had created standard tables of organization (T/O), templates to use as a starting point for building all defense battalions. The standards called for a unit of about 900 men in 5-inch coast defense gun batteries, 3-inch antiaircraft gun batteries, a sound locator and searchlight battery (radar came to the Marine Corps in the late 1930s but it was classified and therefore not openly discussed). To these were added a battery of .50-caliber antiaircraft machine guns and a battery of heavy, water-cooled .30-caliber machine guns for beach defenses.[2] Necessary changes to this standard — men, equipment, and guns — depended on where a battalion was going. Heavy firepower was a common trait of all defense battalions.

A Formidable Unit

The firepower of the 51st Composite Defense Battalion would be considerable. The D-157 Table of Organization (T/O) for the black combat unit, including notations for major armaments, is shown in the following Figure 1.[3]

Battery "A" Is Activated for Training

Things moved quickly. On August 26, eight days after the 51st Composite Defense Battalion came into being, Battery "A" activated. An administrative and training unit rather than a tactical war-fighting unit, Battery "A" would form black recruits into 40-man platoons.[4] Each platoon would go through about seven weeks of basic training. Platoons were numbered sequentially as they formed. The battery staff took care of administrative records and provided basic training for the men.

The First Blacks Arrive

The same day Battery "A" activated, thirteen of the first twenty-four black recruits, some of the truck drivers, typists, and cooks, arrived at Jacksonville, North Carolina, the town just outside the borders of the military reservation, for further transportation the short distance to Montford Point Camp. Jacksonville, sharply split along racial lines, was typical of many small southern towns of the early 1940s. Railroad tracks made a tangible dividing line, with whites here, blacks over yonder. On August 26, 1942, Howard P. Perry, originally from Charlotte, North Carolina, was the first black recruit to pass through the gates at Montford Point

COMPOSITE DEFENSE BATTALION
TABLE OF ORGANIZATION D-157
APPROVED 7 MAY 1942

41 OFFICERS USMC & USN
8 WARRENT OFFICERS USMC
1041 ENLISTED MEN USMC & USN

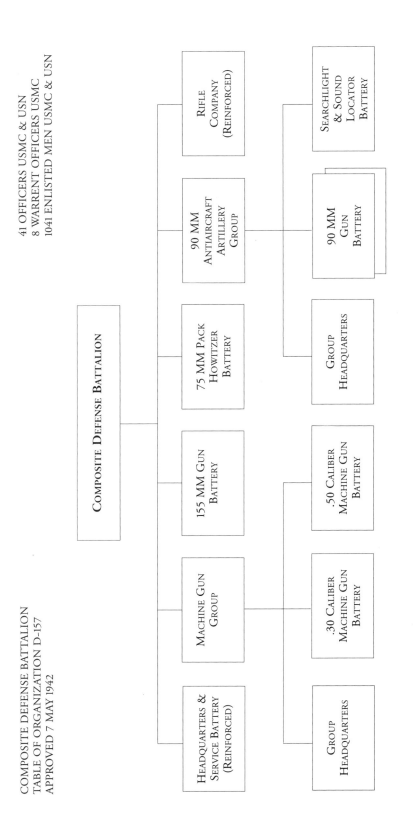

COMPOSITE DEFENSE BATTALION

HEADQUARTERS & SERVICE BATTERY (REINFORCED)

MACHINE GUN GROUP

155 MM GUN BATTERY

75 MM PACK HOWITZER BATTERY

90 MM ANTIAIRCRAFT ARTILLERY GROUP

RIFLE COMPANY (REINFORCED)

GROUP HEADQUARTERS

.30 CALIBER MACHINE GUN BATTERY

.50 CALIBER MACHINE GUN BATTERY

GROUP HEADQUARTERS

90 MM GUN BATTERY

SEARCHLIGHT & SOUND LOCATOR BATTERY

MAJOR ARMAMENT: 4 155 MM GUNS, 8 90MM ANTIAIRCRAFT GUNS, 20 .50-CALIBER ANTIAIRCRAFT MACHINE GUNS, 30 .30-CALIBER ANTIAIRCRAFT MACHINE-GUNS, 2 81 MM MORTARS, 2 .30-CALIBER LIGHT MACHINE GUNS, 5 LIGHT TANKS (AUTHOR'S NOTE: NO DESCRIPTION FOR THE 75 MM PACK HOWITZERS WAS INCLUDED ON THE ORIGINAL T/O ARMAMENTS LIST.)

Camp. Perry was to become a member of the special duty platoon slated for camp operation duty.[5]

Perry had studied law at Lincoln University in Missouri and enlisted in Detroit, Michigan, where he worked. A deter-mined-looking Perry, with a close-cropped "boot" haircut, clad in dungarees and holding a sun helmet with eagle, globe, and anchor device, appeared in a photograph that accompanied a September newspaper article about black recruit training in the *Philadelphia Tribune*. The photo caption in bold print proclaims "First Negro Marine."[6] In Washington DC, at the recently established Division of Press Intelligence in the Office of War Information (OWI), an unknown clerk responsible for preparing summaries and digests of press and radio comments clipped the article from the paper and tagged and routed it though the bureaucracy. (The OWI was a government agency created by Executive Order

"Breaking a tradition of 167 years, the U.S. Marine Corps started enlisting Negroes on June 1, 1942. The first class of 1,200 Negro volunteers began their training 3 months later as members of the 51st Composite Defense Battalion at Montford Point, a section of the 200-square-mile Marine Base, Camp Lejeune, at New River, NC. The first Negro to enlist was Howard P. Perry shown here." He became a member of the special duty platoon for camp operation duty. At the time of this photograph, Perry wore the single stripe of a Private First Class on the left sleeve of his uniform blouse. No date. Roger Smith; Still Picture Branch (NNSP), National Archives, Washington, DC.

9182 on June 13, 1942. Its purpose was to consolidate war information functions.) The clipping made its way from 14th Street N.W. across the Potomac River to the Navy Annex and Headquarters Marine Corps where it ended up at Central Files in a catchall folder labeled "Negroes in the Armed Services."[7] It was the first of many such clippings, for the Marine Corps was concerned about how the black press perceived and reported on black Marines.

Three training platoons formed when enough black recruits had reported to camp. The men, with justifiable pride, called these the "Mighty" 1st, 2d, and 3d.[8]

"Newly-arrived recruits shoulder seabags outside a supply shed at the Montford Point Camp." No date. Used with permission of the Montford Point Marine Museum, Camp Lejeune, NC.

Soon afterward six additional platoons formed to begin the Marine Corps's first training cycle for blacks. These new recruits, all Privates, endured a reception experience common to all Marines. Recruits were confused, bewildered at new surroundings and new ways of doing things. Impatient white men who seemed to be angry about everything shouted orders at the black youths. Physical examinations required even the shy men to strip to their drawers. They lined up and filed between unsmiling, businesslike sailors who stabbed inoculations into their arms. They managed a hurried lunch, which they called "noon chow." Haircuts came next, then piles of new clothing, and all of it done with a group of people who were complete strangers just 24 hours ago in the humid heat of eastern North Carolina's coastal plain.

Private Herbert Lawrence Brewer was one of the first of those highly qualified new recruits, called "skinheads," to experience the shock of Marine culture. On his first night at Montford Point, a white drill instructor (DI) conducted an inspection "just before we went to bed. One of the fellows from Chicago had on a pair of pink silk pajamas — that was when we slept in our underwear and he had these pinks on. He got quite a lecture on that. The sergeant said, 'I want those things in

"...Although a dress uniform is not a part of the regular equipment, most of the Negro Marines spend $54 out of their pay for what is generally considered the snappiest uniform in the armed services... Photo shows a group of the Negro volunteers in their dress uniforms." Ca. May 1943. Roger Smith. Still Picture Branch (NNSP), National Archives, Washington DC.

the mail first thing in the morning.' One fellow didn't have any shoes, his feet were so big, and he sat around several weeks until they could get shoes for him. He was from Alabama. I don't think he completed boot camp because he had some problem with his ability with the manual of arms."[9] Brewer, and all the new recruits, quickly learned that the Corps does not create fully trained combat-ready Marines in boot camp, but basic Marines, ready to be further trained in war fighting skills when they arrive in their Fleet Marine Force (FMF) units.

Prior to World War II Marines wore either the summer service cotton khaki uniform or one piece blue denim coveralls with a field hat (a flat-brimmed hat with a peaked crown, later known as a campaign cover or "Smokey the Bear" hat) when training in the field. The Montford Point Marines received the newly introduced two-piece field uniform made of sage-green herringbone twill cotton to replace the denim coveralls. The loose fitting jacket had three pockets, one on the left breast and two in front below the waist on either side, without flaps or closures. Stenciled on the breast pocket were an eagle, globe and anchor and the letters USMC (this is the uniform Howard Perry wore in the *Tribune* photograph). A field cap of the same material came in 1943, but in the interim Marines wore either sun helmets or garrison caps (a small cap with no bill, later called a "fore and aft cover" or "piss-cutter") with the dungarees. Those hoping for a dress blue uniform would have to wait, for it was not a part of the basic uniform issue. After completion of boot camp the men would have the opportunity to purchase a set of "blues."

Classification Testing

Early in their boot camp experience the men were given a series of written tests, the General Classification Test (GCT), an aid to assigning an occupational specialty. Records of how the men fared no longer exist. However, an internal HQMC Division of Plans and Policies memorandum, classified SECRET, shows the kind of test scores personnel planners expected from black Marine recruits. Dated December 26, 1942, under the subject "Colored personnel" the memo presented a score sampling from both black and white draftees prepared by the U.S. Army. The scores were[10]:

	Class:	*Negro Percent*	*White Percent*
I	Superior	0.6	7.6
II	Above Average	5.0	29.2
III	Average	16.5	32.7
IV	Below Average	30.4	21.6
V	Inferior	47.5	21.6

If those figures could be accurately applied to the approximately 19,168 blacks who served as Marines in World War II, then almost 78 percent, or about 14,900 men, may have scored in the two lowest classes. The Marine Corps's strength in World War II peaked at 485,113, so those same figures would indicate that approximately 140,000 white Marines also scored in the two lowest classes.[11]

The problem was this: While the whites from the two lowest classes could be assigned throughout many units around the Corps, the blacks from the same classes, because of segregation, were concentrated in only a few units. Marine officers planned from the outset to limit the military occupations blacks could hold and the type of units in which they could serve, so the numbers have little meaning. Limited opportunity meant that a high school graduate could manhandle boxes of supplies alongside a man who never completed the seventh grade.

Rank and Pay

As privates, they were at the lowest rank and rated no rank chevron on the sleeve of their uniforms. The rank structure had been in place since 1937 when it

"Three of the first black recruits strike a martial pose at the Montford Point Camp. The bolt-action Springfield M1903 rifles and the sun helmets indicate this photo probably dates to early autumn, 1942." Used with permission of the Montford Point Marine Museum, Camp Lejeune, NC.

was set up according to an earlier delineation of pay grades, and with minor changes it continued in effect until after the war (see appendix B, Marine Corps Rank and Pay Structure in 1942). However, some adjustments were necessary. In 1943 the rank of first sergeant moved up to the first pay grade to reflect changes in the way first sergeants were used, and ranks such as Steward and Steward's Assistant were added when the Marine Corps incorporated such duties.[12]

The men were paid according to an Enlisted Pay Grade Table established in 1922. Pay grade E-7 was the lowest and E-1 the highest. The new black recruits were at the seventh pay grade and they earned $21.00 per month, paid with small ceremony at the end of the month. The pay was not much, and for all servicemen the years between 1922 and 1942 represented a long time without a pay raise, but at least it was not taxed.[13]

White Drill Instructors

The drill instructors (DIs) were professional Marines. They used shock — loud voices, feigned anger, impatience, and hurry — to keep the boots off balance and on the run, hammering them psychologically day and night through physically demanding training. A DI told Private Huff, "I'm going to make you wish you never had joined this damn Marine Corps."[14] The recruits' best effort was never good enough for the DIs, for they demanded perfection and accepted nothing less. The goal of such training was not to drive them out of the Corps, but to meld the young black men into a unit, a platoon, rather than a collection of loosely associated, undisciplined individuals. Private Gilbert Johnson had served in the army and the navy before becoming a Marine. No stranger to the hardships of military duty, he had served on the Mexican border with the army's 25th Infantry Regiment in the 1920s. Johnson was glad his DIs "were not against the Negro being a Marine, and had it been otherwise, why I'm afraid that we would have all left the first week. Some of us, probably, the first night."[15] One of the most important lessons the men learned during recruit training was how to live with other men as part of a unit. The forced togetherness fostered a sense of belonging, where friendships were born of shared difficulties.

Why So Tough?

What is the reason for the rugged training all Marines, white or black, endured? The Marine "club" has rigid entrance requirements for any man who accepts the challenge. It is, physically and mentally, a demanding process to toughen young Americans to endure the horrors of war yet prevail against the enemy. Marines must have confidence in themselves and their fellow Marines, for each must depend on all other Marines of his unit in battle. If any man cannot follow orders, if he quails under minor discomforts in the safety of garrison life then he will likely falter on the harsh, unforgiving battlefield where failure to follow orders might get a man killed, or worse, cause the death of a buddy, a fellow Marine. Marine recruit training *by design* weeds out the weak before they ever get to the battlefield.

9

Training the First Black Recruits

A New Language

Because the Corps came under the Navy Department and specialized in attacks from the sea, all Marines could expect duty aboard ship. "Skinheads" learned to speak a language where rumors became "scuttlebutt," but for some odd reason the same name applied to a water fountain; bathrooms were called "heads," a term left over from the days of sail. Walls were "bulkheads" and a man entered a room through a "hatch" instead of a door. A floor or the ground was the "deck" and the ceiling an "overhead." Left was "port" and right was "starboard," upstairs was "topside" and downstairs was "below." A mop was a "swab." There were more expressions to be mastered, some uniquely Marine in usage. The men wore high top field shoes called "boondockers" with their "dungarees," the new herringbone twill work uniforms. The deep woods were "the boondocks." They learned that a Navy man was a "swabbie" and a soldier was a "dog face," but neither of them could ever measure up as a Marine.

The first black recruits to arrive at Montford Point were issued a .30 caliber, bolt-operated Model 1903 rifle made by the Springfield Armory in Massachusetts, the legendary and highly accurate "'03 Springfield." First issued to Marines in 1908, the '03 was soon to be replaced in general issue by the U.S. Rifle, Caliber .30, M-1. In fact, all Montford Point Marines fired the M-1 for qualification on the rifle range; even those initially issued the '03. That M1903 Springfield rifle was a "piece" but it was never a "gun." The young men had a dizzying amount of new terms and material to learn, all of which they were expected to have learned yesterday.

If a boot dropped his piece, absolution could only come from sleeping with the piece when the miscreant hit the "sack" that night. There was a reason for sentencing a man to a very uncomfortable night. DIs believed that if a man dropped his piece, the front sight blade might be knocked off true, affecting the accuracy of the weapon. A fact, maybe, but the '03 was a sturdy weapon and besides, the Springfield rifles issued to the men had hooded front sights to keep that from happening; but there is no doubt that the DIs were intent on instilling in the men respect for their equipment, especially equipment that a man needed to survive in battle.

Home Sweet Home

"We had 10-man huts, made out of, I wouldn't say cardboard, but it was a similar material, and the huts had wooden floors and big windows for plenty of air. Ten men per hut, so we had four huts per platoon."[1]

The thin-walled "homosote" huts where recruits lived while undergoing training were painted green, unheated and had no running water. Nearby were six heads (white-painted wooden bathroom buildings) separate from the huts. Each head had thirty-four sinks with mirrors, a row of ten commodes lined one wall (there were no partitions for privacy) and there was a single three-foot long "gang" urinal. Recruits standing guard duty fed a coal-burning furnace in the head that supplied both heat and hot water. Each head accommodated 75 men, who got barely five minutes in the morning to relieve themselves, brush their teeth and shave.

Discipline, the Hard Way

The men were now subject to the "Articles for the Government of the United States Navy, 1930"—military laws, many of which were unchanged from the nineteenth century, known to the men as "Rocks and Shoals." The laws ensured good order and discipline in the navy and Marine Corps. For example, Article 8[2] (there were seventy articles in all) warned the men that, among other things, anyone:

1. Who is guilty of profane swearing, falsehood, drunkenness, gambling, fraud, theft, or any other scandalous conduct tending to the destruction of good morals;
2. Or is guilty of cruelty toward or oppression or maltreatment of any person subject to his orders;
3. Or quarrels with, strikes, or assaults, or uses provoking or reproachful words, gestures, or menaces toward any person in the Navy ... could be awarded a court-martial.

In spite of the prohibition against swearing, some of the "old salts" at the time were notorious for their profanity and demonstrated daily that the term "cuss like a sailor" applied to Marines as well. The language came as quite a shock to young men reared in church-going families, but others took up the habit, believing it made them appear tough and manly.

The men learned of the "Rocks and Shoals" in classes and had to conform to the articles. These were harsh, and an individual's rights were a distant second concern in matters of discipline. (The more modern Uniform Code of Military Justice replaced the Rocks and Shoals in May 1950.)

Private Brewer's platoon had three white drill instructors: an experienced platoon sergeant, a corporal, and a private first class. While on a conditioning hike in the early stages of the training, Private Brewer's platoon, with the drill instructors marching alongside the column, came to a low-lying swampy area of standing water. Sensibly, as a civilian would think, the boot at the front of the platoon's file naturally turned to walk around the swamp. The drill instructor stormed to the front shouting, "Who told you to walk around that pond? You come back here and walk through it."[3] The drill instructor led the entire platoon into the swamp. When they got in the middle, he gave the command to "Halt." Then he had the men do exercises, including push-ups, in that water until everyone was soaking wet. It was the Marine Corps's way. When ordered to march in a certain direction, a Marine must learn to do exactly that. There was some consolation for the men because the DI caught a cold and was hoarse for several weeks.

During one of many close order drill periods, Private Brewer's platoon was marched to a paved area of the camp. Their manual of arms with the rifles had been sloppy, not up to standards, in the DI's eyes. When recruits, black or white, executing the manual failed to move with the desired snap, their hands smartly and audibly striking the wooden stocks of their rifles, DIs were not pleased. All DIs have a fix for such poor performance, and Private Brewer's were no different. His DI ordered the men to ground their pieces, get on their knees and beat the pavement with their bare hands. Private Brewer said that was when "I lost my nice high school class ring." DIs are *very impatient.* "I felt I didn't have time to take that ring off and put it in my pocket, because that would just cause more trouble; it tore up my ring."[4] The men learned, took another step toward becoming Marines.

After noon chow, the recruits usually had a small amount of free time in their huts before training resumed. Since they were early in the training cycle, they still had much to learn. After the recruits fell out for afternoon training, drill instructors routinely inspected their huts to see if everything was "squared away" (neat and orderly) and no personal property was adrift. In the 1940s many black men wore hair grease to keep their hair down, and one recruit in Private Brewer's platoon had left his can of hair grease on his sack after the noon break. He had simply forgotten to stow it (put something away) properly. All DIs were firm believers in the beneficial effects of fresh air so open windows were SOP (Standing Operating Procedure) for the huts. However, Montford Point lay on the banks of the New River in the coastal plain and there was sand everywhere; the camp was very dusty. Not only had the young man left a can of hair grease on his blanket, he had failed to clean the dust off his sack.

An unhappy drill instructor burst from the hut. As a lesson for all the recruits, as in "*You will stow all personal gear as instructed!*" the DI made the young man take the can of hair grease and a handful of sand, mix them together, rub the mess in his hair and wear that for the rest of the day.[5]

Humor, DI Style

After high school, Private Brewer had had a year of ROTC at Tuskegee Institute where he learned the manual of arms and close order drill. Some of his fellow recruits had little if any exposure to drill so the DIs had them practice the manual of arms while facing each other, often for an hour or more. Two recruits in particular had trouble with the manual so the drill instructor positioned them in the company street and told them to argue as loudly as they could, about who was the worst Marine. One shouted, "I'm the *worst* Marine in this whole Corps!" and the other would shout back, "No, you're not! *I'm* the worst!" Watching their performance, Private Brewer, still in ranks, laughed aloud. His drill instructor heard, swiveled his head around, eyes fixed on Brewer as he called out so everyone could hear, "Oh, you're laughing, Marine. We got a laughing boy here!" Then came the words no recruit ever wanted to hear, "Come on out here." So, while the two recruits continued to argue in the company street, Private Brewer took a personal tour of Montford Point Camp, running at double-time, with his eight and a half pound '03 Springfield held at high port, for an hour. The only time Private Brewer ever got in trouble in the Marine Corps was for laughing at those two recruits.[6]

Recruiting Problems Worsen

In September, there were 239 blacks at Montford Point. By the end of October, only 647 of the planned 1,200 black recruits had volunteered and of those only 428 were now on active duty. At Marine Corps Headquarters Brigadier General (Brig. Gen.) Keller E. Rockey, Director, Division of Plans and Policies, told the Lieutenant General Commandant that the strict occupational qualifications Headquarters placed on potential black enlistees, that is, trying to enlist only men who already had the skills needed in a defense battalion, were to blame. General Rockey wrote that it was "doubtful if even white recruits" could be enlisted under such rigid restrictions. He proposed a modified program for black recruits. Blacks would be enlisted for general duty, and upon completing boot camp would be sent to specialist schools only if a "colored school" was available; otherwise, instructors would come to Montford Point Camp to conduct the special schools required. Holcomb agreed to relax the standards for admitting black recruits; the new standards became *the same as for whites* (emphasis added).[7]

Training Toughens

The men learned to negotiate the obstacle course, hand-to-hand fighting and the use of the rifle other than shooting while getting more physical education training interspersed with many lectures on combat. Arriving in October, Private Arvin

"...Recruits in training to take their places as fighting Leathernecks in the U.S. Marine Corps, run the rugged obstacle course at Camp Lejeune, NC [Montford Point Camp]. The Marine recruits have shown such excellent results in their aptitudes and leadership capacities that an expanded Navy recruiting program is now underway." April 1943. Pat Terry. Still Picture Branch (NNSP), National Archives, Washington, DC.

L. "Tony" Ghazlo, a jujitsu instructor in civilian life, quickly became the hand-to-hand combat instructor for the camp. Another Private, Ernest "Judo" Jones, joined with Ghazlo to demonstrate jujitsu moves and teach classes to the recruits.[8]

Rifle Qualification

The Corps has tried over the years, with varying levels of success, to hold to the creed that every Marine is a rifleman, regardless of his job specialty. For Privates, the lowest rank and at the lowest pay grade, E–7, earning only $21.00 per month, there were compensation incentives for a man to fire well. A $5.00 boost in pay each month was given to those men qualifying as experts and $3.00 additional for those qualifying as sharpshooters; marksman, the lowest qualification, got no pay boost.[9] A "new" rifle marksmanship course implemented in 1940 governed the training of all Marines.[10] Those who qualified earned the right to wear a shooting badge on their uniform blouses.

In fact, numbers from that time claim that the Corps's marksmanship program succeeded in making *most* Marines into riflemen. Qualification figures for the year 1942 at the famous West Coast rifle range at Camp Matthews show that 88 percent of the 70,000 men who fired the new marksmanship course qualified with the rifle. (The numbers include soldiers from the U.S. Army's nearby Camp Callan as well.)[11] The 88 percent qualification rate for recruits might legitimately raise eyebrows today. Were the rifle range personnel at Camp Matthews too lenient with alibis, allowing extra time or extra rounds for weak shooters? Did the men in the butts (target pits) who marked each shot on the target allow claims that rounds were key holed (two bullets through one hole) rather than disking a miss? We have no way of knowing. However, a generation later, the qualification rate for recruits at one depot was a dismal 35 percent, and it took a new, hard-eyed Weapons Battalion commander who brooked neither excuses nor unprofessional conduct to bring the qualification rate for recruits up to an acceptable 80 percent.[12]

The first Montford Point recruits drilled and trained with the bolt-action M1903 Springfield rifle. In November, after preliminary (non-firing) marksmanship training at Montford Point, Private Brewer's platoon was ready for the intensive live firing course on the rifle range located on the south shore downriver at Stone Bay, the same ranges used by all Marines at New River. Some of the men had never fired a rifle.

In accordance with the prescribed course of fire, before stepping onto a .30 caliber range, reservists (and every one of the black recruits were reservists) were required to fire a 50-foot course with .22 caliber rifles to learn the basic techniques of sight alignment and trigger squeeze. However, the blacks did not shoot on the .22 caliber course but went directly to the .30 caliber course.[13] The decision to do so may have been made for the same reason black Marines received no training in handling rocket launchers, satchel charges, flame throwers, or hand grenades, and no

"Judo instruction is one of the high spots in the life of the latest addition to the Leatherneck Marines here. An instructor shows a recruit how to make the enemy's bayonet useless. Cpl. Arvin Lou Ghazlo, USMC, giving judo instruction to Pvt. Ernest C. Jones, USMCR." (L-R: Jones, Ghazlo.) Montford Point Camp, NC, April 1943. Still Picture Branch (NNSP), National Archives, Washington, DC.

training in rifle squad tactics. The blanket rationale — the author found it nowhere in writing — seems to have been this: Black Marines will not fight as riflemen, therefore there is no need for that training. It was a policy that would later cause the Corps some embarrassment in the press.

The Montford Point men did not stay at Stone Bay overnight because segregation required separate barracks, and there were none at Stone Bay. Therefore, trucks transported the blacks of the first recruit platoons to the rifle range early every morning and brought them back at the end of each day.[14]

To qualify with the .30 caliber rifle, the black recruits, all Class III Reserves, fired the "D" course at Able and Dog targets from a range of 200 yards. The "D" course is shown in Figure 2.

Range (yd)	Type of fire	Time	Shots	Target	Position	Sling
200	Slow	No limit	10	A	Prone	Loop
200	Slow	No limit	10	A	5 Kneeling 5 Sitting	Loop
200	Slow	No limit	10	A	Standing	Loop
200	Rapid	60 sec	10	D	Prone from Standing	Hasty
200	Rapid	60 sec	10	D	Sitting from Standing	Loop

Figure 2: "D" Course of fire

On the Able target, a shot dead center in the bulls-eye (indicated by a circular white disk placed by the men of the pit crew in the bullet hole through the bulls-eye) was worth five points, and point value decreased as black disks covered bullet holes in the concentric rings more distant from the bull. A complete miss ("Maggie's Drawers," a red flag waved across the front of the target by the pit crew) earned no points. A score of 226 or better (250 points were possible) earned a man the coveted Expert badge; 215 to 225 earned a Sharpshooter's badge, and 195 to 214 got the shooter a Marksman's badge.[15] While the men were on the firing line each had a Marine sitting by him to act as coach. The coach spotted the location of the recruit's shots and then advised the shooter how to adjust his sights to hit the bulls-eye. Unfortunately for Private Brewer's platoon, at the range their '03s were taken away and replaced by the new and unfamiliar semi-automatic M-1. "When he [the coach] told me to make a certain change, I did and it was worse because the sights were different on the two rifles."[16] The first time on the range Private Brewer, an outstanding competition shooter at Tuskegee Institute, did not qualify because on record day he had to fire an unfamiliar rifle.

"Acting Jacks"

Before the first black recruits completed training, the white drill instructors sought out men who showed an ability to learn quickly, men with the maturity and self-confidence to take on a leadership role. Selected men worked as assistants to the drill instructors in their own platoons. The recruits called them "acting Jacks."[17] This was a first step in developing black noncommissioned officers (NCOs), the corporals and sergeants who would eventually take over and train other blacks. In peacetime, that process might take years. In the pre-war Marine Corps it was not uncommon to see a private first class with a four-year service stripe (hash mark) on his sleeve.

However, the Marine Corps was fielding a black defense battalion with a wide range of job specialties, including cooks, administrative clerks, mechanics, drivers, radio and radar operators, telephone wiremen, gunners, armorers, fire control technicians, sound detector equipment operators, and more. Some of the billets called for seasoned NCOs with twelve or more years' experience. There was a sense of urgency as men began training, preparing as quickly as they could complete boot camp. Plans required that eventually all of the enlisted men in the battalion would be black, from the battalion sergeant major to the lowest private. Promotions depended on a man's demonstrated ability. For some, promotion would come rapidly.

Col. Woods, the battalion commanding officer, wrote to the Marine Corps's Director of Recruiting:

> *Thank you for getting us some excellent recruits. They are doing fine and are most enthusiastic and I am sure they are doing their level best to make good. We have to train the organization to operate, maintain, and repair the equipment that belongs to the Composite Battalion, therefore have to run our own schools.*
>
> *The men recruited have, in general, shown splendid aptitude for the service.... At present we have six probable rejections, but so far none of these has been for inaptitude.*[18]

The first black Marines had passed their trial period, at least in Col. Woods's eyes. They opened the door for others of their race.

With Graduation Comes Further Change

At the end of November 1942, soon after completion of their marksmanship training, 198 Montford Point Marines graduated from boot camp as full-fledged Marines. They were the first of their race to complete the most difficult military service's rite of passage into manhood. Only weeks earlier they came to Montford Point by ones and twos, civilians from different backgrounds and parts of the country. They were men who shared little more than the common desire to become Marines. Now they had achieved that goal. They entered into a fellowship of arms that had heretofore been the sole province of white males. The experience of shared hardships bound them forever to each other and to every man, regardless of race, who ever claimed the title "U.S. Marine." Men would try, and for years refuse, to acknowledge them as equals, but no one could deny the fact of their accomplishment, nor take it away. To this day, their confidence and deep pride is an almost tangible thing.

A few sewed on the single chevron of a private first class, an assistant cook, a drummer or a trumpeter. Looking back on his boot camp experience, Brewer said, "I think the Marine Corps did a good job in selecting the drill instructors and officers that were sent there to train us because I never really experienced or noticed any racial overtones. They were tough, tough but fair."[19]

The Rifle Company (Reinforced) of the 51st Composite Defense Battalion was activated by Battalion General Order No. 6–42 on December 1, 1942, with 2d Lt. Cade Strickland as company commander, not as a combat unit but as an administrative organization for the men who would be trained as cooks, bandsmen, clerks, truck drivers or communicators. By the end of December, there were 14 PFCs and 165 privates in the company. A General Support Battery with 155mm guns and the 90mm antiaircraft group activated as well on the same date.

The men responsible for making assignments for the new Marines matched ability with the job in the case of newly promoted Private First Class (PFC) Herb Brewer. He went to the 90mm antiaircraft group. "I had had some surveying at Tuskegee

"One of the first black Marines to graduate from recruit training at Montford Point Camp stands in front of one of the one hundred and eight "homosote" huts where blacks were billeted at the camp. Note the hooded front sight blades on the Springfield M1903 rifles. Photo probably dates to late autumn, 1942, before M-1 Garand semi-automatic rifles became standard issue for the black Marines." Used with permission of the Montford Point Marine Museum, Camp Lejeune, NC.

Institute learning about angles and things like that, so I was assigned to the fire control section in one of the [90mm antiaircraft gun] batteries there. Our job was to aim the guns. At that time we didn't have radar [black operators and repair technicians had yet to be trained]." However, Brewer's battery did have "a device called a director and we had a range finder so that by observing the plane we could compute its range and then the director would estimate its speed and calculate the firing lead necessary to hit the plane. So that's what became my assignment: a fire control technician."[20]

These new black Marines welcomed their first off-base liberty and a chance to go into town, relax and socialize now that the pressure of boot camp was behind them. They were young men, physically fit and bursting with excitement and full of energy and life, for they had been too long away from the pleasures of a town, any town. They were ready to catch up on good times they had missed.

No blacks had ever proven themselves by enduring Marine boot camp to earn the right to wear the eagle, globe and anchor device on their lapels. They wore sharply pressed forest green uniforms with the black leather belt and brass buckle, shoes polished and gleaming. Some spent fifty-four dollars to buy the dress blue uniform to wear on liberty. They were proud to be Marines, serving their country in time of war.

The Enlisted Club at Montford Point Camp. Also called "the slop chute," it was a place where the men could relax and socialize with a soda or cold beer after normal duty hours. The sailor in the foreground is a Medical Corpsman. No date. Used with permission of the Montford Point Marine Museum, Camp Lejeune, NC.

They were about to meet people for whom that meant nothing.

There were problems. Brewer said, "I didn't go anywhere because the leave was just for a few days and it was too far to come back to Texas. Some of the fellows did get into trouble because they were seen [in uniform] on leave and accused of impersonating Marines. A lot of people weren't familiar with the fact that the Marine Corps had accepted us. Several Marines were arrested off base and held and had to call the camp."[21]

When the 1st Marine Division came to Marine Barracks New River in 1941 to train for war, locals soon threw up many "joints" across Highway 24 outside the military reservation. Some were little more than tents or shanties, all beckoning to young Marines in search of a little fun while on liberty. Selling beer and sometimes rotgut moonshine liquor, their main reason for being was to separate the young men from their money. Fortunately, in this case, they catered to whites only.

December 21 saw the activation of the 75mm pack howitzer battery. The battalion was taking shape.

Racial Attitudes On-base and Off-base

The new Marines soon learned that travel alone to any other part of the sprawling New River base, now re-named Camp John A. Lejeune, was not permitted. As Turner Blount said, "You wasn't allowed to go to mainside. That's off limits."[22] To go to mainside, black Marines had to be in the company of a white Marine. There were outdoor movie theatres at mainside, but black Marines had to sit or stand in the back. There was commercial bus service with stops on the highways outside the base to Jacksonville. Black Marines had to sit in the back of those buses *if* the bus stopped to pick them up or if the bus did not pull away after white Marines filed aboard (whites waited in one line, blacks in another), and providing there was room (at times drivers would ignore black Marines waiting at the stops and speed past them).

When the black Marines arrived in town, even if only passing through to take the bus to nearby Kinston, Wilmington, or New Bern, they found that many of the residents of Jacksonville and in surrounding areas openly expressed their racist feelings toward them. There were exceptions, for the men met some whites who treated them fairly and with the same respect due any man.

The black Marines believed (then and today) that white civilians in Onslow County were apprehensive about truckloads of blacks carrying rifles on state highways to get to the rifle range at Stone Bay. That procedure changed in 1943 when blacks going to the rifle range marched to the boat landing at Montford Point and boarded landing craft that motored a few miles down New River to rifle ranges. At the end of the day, the men loaded back aboard the boats to return to camp. Glenn J. White recalls, "They said we might want to take off on the way out" if they were on trucks, so the men traveled by landing craft downriver to the ranges.[23]

10

Changes Come Quickly

The President Intercedes

Great change was in the offing. President Roosevelt decided to abolish volunteer enlistments in the armed forces for men between the ages of 18 to 37, on December 5, 1942. Starting in January 1943, all men in that age bracket were subject to call-up through the Selective Service System. Subsequently, the navy, Marine Corps, and Coast Guard established a quota—10 percent of all new accessions—for black recruits. For the year 1943, a quota of ten percent of its new recruits could mean the addition of as many as 15,400 more blacks in the Corps.[1] However, at the same time, the Marine Corps was permitted to continue to enlist 17-year-old volunteers and to encourage draftees to volunteer for the Corps.[2]

Token Compliance

If anyone in the Marine Corps expected that the composite battalion announced in the May 1942 press release would mark the extent of black service in the Corps, one token battalion of about 1,200 men, then those hopes were dashed by the President's decision. The Lt. Gen. Commandant knew the decision was coming. A December 26, 1942, memorandum to the director, Division of Plans & Policies, listed proposed assignments for black Marines according to

the type of duty which can best be performed by colored personnel and at the same time disturb the Marine Corps as little as possible from mingling with Negroes:
  (a) Composite battalions (up to twelve hundred a year)
  (b) Messmen's branch (about thirty-five hundred)
  (c) Large Marine Corps bases for assignment to the following duties: (1) messmen in large general messes; (2) chauffeurs; (3) messengers, post exchange clerks, and janitors: (4) maintenance and policing.[3]

As a first step, the all-white Mess Branch became the Commissary Branch, and a Messman's Branch was created for black volunteers.[4] Patterning it after the navy's

Steward Branch, Headquarters even changed the name of the branch from Messman to Steward. Melvin Borden, one of the later stewards, said he "worked with generals a lot," and his duties generally included "cooking and baking, serving food and drink, working at clubs and parties."[5] Plans were made to assign one steward for every six officers, but it soon became clear that there were not enough volunteers. The ratio of stewards to officers was cut back drastically.

Overwhelming Numbers

Could the Marine Corps train and assign over 15,000 blacks while ensuring they remained segregated? At Headquarters Marine Corps, the Division of Plans and Policies scrambled to solve this problem. Headquarters had expected that composite defense battalions would receive their full complements of black enlisted men, about 1,200 men. However, after Roosevelt's decision, there remained the unanswered question of what to do with the remainder of the 15,000 black draftees that 1943 would bring. Some of the men would necessarily become permanent party at the training camp, but in what other units might large numbers be assigned? In a March 20 memorandum, Major General (Maj. Gen.) Harry Schmidt, acting as commandant in Lt. Gen. Holcomb's absence, outlined plans to assign the influx of black Marines as follows:

> Messman branch
>   Officers' Messes (combat units)
>   General Officers' quarters (public)
> Organized Combat Units
>   Composite Defense Battalions, Fleet Marine Force
>   Separate Infantry Battalions, Fleet Marine Force
> Depot Companies (including Fleet Marine Force units)
> Motor Transport units (including Fleet Marine Force units)
> Special Detachments, Marine Corps Activities in U.S.
> Guard Detachments, U.S. Naval Activities[6]

A full-strength infantry battalion at that time called for almost 900 men, so Maj. Gen. Schmidt clearly intended to use the maximum practicable number of black Marines in combat units. However, he went on to identify the lack of noncommissioned officers as the most serious chokepoint to forming and training blacks. Schmidt appears to have been aware of the army's experience with blacks in World War I, where "in nearly all cases to intermingle colored and white enlisted personnel in the same organization" led to "trouble and disorder." Schmidt advised Marine commanders that black units should be commanded by men "who thoroughly knew their [Negroes'] individual and racial characteristics and temperaments."[7]

Was it feasible to create additional defense battalions for that many blacks? No. One reason, as explained by Maj. Gen. Schmidt in his March 20 memo, was the lack of black noncommissioned officers (NCOs) for that many battalions.

Besides, existing plans called for only six additional white defense battalions and for one additional black defense battalion to be activated in late 1943 or early 1944. In actuality, there was no need to activate the units proposed by Maj. Gen. Schmidt because the monthly Selective Service draft calls never met the quota. By December 1943, the Marine Corps had only 12,400 blacks on active duty (there were 2,484 volunteers and 9,916 Selective Service accessions in that month), far fewer than the expected 15,400 black inductions through the draft for 1943 alone.[8]

In the same March 20 memo, Maj. Gen. Schmidt also wrote that the Marine Corps must consider the black press. "Every possible step should be taken to prevent the publication of inflammatory articles by the Negro press. Such control is largely outside the province of the Marine Corps, but the Marine Corps can, by supplying the Negro press with suitable material for publication and offering them the cooperation of our Public Relations Division, properly encourage a better standard of articles on the Negro in the military service."[9] Soon, photographers from the Office of War Information descended upon the 51st Composite Defense Battalion to help provide suitable material. Now held in the Library of Congress, they show newly arrived recruits drawing equipment, practicing saluting, going through a wide range of training activities. The men are shown at gun drills and live fire training on a variety of weapons such as M-3 "Stuart" light tanks, World War I era French guns, the M1918 *Grande Puissance Filloux* (GPF) 155mm artillery pieces, and machine guns. Others show men operating field radios, exiting the camp chapel (which is still standing and in use in 2006) and posing stiffly in an administrative office. Overall, the Corps tried to show the new camp and the new Marines in the most positive possible manner.

Black Press Response

Black newspapers across the country picked up the OWI photos, several of which are included in this book, and took a patriotically supportive tone in articles accompanying the photos. Two informative examples of early reporting by the black press are the *Philadelphia Tribune*'s "Negro Recruit Training Now in Progress" article (see chapter 8) and "Civilians Made into Marines at LeJeune," which appeared in November 1943 in the widely circulated *Baltimore Afro-American*.[10] Like the *Tribune*'s article, the latter was supportive and emphasized the difficulty of the training for black Marines. Patriotic newspaper articles about black Marines continued throughout the war, but by 1944 black correspondents and editorial writers took a more critical position.

Critical Problems in the Pacific

At the same time the Division of Plans & Policies prepared for massive numbers of black draftees, the critical supply lessons learned in August of the previous

"Two recruits in a light tank during training in mechanized warfare at Montford Point Camp, NC. April 1943." The tank was one of the 51st Composite Defense Battalion's M-3 Stuart tanks. Pat Terry. Still Picture Branch (NNSP), National Archives, Washington, DC.

year on the confused beaches of Guadalcanal demanded attention and resolution. The supplies and equipment needed by the 19,000 Marines at Guadalcanal had been winched out of the deep holds of large transports and cargo ships, hoisted over the side and loaded into small landing craft bobbing like corks on the long swells in the transport area off the beachhead. After the supplies arrived at the water's edge, everything had to be hand-lifted and then piled onto the beaches by long lines of sailors and Marines.

Navy concerns for the problem were evident. COMTRANSDIV Eight (Commander, Transport Division 8) wrote in a November 1942 letter to COMPHIB-FORSOPAC (Commander of Amphibious Forces, Southern Pacific), "The bottleneck of unloading is still in the Shore Party.... Unloading boats on a beach is extremely strenuous physical labor and the Shore Party must be organized into reliefs if the unloading is to extend over 12 hours."[11]

The supply system desperately needed improvement in the ship-to-shore transfer of massive amounts of essential supplies but especially in the subsequent shifting, sorting and stockpiling in dumps ashore. From dumps, the supplies, all of the "beans, bullets, and bandages" that kept the riflemen moving, had to get into the hands of the Marines on the front lines. Navy and Marine planners were learning day by day from their mistakes, and they forged ahead in developing the boats and craft needed in the ship to shore movement, refining procedures, and streamlining procedures at supply depots in the theatre of operations. Headquarters Marine Corps recognized the need for more manpower to move supplies from the high water mark, the laborious work of stevedores.

SECTION III

1943

11

Proving Amphibious Doctrine

A Pivotal Event

The island of Guadalcanal was declared "secure" on February 9, 1943. It was the longest of the Marines' island battles, and it marked a critical turning point in the war. Lt. Gen. Vandegrift, awarded the Medal of Honor for leading the 1st Marine Division to victory, wrote about Guadalcanal, "We were as well trained and as well armed as time and our peacetime experience allowed us to be. We needed combat to tell us how effective our training, our doctrines, and our weapons had been. We tested them against the enemy, and we found that they worked. From that moment in 1942, the tide turned, and the Japanese never again advanced."[1] So began the shift away from a defensive way of thinking that would change the organization and even the names of the defense battalions. The Marines were poised to begin an offensive toward the Central Pacific that would continue until the Japanese were defeated.

Amphibious Training

The Marine Corps's amphibious mission to attack from the sea to seize advanced naval bases was still evolving. In order for Marines to force their way ashore to seize, garrison and defend their objective, the navy had to first *get them there*. In the pre-war navy, strapped for funds by an isolationist Congress, ships to haul Marines were at the bottom of every blue-suiter's list of critical needs. In 1943, involved in a two-ocean war, the navy was hurriedly rebuilding after Pearl Harbor. But internal power struggles between old-line admirals who wanted to build more battleships and young upstart admirals who saw the future in aircraft carriers overshadowed Marine Corps needs. With the nation fully on a war footing, Congress loosened the purse strings for funding new ships and the navy's Bureau of Ships in Washington was playing a game of catch up in finding the right numbers and mix of amphibious ships to do the job.

73

As a result of lessons learned in the pre-war Fleet Landing Exercises, existing ships and craft left over from the post–World War I navy failed to accommodate advances in amphibious doctrine. However, new ships had to be funded, designed and built, so what could the navy and Marine Corps use in the interim until the right ships slid down the ways? The high-speed transport serves as a good example of a kind of "make do" expedient employed at the time.

As early as 1937 Marine officers suggested that destroyers might solve the problems of a shortage of both amphibious transports and naval gunfire support ships. Here the Marines had their eyes not on any of the navy's coveted modern ships (which Marines had not a prayer of getting), but on ships in the mothballed fleet of old four-stack flush deck destroyers from World War I. From modified destroyers, the Marines said, "troops could move quickly close into shore and disembark under protection of the ships' guns." The USS *Manley* (DD 74), an old flush-deck, four-stack destroyer built during World War I, became the test ship. Shipyard workers removed all torpedo tubes, one gun, two boilers and their stacks to create a hold amidships for cargo and troops. After testing the ship in a Caribbean exercise in 1940, the navy re-designated *Manley* as the lead ship of a new class, APD-1 (the APD designation meant she was a high-speed transport: "A" denotes amphibious, "P" indicates transport while "D" is for destroyer, and the number one is for the first ship of the class). Five of *Manley's* sister ships also became APDs.

Typically, the navy overlooked all but the most basic amenities for embarked Marines so the troop compartment below decks was nothing more than an empty space. There was no ventilation, no bunks (steel decks were deemed good enough for the Marines to sleep on), and only four washbasins to accommodate 130 men! It took a high-level investigation, launched by one Marine's letter to his congressional representative, to get the berthing space upgraded. At any rate the expedient APD worked, and before the war was over the navy converted another 133 destroyers and destroyer escorts to the transport role.[2]

Like their white counterparts, the black Marines of the 51st had to learn the basics of how to get ashore from a variety of different types and sizes of ships such as the high-speed transports (APD), cargo (AP), attack transport (AK), and other landing ships and craft. In order for Marines loaded with their combat gear to transfer from the attack transports into landing craft bobbing alongside some 20 or 30 feet below, the men had to climb down cargo nets draped over the sides of the ships.

From a new type ship, a Landing Ship, Dock (LSD), Marines might load into smaller landing craft carried inside the ship in the well deck without having to negotiate a cargo net. An LSD's squared-off stern was actually a gate that, when the ship took on seawater to ballast down her stern, opened to the sea so the smaller craft could enter and exit though the gate.

Among other new craft were the versatile seagoing, shallow-draft, diesel powered landing craft, infantry (LCI). These could carry 200 men and 30 tons of cargo and discharged the men directly onto the beach from twin ladders on either side of the bow. The landing ship, tank (LST), also called "Long, Slow Target," had a shallow forward draft, was ram-equipped and capable of beaching to unload men and equipment directly on the shore. Smaller craft, not fully seaworthy, were the landing craft, tank (LCT) capable of carrying four medium tanks or 150 tons of cargo, the 50-foot long landing craft, medium (LCM) and the 36-foot long landing craft, vehicle and personnel (LCVP).[3]

Finally, the vehicle that would play a vital role in World War II amphibious operations was the Landing Vehicle, Tracked (LVT), also called "Alligator" and later "amtrac," short for amphibian tractor. Unarmed, the early LVT (1) weighed 17,300 pounds, could travel at 25 miles per hour on land and nine miles per hour in water. It was a track-laying vehicle propelled afloat not by a propeller, but by flanges attached to the tracks.[4] While LSTs, LCTs, LCMs, and LCVPs could not cross shallow water over a reef, the LVT had no such limitation and could easily traverse such an obstacle.

The Pacific Offensive Begins

Driven from Guadalcanal, the Japanese shifted their operations to Munda airfield on New Georgia in the Central Solomon Islands. Late in February 1943, an army division, accompanied by the 3d Marine Raider Battalion, took the Russells Group, a cluster of islands about 12 miles from the northwest tip of Guadalcanal, against no opposition. By constructing an airfield there, and installing early warning radars, the Russells became not only an early warning station for Guadalcanal but also a stepping-stone in the advance on Rabaul.

The second stage of the offensive against Rabaul began in late June 1943. In the first of a series of three amphibious operations, units of the I Marine Amphibious Corps (IMAC) landed on the island of New Georgia in the Central Solomons to secure air bases to support further advances in a two-pronged drive up the Solomons toward Rabaul. A compact maze of islands of volcanic origin, the twelve major islands of the New Georgia Group lie between Bougainville to the northwest and Guadalcanal to the southeast. The Japanese airfield at Munda on New Georgia fell to the Marines on August 5. The northward advance up the Solomon Islands chain continued with landings in August and again in October.

The Central Solomons campaign demonstrated improvements in amphibious landing techniques. Large numbers of troops and vast amounts of supplies arrived on the beaches quickly. This was due in part to the increased availability of the right kinds of ships and landing craft, the new LCIs, LSTs, and LCMs needed to move the men and equipment.

Marines and soldiers attacked the last major island in the Northern Solomons, Bougainville, in November. The operation highlighted an old but familiar problem with supplies on the beaches; still more improvements were needed.

Developing the Supply Service

War-fighting supplies and materiel flowed from depots and ports in the United States to war theatres in the Pacific. There it was offloaded, sorted, and stored in dumps at major Base Depots on islands some distance from the fighting until needed (for locations and strengths of these units, see appendix C — Supply Service Base and Field Depots — August 31, 1944). Then the supplies went to Field Depots in the forward operational areas for use by combat units in amphibious operations. The Field Depots received and repaired equipment damaged in the island fighting and then returned the equipment to the owning units. The depots shared bases with Allies and the other services, first in the Territory of Hawaii, and then New Zealand, and as the war progressed, on New Caledonia, Guadalcanal and other islands.

Marine Base and Field Depots came under the administrative control of a higher headquarters, the Service of Supply. However, in a confusion of administrative and tactical oversight, theatre and area commanders exercised control over them as well. Subordinate to the theatres were IMAC (I Amphibious Corps) and the VAC (V Amphibious Corps). A corps is a fighting organization made up of two or more divisions with supply support provided by corps troops, and an army is likewise a fighting organization made up of two or more corps. Finally, through far-reaching change, some organizational clarity emerged when Headquarters, Fleet Marine Force, Pacific (FMFPac) came into existence in mid–1944, with Supply Service, FMFPac as a major subordinate element.[5]

As the war progressed and amphibious doctrine matured, units from the depots were attached for operational control to the amphibious corps for specific operations, reverting to their parent depot at specified dates after the operation was launched or becoming part of the island garrison when the fighting ceased. It was a manpower intensive system where organizations and procedures were constantly being tested and improved.

Tables of Organization for Marine Divisions included men to muscle boxes of supplies and materiel in and around dumps (see appendix D: Marine Division Service and Supply Units — World War II). Each had Service Battalions that included 455 men in a Service and Supply Company, and an Ordnance Company of 155 men to safely move ammunition across beaches and sort it into dumps and then move it forward to the riflemen and artillerymen, all in addition to the division's 744-man Pioneer Battalions that augmented the Shore Party. However, the divisions were seldom co-located with Field Depots, and a desperate need developed for men back at the Base Depots in the rear areas to satisfy the demand for huge tonnages of supplies that sustained the Pacific island assaults.

The Headquarters Solution

The thousands of blacks expected to come into the Corps through the Selective Service system proved to be an expedient solution for two problems facing

Headquarters. First, what to do with thousands of black draftees, and second, where to find more strong men to handle the tens of thousands of tons of supplies and equipment pouring ashore in an amphibious assault.

The solution: assign black Marines to companies as soon as they completed boot camp. They would work only as "labor troops," so the men needed no specialized training in infantry tactics or weapons. Furthermore, small company-sized units were easy to move from place to place as the need arose. Accordingly, Headquarters named the new unit a "Depot Company" (as in "Field or Base Depot") and prepared a Table of Organization approved February 12, 1943 (appendix E, Depot and Ammunition Companies 1943–1946, shows organizational diagrams). Early Marine Depot Companies consisted of three Marine officers and one hundred and ten enlisted men in a company headquarters element and two platoons.[6]

12

Segregation Is Still the Rule

Hit 'em Where It Hurts

As more black Marines graduated and received off-base liberty, there were more liberty incidents involving blacks and white bus drivers. Of course, the complaints about black Marines reached the base and Col. Woods. Herb Brewer said,

> Some of the people from the bus company called and complained that some of our people weren't sitting where they were supposed to sit. So the Commanding Officer, Colonel Woods, a very nice fellow from South Carolina, ordered Marine Corps trucks [from the 51st Composite Defense Battalion's Motor Transport Company] to go pick up our people. Colonel Woods said, "I don't want my Marines going through that." He was a very fair, very professional Marine. It was a help to have somebody like that in charge.[1]

Every time a Marine Corps truck loaded with black Marines came and went from Jacksonville, the bus companies lost fares. Col. Woods had hit that part of a booming war economy where it hurt most, and shortly the bus drivers got the message to pick up and discharge black Marines the same as whites.

The First Black DIs

Experienced white noncommissioned officers (NCOs), *any* experienced Marines, actually, were in very short supply. The Corps had expanded rapidly, and many of the old salts, the small but solid cadre of pre-war professional Marines, had been promoted to NCO ranks or commissioned as officers to fill the new infantry battalions in the FMF. When activating new units it was Standing Operating Procedure (SOP) in the Marine Corps to pull experienced men from existing units and replace them with newly trained men. The experienced men then formed a solid core for the new unit. Of course, the overall battle readiness of the unit giving up men suffered from the loss of trained, experienced members.

New units activating around the Corps needed such a leavening of experience.

This happened not only to the black units but occurred throughout the Corps. In March 1942, Headquarters Marine Corps broke one group of the 1st Marine Aircraft Wing, Marine Air Group (MAG) 11, into MAGs 12, 13, 14, and 15.[2] On the ground side, the 4th Marine Division had its roots in the shifting and redesignation of several other units. The 23d Marines began as infantry detached from the still-forming and training 3d Marine Division in February 1943, the same month that an artillery battalion became the genesis of the 14th Marines and engineer elements of the 19th Marines formed the start of the 20th Marines. In March the 24th Marines was organized, and then in May it was split in two to supply the men for the 25th Marines. The "old Salts" were spread very thin indeed.

Because of the competing demands for experienced white Marines, it was important that qualified blacks train as drill instructors at Montford Point as soon as possible. Therefore, six men were selected for training as drill instructors. Gilbert H. "Hashmark" Johnson and Edgar R. Huff were among several of the newly promoted privates first class that would become drill instructors.

A More Functional Organization

Col. Woods knew that the 51st Composite Defense Battalion, a combat unit, could not long continue all the functions required of a recruit depot. Headquarters Marine Corps (HQMC) approved his plan for a more workable organization at Montford Point in January. Other plans called for an eight-week-long Mess Attendant School and a sixteen-week-long Officers' Cooks and Stewards School at Montford Point.

Col. Woods implemented the many facets of his plan in early March 1942. The first change came with the standup of Headquarters and Service (H&S) Company, Headquarters Battalion (HQBN), Montford Point Camp, the organization responsible for all the "housekeeping" duties required of a satellite camp under the larger umbrella of the Camp Lejeune complex. Col. Woods became camp commander while Lieutenant Colonel (Lt. Col.) W. Bayard Onley took command of the 51st.

A Recruit Depot Battalion, commanded by the former Executive Officer (XO) of the 51st, Lt. Col. Theodore A. Holdahl, formed with the responsibility for all black boot camp training; thus, the 51st Composite Defense Battalion relinquished its recruit training responsibilities. Battery A of the 51st and all Marines in it became Company A, Recruit Depot Battalion.

Unfortunately, the 51st, preparing for war, became a manpower pool to draw upon when there was a billet to be filled that called for black Marines. For those other needs, such as security guards at the Naval Ammunition Depot, McAlester, Oklahoma, or at the Philadelphia Depot of Supplies, HQMC knew where to look.

On April 1, Headquarters Company, Messman Branch Battalion, came into being and two weeks later, that battalion became the Stewards Branch Battalion.

"A platoon of Negro 'boot recruits' listen to their drill instructor [Sgt. Gilbert Hubert Johnson] whose job is to turn them into finished Marines." This is "Hashmark" Johnson. Montford Point Camp was renamed Camp Gilbert H. Johnson at Camp Lejeune in his honor. Montford Point Camp, NC, ca. April 1943. Still Picture Branch (NNSP), National Archives, Washington, DC.

Company A (Assistant Stewards School) and Company B (Stewards Cook School) completed the Stewards Branch Battalion.

Along with the organizational changes came changes in building allocations within the camp area itself when areas of Montford Point Camp were designated as Camps No. 2 and 2A. The Stewards Branch Battalion occupied Camp 2 along Company Street West. Depot companies lived in barracks located along Company Street East. Camp 2A housed white officers and enlisted men. At the same time, HQMC authorized Col. Woods "to designate qualified colored personnel as band personnel, quartermaster personnel, engineer personnel, and commissary personnel."[3]

The 1st Marine Depot Company Activates

HQMC continued to work with FMF units to refine the supply system in the Pacific. The same manpower shortfalls identified in Shore Party operations before the war and in early operations in the Pacific still plagued the Marine supply system. In the Pacific, the men and material to fight the war moved by ship, and administrative loading or combat loading called for stevedores. The need for labor units, stevedores on the docks, strong backs and brute force muscle in the supply dumps, and hauling water, rations, and ammunition to the men fighting in the front lines was a problem with a solution at hand. After Guadalcanal, 1st Marine Division officers had reported that they needed at least 100 men for each vessel discharging cargo and someone at HQMC listened.

In the midst of the major changes taking place at Montford Point, a milestone event occurred. While the 51st had hardly begun training as the first black combat unit in the Corps, the 1st Marine Depot Company activated on March 8, 1943, under T/O E-701 with three officers (a company commander and two platoon leaders) and 110 enlisted. The senior NCOs were white. The other enlisted men were 101 black Marines at the lowest pay grades, privates (no rank chevron on their sleeves) in the seventh pay grade or privates first class (one rank chevron) in the sixth pay grade, all fresh from boot camp. One of the men became an Assistant Cook, sixth pay grade. Grouped into a headquarters element and two platoons, this was the first of the labor units so sorely needed in the Pacific.

As a labor unit, the men received no additional training in the use of weapons or tactics. One Marine later described the lot of the men assigned to a depot company: "There was no training" after boot camp, just "a hell of a lot of drilling. They were the drillingest people that you'd ever seen in your life."[4] The black Marines of the 1st Marine Depot Company left Montford Point in early April for San Diego, California, arriving on April 5. There they boarded a transport on April 16, 1943, and two days later sailed for Noumea on New Caledonia.

One source indicates the men sailed on the USS *HUNT* (DD-674), an error that needs to be rectified. The *Dictionary of American Naval Fighting Ships*, published by the Naval History Division of the Office of the Chief of Naval Operations, lists two destroyers with that name. Commissioned in 1920, the first USS *Hunt*, a Clemson class "flush decker," was transferred in 1940 to the United Kingdom where she was renamed HMS *Broadway*. Not until August 1, 1943, did the Fletcher class USS *Hunt* (DD-674) slide down the ways at Federal Shipbuilding & Drydock, Kearny, New Jersey. After its commissioning on September 22, Commander Frank P. Mitchell took *Hunt* out to Bermuda for shakedown followed by final alterations in the New York Navy Yard. *Hunt* cleared Norfolk for the Pacific on December 2, 1943, where she joined Vice Adm. Marc Mitscher's Fast Carrier Task Force 58.[5] While neither *Hunt* was in commission in April 1943, I have not been able to determine the correct name of the ship that took the company to the Pacific.

Understaffed Supply Units

Located northeast of Australia in the island area of the South Pacific known as Melanesia, the island of New Caledonia was a French possession with a French governor since 1853. Bordered on the east by the Coral Sea, the island is just over 200 miles in length and its widest point is less than 50 miles. Melanesia includes the Solomon Islands and the major island of New Guinea. The population is mainly Melanesian and European, with small groups of Wallisians, Tahitians, Indonesians, and Vietnamese. The main island is divided by a central mountain range creating a wet tropical east and a dry west side, with Noumea as its only city.

Located at Noumea were the I Marine Amphibious Corps (IMAC) and the headquarters of Marine Aircraft South Pacific (MASP), neither of which had any significant tactical function. Both were administrative headquarters responsible for training FMF Marines in the South Pacific and for providing supply support.[6] Maj. Gen. Charles F.B. Price's Samoan Defense Command was a third major headquarters for FMF Marines in the South Pacific. His command garrisoned American and British Samoa, Wallis Island, and Funafuti in the Ellice Group.

At New Caledonia were vast compounds of supplies, tank farms for fuel storage along with many maintenance, repair, and service facilities. Supply support for the Central Solomons campaign was to have come from facilities at Noumea, but an understaffed corps of laborers failed to maintain a smooth and uninterrupted flow of necessary supplies. The result was a confused backlog of equipment and supplies at New Caledonia and Guadalcanal that almost sidelined the New Georgia operation. Help, however slight, in the form of the black Marines of the 1st Marine Depot Company, was on the way.

These first black Marines arrived at Noumea and reported to the 1st Base Depot. Prior to their arrival, not even wounded men recovering at the Base Depot hospitals were exempt from serving in working parties loading and unloading ships! The Depot's unit history recorded that "these troops offered the first solution to the depot's labor problem." Back at Montford Point, the 2d and 3d Marine Depot

Companies stood up on April 23 and quickly shipped out for the Pacific. Also during April, the Marine Corps formed a new supply unit in the Pacific, the 4th Base Depot, using the usual procedure of taking the core of the new unit from existing units, in this case the 1st Base Depot on Noumea, and from the 2d and the 3d Base Depots on New Zealand.

The 4th Base Depot moved forward to Guadalcanal to help relieve the congestion and to bring order out of the general confusion. Its mission was to receive and store all supplies for the New Georgia operation and the Russells garrison. The 4th Base Depot would maintain a 60-day level of supplies for TOENAILS (codename for the operation to seize and occupy New Georgia in the Solomon Islands) and handle and load aboard ships all supplies for the (Army's) 43d Division and supporting troops on New Georgia.[7]

Growing Pains in the 51st

The 51st welcomed 1943 short of equipment, short of men qualified to act as instructors, and short on experienced men to act as the cadre for building a unit. The 51st had become a pool to draw on for men needed in the rapid expansion of other units at Montford Point. After a very short tenure as battalion commander, Lt. Col. Onley gave up command to Lt. Col. Floyd A. Stephenson, a veteran of the 4th Defense Battalion recently returned from the Pacific. Onley took command of HQBN, Montford Point Camp, and served as Col. Woods' executive officer.

Stephenson took command of the 51st but said later that he received no briefing on "the Negro program in the Marine Corps." He was a Southerner, a Texan, "where matters relating to Negroes are normally given the closest critical scrutiny."[8]

Stephenson may not have been aware at the time, but on Christmas Eve, 1942, the commandant had approved a surprising and somewhat premature study made by the Director, Division of Plans & Policies. The paper recommended the "authority of the Commander in Chief be obtained for the transfer of the 51st Composite Defense Battalion, by echelons, to the South Pacific beginning 1 April 1943."[9] Realistically, there was no way the battalion could have been ready for overseas deployment so soon.

Stephenson knew that the situation in the Pacific had changed, and there was no longer a need for composite defense battalions. He recommended that HQMC reorganize the 51st as a regular defense battalion according to T/O D-155A.[10] Col. Woods favorably endorsed the plan and HQMC approved it at the end of May. A Special Weapons Group replaced the Machine Gun Group. The new T/O included an artillery group made up of two batteries of four 155mm howitzers each to battle enemy ships. But the infantry and pack howitzers were taken from the battalion.

To defend against high-altitude enemy planes the anti-aircraft artillery group had three batteries of four 90mm guns each. The Special Weapons Group, made up of three large batteries, would deal with low flying enemy planes. These were:

DEFENSE BATTALION
TABLE OF ORGANIZATION D-155A
APPROVED 25 MAY 1942

43 OFFICERS USMC & USN
6 WARRANT OFFICERS USMC
1122 ENLISTED MEN USMC & USN

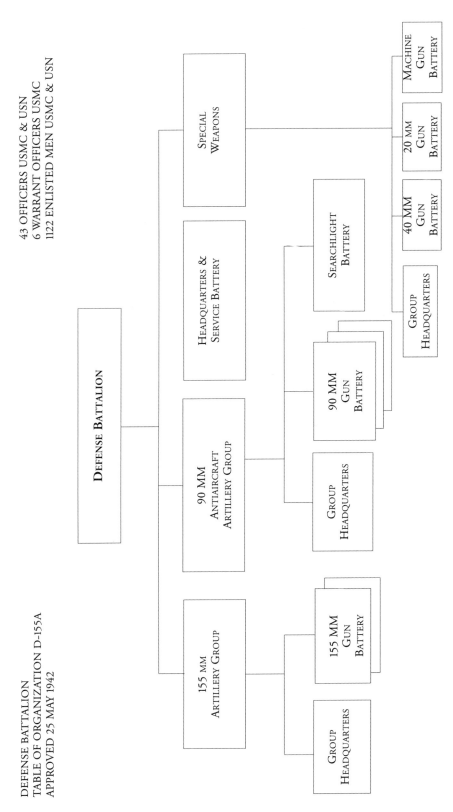

MAJOR ARMAMENT: 8 155 MM GUNS, 12 90 MM ANTIAIRCRAFT GUNS, 12 40 MM ANTIAIRCRAFT GUNS, 16 .50-CALIBER ANTIAIRCRAFT MACHINE GUNS, 30 .30-CALIBER ANTIAIRCRAFT MACHINE GUNS

- A 40mm Anti-aircraft (AA) Gun Battery of twelve Bofors "light" antiaircraft artillery (AAA) guns
- A 20mm Anti-aircraft Gun Battery of twelve Oerlikon "heavy" machine guns
- A Machine Gun Battery of sixteen .50-caliber "heavy" anti-aircraft machine guns and thirty .30-caliber anti-aircraft machine guns

The men knew nothing of the reason for the organizational changes, and the result was a growing anxiety. Did the loss of the rifle company and the 75mm pack howitzers, coming soon after the loss of the M-3 light tanks, mean that they would lose their status as a combat unit and be assigned to depot companies or as officers' stewards?[11] The D-155A T/O is shown in the preceding figure.[12]

The Camp Expands

The camp infrastructure continued to grow with the addition of a Schools Company and a Motor Transport Company to the Montford Point Camp HQBN. The 51st Composite Defense Battalion's Rifle Company (Rein) continued in existence but not as an infantry organization. Its new purpose was in forming depot companies for further transfer to the Pacific.

Of course, new recruit companies, numbered serially, continued to form at a rapid pace. By the end of April 1943, almost all DIs overseeing training of the eight recruit platoons were black sergeants and corporals. Among the DIs were Johnson and Huff, two men destined to become well known throughout the Corps in the coming years. The last white DI transferred in late May, and "Hashmark" Johnson took over as the recruit training battalion's field sergeant major. From that time forward, black NCOs conducted all recruit training at Montford Point.

A Preacher's Son Gets Drafted

Twenty-one-year-old Frederick Clinton Branch was the son of an African Methodist Episcopal Zion minister. Born in Hamlet, North Carolina, he was the fourth of seven sons. He graduated from high school in Mamaroneck NY and attended Johnson C. Smith University in Charlotte, North Carolina, before transferring to Temple University in Philadelphia in 1942.[13] His studies were interrupted when he was drafted in May 1943.[14]

Branch reported for induction at the army's Fort Bragg, near Fayetteville, North Carolina. A white Marine sergeant at the induction center chose Branch to

Opposite: Figure 1: The second Table of Organization approved for the 51st Defense Battalion. The 52d Defense Battalion formed under this T/O.

become a Marine, and he was sent to Montford Point Camp, arriving about the time when last white DI was transferred out of Montford Point. During his recruit training, Branch decided he could become a leader. After graduation he was assigned to the 51st Defense Battalion. "I read all the requirements to be an officer," he said, "and nowhere in there did it say anything about race." Branch wanted to become an officer, but he was black, and there were no black Marine officers. He said, "I was stubborn."[15]

An Alabaman Gets Called Up

Eugene Smith of Birmingham, Alabama, was too old to volunteer at nineteen. He was drafted. When he passed his induction physical, he learned that the Marine Corps had not met its quota for that month so Smith would become a Marine. He arrived at Jacksonville, North Carolina, on May 26, 1943. "A hick town full of hate for us" was his lasting impression of Jacksonville. Taken by truck out to the Montford Point Camp, Smith got the "rough" reception common to all recruits. To Smith the drill instructors' harsh demands during the early days were a "humiliating" experience, their intent to change the civilians into Marines as quickly as possible not immediately clear to the young man. "When I was in boot camp, no matter what was imposed on you, there was no one to complain to other than receive a TS (Tough Shit) slip and go see the chaplain." After his receiving experience, Smith joined the 74th recruit platoon and called one of the "little green huts" home for the next seven weeks. The training gave Smith no problems, and like countless other Marines before and after him, Smith's keepsakes today include a photograph of the 48 Marines of his boot camp platoon. The young men, posed on a bleacher, stand at attention in their khaki uniforms, faces stern, M-1 rifles at the order arms position. Clearly written on the photo are all the names so Smith will remember them. Smith still comments on the open racism he encountered as a "skinhead," in particular the camp's white Marines' use of the demeaning term "you people" when addressing black recruits. For all that, his boot camp experience was a good one, for he found the kind of discipline that would serve him well in the future.[16]

Managing the "New Departure"

Decision makers in the field needed clear guidance from up the chain of command on their dealings with the influx of blacks. A year after the announcement that opened the Corps to black enlistments, the guidance came down. Lt. Gen. Holcomb issued Letter of Instruction Number 421, classified "CONFIDENTIAL," to all Marine commanders in May 1943. "Since the inclusion of colored personnel in Marine Corps organizations is a new departure," Holcomb offered white Marines information and guidance for handling black Marines. Regarding the promotion of blacks he wrote, "While rapid promotion, when deserved, is necessary, it is essential that in no case shall there be colored noncommissioned officers senior to white men in the same unit, and desirable that few, if any, be of the same rank." In segregated America, few, if any, white men would work under a black supervisor. In fact, this policy was already in place at Montford Point Camp. By the end of May, the drill instructors at Montford Point were all black.

Holcomb concluded his letter with an admonition to his commanders. "All marines are entitled to the same rights and privileges under Navy Regulations. The colored marines have been carefully trained and indoctrinated. They can be expected to conduct themselves with propriety and become a credit to the Marine Corps. All men must be made to understand that it is their duty to guide and assist these men to conduct themselves properly, and to set them an example in conduct and deportment." Holcomb concluded by directing his officers to "see that all men are properly indoctrinated" in his instructions, "particularly when Negro troops are serving in the vicinity."[17]

By "all men," was Holcomb not referring to white Marines only? Did Holcomb believe that by simply writing a letter of instruction he could change deeply ingrained attitudes? That men who were born and grew up in America, living all their years in a Jim Crow society, could suddenly do an about face? Was that not expecting too much from even the stoutest, most disciplined Marines, some of whom the Corps had sent out only a few years earlier to bash their "little brown brothers?"

No black Marines ever saw Instruction No. 421 during the war, but promotion and reassignment policy caused some to suspect the existence of such a directive. Not until 1946 did the public learn of the existence of the instruction, and the black press took Brigadier General Franklin A. Harte, Director, Division of Public Information at Headquarters Marine Corps, to task in a series of scathing articles.[18]

Training Begins in Earnest for the 51st

The Montford Point Camp bustled with activity. By June the influx of draftees brought the total of blacks in the Corps to over 4,000, and the 51st, numbering nearly 1,000 men, had almost doubled in size and was nearly up to strength. Gone was the term "Composite" from the unit name. Although the men did not know it, HQMC planned to send the 51st to the Pacific by early 1944 — little more than six months in the future.

Lt. Col. Stephenson proposed a pre-deployment training schedule to take the men from the basics of managing their equipment and duties through the advanced work needed to qualify them in their military specialties, and HQMC approved it.[19] Equipment was on hand and white NCOs began training the men on the vast array of weapons and equipment found in a defense battalion. The amount of training to prepare the battalion was formidable, for *none* of the young black Marines had completed their first full year of active service. At that time, any black Marine who was six months out of boot camp could rightly be considered a seasoned veteran. When any newly formed battalion begins its training cycle two things have to happen: First, the men assigned must be physically and mentally able to perform the duties required in the unit, and second, personnel assignments must be stabilized.

As was shown earlier, the first black volunteers for service in 1942 were physically and mentally a select group with considerable ability, and these formed perhaps one third of the 51st. Starting in 1943, the draft brought a small percentage of equally fine men, but also many men of lesser mental ability; the Corps could no longer exercise its old levels of selectivity and so filled the battalion with draftees. Now the earlier decision to limit blacks to certain occupational fields, even though some of those fields required the high degree of technical skills found in a defense battalion, would greatly affect the "new departure" (HQMC's euphemism for blacks in the Marine Corps).

Stability in personnel assignments was needed. The less turmoil caused by transfers and reassignments, the better for the men and the unit. Men should remain in their assigned jobs long enough to be thoroughly trained. Unfortunately, the 51st was *the* pool of black Marines to draw upon to form other units (that was how the Corps worked). In many cases replacements arrived in the battalion who had not completed boot camp; inexcusably, some had *no* boot camp training.[20] Very shortly, it would become evident that seemingly sound decisions made in 1942 virtually guaranteed a rough time for the 51st in 1943.

Maj. Gen. Larsen Speaks his Mind

Training at Montford Point was progressing, and time was set aside for relaxation and entertainment after normal working hours. The camp had a "slop chute" where men could relax over a beer or a soda and listen to music from a jukebox. Boxing smokers were popular among the men and well attended. Maj. Gen. Henry L. Larsen, the new commanding general at Camp Lejeune who had recently returned from duty in the Pacific, attended one early summer smoker. He chose to address the assembled black Marines, and while no one can quote his exact words, Herb Brewer was there and recalls, "He spoke to us and said something to the effect that 'When I saw you people wearing my uniform then I realized that we were really in a war; things must be rough.' It was very inappropriate to say something like that."[21] Some claim a full-fledged race riot ensued with the general being knocked off the stage by a thrown soft drink bottle. However, Brewer continues, "I remember some people hissing the general, things like that; he couldn't do much about it because you couldn't tell just who it was" making the noise.[22] The speech ended quickly. Whatever Larsen's words, the black Marines who were there, and all those who heard about it later, remember the incident even now. It would seem that Lt. Gen. Holcomb's Letter of Instruction Number 421 regarding the treatment of black Marines might not have been as widely disseminated as he had intended.

Different Treatment from a White Officer

Herb Brewer learned about three of the antiaircraft guns in the battalion, the 20mm, 40mm, and 90mm guns. Captain R.H. Twisdale, an Annapolis graduate, was Brewer's Battery Commander. Twisdale, Herb recalls, "went out of his way to take us to learn to sail. He took us out in a sailboat from the main camp at Lejeune and showed us how to operate the sails. All the officers were Anglos, and as I said, I think the Marine Corps did a good job in their selection."[23]

Another white officer well respected by the black Marines was Lieutenant Robert W. "Bobby" Troup, later Commanding Officer of the 6th Marine Ammunition Company. Troup was a well-known musician before becoming a Marine. His duties at Montford Point included an assignment as Camp Recreation Officer where he formed a band. Troup wrote a song, "Take Me Away from Jacksonville," that summed up the feelings of black Marines and became very popular around the camp. A few lines from the song are:

> *Take me away from Jacksonville, 'cause I've had my fill and that's no lie, Take me away from Jacksonville, keep me away from Jacksonville until I die, Jacksonville stood still while the rest of the world passed by.*[24]

Some of the lieutenants at Montford Point were not happy to be with the depot companies and serving with blacks. However, there were exceptions. Two of the white lieutenants, platoon commanders Kenneth Graham and John D'Angelo were the kind of officers who looked out for their men. They could often be seen patrolling Jacksonville's streets when their black Marines were on liberty, ready to intercede on their behalf when locals harassed them.[25] Another officer, Captain John R. Blackett, a "mustang," set a high standard for behavior and attitude. At a company formation "he spoke out long and loud about his uncompromising stand that under no circumstance would the staff or anyone else under his command support racism, prejudice, discrimination or oppression."[26]

13

Training with the Guns

Will They Be Ready?

The training methods used in the 51st were in the proven and effective military style, introducing the subject, whether general military subjects or technical skills, at the lowest level and progressing in complexity. It was a challenge for the instructors, novice NCOs trying to adjust to their new positions, and for the students as well. The men in the battalion represented the wide range of reading, writing, and learning abilities, from college men who scored in Class I on the GCT and did well in mechanical aptitude tests, to those who never made it out of grade school or scored in the lowest classes. The final test would come in the field, the training areas and firing ranges at Onslow Beach. One question on everyone's mind from HQMC down to the battalion's headquarters at Montford Point was this: Could the men set up and operate every part of the battalion, trucks, jeeps and generators, properly dispersed and emplaced guns, fire control centers, searchlights, telephone networks and switchboards, radios — everything as it ought to be done on some Pacific island? Finally, the big one: Could the men *hit* the targets when they fired the guns?

Other defense battalions made up of volunteers and draftees were going through similar training. White Marines, many with little, if any, more time in the Corps than the black Marines of the 51st, filled the other defense battalions being formed. The stakes for all were nothing less than success on the battlefield, to kill your enemy before he killed you or some other Marine. Blacks at Montford Point, however, struggled with the additional burden of having to prove themselves as Marines. They learned from Maj. Gen. Larsen's remarks that they were *still* not full-fledged members of the club.

What did it take to become fully accepted? What lay before them? Long hours of study, practice, and work in the field. An overview of what was involved best reveals what the men needed to accomplish.

Special Weapons Group (Light Antiaircraft Guns)

In garrison, the men who would defend against low-flying enemy aircraft with their smaller caliber guns received classroom instruction in their new job assignments. From the classrooms, they progressed to hands-on drills. For example, the men assigned to the Machine Gun Battery as gunners and assistant gunners learned the basic nomenclature and functioning of every part of the battalion's thirty M1917 .30-caliber water-cooled machine guns. They learned how to take the guns apart and put them back together again, drilling endlessly until it became second-nature.[1] After they learned their assignments as gunner or assistant gunner they loaded the guns on boats for the trip downriver and on the ranges near Onslow Beach conducted live firing exercises. They learned how to place the guns to defend an assigned sector.

Crews for the water-cooled .50-caliber antiaircraft machine guns went through the same process, as did crews for the foreign-designed antiaircraft guns, the 20mm Oerlikon and the 40mm Bofors. Both of the latter were new to navy and the Marine Corps.

.50-caliber Antiaircraft Machine Gun

As an antiaircraft weapon, the battalion's sixteen water-cooled .50-caliber guns were mounted on heavy tripods.[2] In production since 1932, these recoil-operated guns were belt-fed from an ammunition can attached to the left side of the gun. It had a sustained rate of fire of 550 rounds per minute and an effective range of 2,000 yards. The gun fired ball, armor piercing, or tracer ammunition; later in the war API rounds were introduced (armor piercing incendiary). Normal loading in an ammunition belt called for every fifth round to be a tracer so the gunner could observe the trajectory of his fire. A gunner, a spotter and a loader operated each weapon.

Each gun had an open circular ring-type rear sight at eye level. The small inner circle was parallel to the bore. Outer rings represented target speeds. The gunners learned to get the target in the sight flying toward the center ring at an estimated speed ring away. A gunner had to be a good judge of aircraft speeds, which was a difficult skill to acquire. When he fired, the gunner and the spotter watched the tracers and adjusted the position of the target in his sight. Gunners could fire rounds in short bursts or continuously.

20mm Oerlikon Gun

The 20mm Oerlikon guns came into service in 1942. The 51st had a battery of twelve of these guns in three sections of 4 guns each.[3] Crews consisted of three

men: a gunner, sight (range) setter, and a loader for the gun. The 20mm was originally designed in Switzerland by the Oerlikon Company, hence the metric designation. It was an inertia-operated (blowback, or recoil operated) gun capable of
getting into action quicker than larger caliber weapons. Ammunition fed from sixty
round drums that fitted on top of the breeches. After long periods of firing (about
240 rounds) the barrel had to be changed by loaders wearing asbestos gloves.
Although rated at 430–480 rounds per minute, this rate could never be achieved
because of the small magazine capacities.[4]

40mm Bofors Gun

Designed in Sweden by the Bofors company, the M1 40mm was manufactured
in the United States by Blaw-Knox, Chrysler, and York Safe & Lock. The M1 was
inertia operated and was a dual-purpose gun; that is, it was effective against either
air or ground targets. The gun fired a projectile loaded from the top in a four-round
clip. Each round weighed about two pounds and had a hole in the nose that exploded
the round when it hit something.

The battalion's 40mm Gun Battery consisted of twelve Bofors guns mounted
on towed carriages.[5] A well-trained crew could bring a gun to firing position in as
little as 25 seconds. The gun had "tractor" seats and speed ring sights for the azimuth
and elevation trackers on each side of the gun and a platform for the rest of the
crew. The speed ring sights to aim the gun were made of rings representing speeds
in increments of one hundred miles per hour for a crossing target. The men who
served as azimuth and elevation trackers aimed the gun by using hand cranks to
point the gun so that the target moved toward the center of the speed rings (the
target was offset by one, two or three speed rings, depending on the angular rate
of the airplane's approach). The elevation tracker operated the trigger, which was
a foot pedal.

90mm Antiaircraft Artillery Group

The 51st Defense Battalion's 90mm Antiaircraft Artillery Group was organized with a Group Headquarters, three 90mm Gun Batteries of four guns each, and
a Searchlight Battery.[6] The crews learned about their guns and gunnery from the
lowest levels, the same as for the lighter antiaircraft guns.

Soon after the war started, the Marine Corps adopted the army's M1 90mm
gun, in production since 1940, and replaced its old 3-inch antiaircraft guns. The
M1 was a great improvement over the obsolete 3-inch gun formerly used by Marine
defense battalions, for when coupled with some of the more advanced radars, it was
capable of automatic target tracking and gun laying.

Designed from the outset for use as an antiaircraft weapon, the M1 gun car-

Looking down the bore of an M1 90mm antiaircraft gun crewed by black defense battalion Marines at Monford Point Camp. Seven of the 10-man crew are visible. No date. Used with permission of the Montford Point Marine Museum, Camp Lejeune, NC.

riage had two road wheels that had to be folded back out of the way and then outrigger spars (stabilizers) emplaced before firing.[7] The gun could not be depressed below zero degrees elevation. It became the standard antiaircraft artillery piece for Marine Corps defense and AAA battalions. After modification, the M1A1 could be towed on a single axle, dual-wheel carriage. It had a distinctive, perforated steel firing platform. It was a dual-purpose gun in that it could be directed against ground targets as well.[8]

The Antiaircraft Artillery Group's Searchlight Battery

The battery used twelve Sperry 60-inch searchlights that threw an 800-million-candlepower light beam out to a slant range of 20,000 yards. The searchlights cost $60,000 each. The 51st Defense Battalion's searchlight crews trained to use them in conjunction with sound locators and later with radar sets to track airborne targets.

The first major operating component of a light was its 180-pound, 60-inch-diameter highly polished mirror, which concentrated the intense light produced from the second major operating component, a one-inch electrical arc. That arc was the heart of the light. The electrical arc was a highly luminous and intensely hot discharge of electricity between the ends of two carbon rods. One rod was attached inside the light and another was fed through a hole in the center of the searchlight lens.

The lights and generators were mounted on a four-wheel chassis and loaded into a trailer for towing. A Hercules flat-head six-cylinder engine coupled to a DC generator supplied the electrical power, and all were either towed directly or placed aboard a trailer.[9]

Antiaircraft Gun Fire Control

The 51st Defense Battalion's Gun Operations Room targeted enemy aircraft using a combination of radar, conventional optical sights, coincidence range finders, sound locaters, and at night, searchlights. Visual sightings and sound detectors worked in conjunction with gun directors to convert tracking data and generate firing data, the trigonometric solutions predicting flight paths. Directors also furnished fuse settings for the 90mm guns.

As a fire control technician, Herb Brewer said, "Our job was to aim the guns."[10] During daylight hours, the fire control men used sound locators. These were giant horn-like "ears" to amplify the faintest sound of the engines of an approaching airplane. The sound locators provided a compass line of bearing to the enemy airplane, but the crews waited until the airplane came into sight in order to track it, and then pass the data to the guns to shoot at it. Before the battalion received radar, a control station and a sound locator directed the searchlights. The cover photo on the December 1941 issue of *Popular Science* magazine showed the latest sound locator in use by the U.S. Army, a large 3-horned receiver with a two-man crew. Instructions were relayed to an analog computer attached to the guns and searchlights, which would track the target, training to the direction where the sound detector indicated. At night, when one or more light beams illuminated the target, the gunners would open fire. During the day, gunners fired when the target came in visual range.

Radar in Defense Battalions

Radar was still classified and closely guarded equipment. Included in the new defense battalion's T/O under the Headquarters and Service Battery was a Radar Section, and Captain Gerald A. Woodruff was the Radar Officer for the 51st. Operators and technicians trained at schools moved to Camp Lejeune from Quantico, Virginia, in October 1942. Radar had come to the Marine Corps in the late 1930s and by May 1943, the Marine Corps (working with the navy) had enough user experience to publish the "book" on how the equipment should be employed. Entitled "Standing Operating Procedure for Radar Air and Surface Warning and Radar Fire Control in the Marine Corps" the CONFIDENTIAL book was a basic guidance tool for responsible officers.[11] It included definitions of terms such as "Searchlight Control System" and "Antiaircraft Gun Control System," with general descriptions and diagrams of how each system worked, as well as how each fit into an overall area air defense system. As with practically every aspect of amphibious warfare, radar and its use was a continually evolving science with a steep learning curve.

Black Marines of the H&S Battery's Radar Section began with a basic operating description of the equipment they would use: Radar consists of a radio transmitter and receiver and a very accurate clock (timer). The directional transmitter sends out radio waves in short pulses for a very small part of every second. Any material body, such as an aircraft or a ship, reflects radio energy pulses that strike them. Knowing the speed of the radio waves, target range is determined by measuring the time interval from the transmission of the radio wave to the time the reflected wave returns to the receiver. This is done by means of a cathode ray tube (CRT or scope) connected between the transmitter and the receiver and calibrated in miles or yards. All radars provide two elements of data on any target, range and direction. Improvements to the early sets soon provided angular heights from which operators could determine a target's altitude. Operating and maintaining the modern, sensitive electronics equipment was a challenging assignment, and no one ever complained that the 51st had problems managing it.

The defense battalions were an integral part of any operations area air defense plan. A drawing taken from a radar technical manual used by the army and Marine Corps in World War II and classified SECRET shows target location by an early radar set (see appendix F, Target Location by Radio set SCR-268).[12] At the time, radars were called "radios," hence the SCR (*Signal Corps Radio*) designation.

Developed in 1937, the SCR-268 was the first radar to track precisely a single target for acquisition by searchlights. Three operators, each with a scope, tracked target azimuth, elevation, and range. The gun control room, guns, radars, searchlights, sound detectors, and generators of an air defense system were widely dispersed across the ground. A network of cables and sound powered telephones and switchboards connected all parts of the system.[13] The wires and cables to make the connections were strung from trees, telephone poles, PO-2 poles (lightweight and man-portable temporary telephone poles), or buried in shallow trenches. In a worst-case hurry-up expedient, all were simply laid on the ground, where much of it was sure to be torn up by passing trucks or men.

As with searchlights, the radar needed electrical power and dedicated generators, which meant even more cable runs and hookups. The men soon learned that it took quite a while to set up and maintain a defense battalion's AAA group.

155mm Gun

The Seacoast Artillerymen of the 51st trained on French-made M1918 *Grand Puissance Filloux* (GPF) 155mm guns, which had split trails, single axles, and twin wheels. These World War I relics deployed to the South Pacific with the early defense battalions. The guns fired a shell that weighed about 90 pounds a distance of 10 miles.

The new M1 155mm "Long Tom" soon replaced the GPF. It used separate loading ammunition comprised of four components: a projectile, a separate bagged propellant charge, a fuse and a primer. The propelling charge consisted of individual bags of powder that could be added or reduced to adjust for the range. Projectiles were shipped in crates or on pallets; the charge was packaged individually in fiber canisters. The 95-pound projectiles had rings in the nose end to assist in handling; these were removed and replaced by fuses when ready to fire. The primers were placed in the breech lock of the gun for firing. The gun had a range of about 15 miles.

A "Long Tom" weighed 30,600 pounds, had a split trail and eight pneumatic tires, was pulled by tractor, and was served by a combined crew of 15 men. It was pedestal mounted on the so-called "Panama" mount for its seacoast defense role. It combined great firepower with high mobility and proved to be a dependable workhorse.[14]

Throughout the battalion, black Marines prepared to wage a very technical war. In gun parks cannoneers learned the intricacies of their 155mm weapons, as did the men who would fire the new M1 90mm antiaircraft guns, the lighter .50-caliber, 20mm and the 40mm guns. Communicators set up radios while wiremen strung tactical telephone links and operated switchboards. Mechanics tinkered with generator motors that would power the huge Sperry searchlights for the Antiaircraft Artillery Group. Drivers and mechanics kept busy learning the mysteries of the many ¼-ton, ¾-ton and 2½-ton trucks and trailers needed to move the battalion. Other men learned how to survive the perils of the supply system, making sure replacement parts were ordered, and administrative clerks took care of morning reports, service records, pay, and promotions.

14

War Is Serious Business

The First Black Casualty

On August 20, men of the 51st Defense Battalion's Seacoast Artillery Group were engaged in amphibious training. The Montford Point boat docks had a tower the height of the main deck of an attack transport ship, and cargo nets hung down to the water. LCVPs idled alongside and the men, loaded with combat gear, filed up stairs to the top of the platform. When ordered, the men made their way over the railing and climbed the 30 feet down to the boats, always being careful to grasp only the vertical strands of the net so the man above them would not step on their hands. Transferring men to the landing craft was, and still is, a dangerous operation even in calm waters.

The training SOP called for the first four men down the nets and into the boats to act as net handlers. These four held the bottom of the net away from the side of the "ship" so that as the LCVP rose and fell on any swells, they controlled the net and any man losing his grip would fall into the boat. If the net were not held inside the gunwales of the LCVP a man might fall and be crushed between the ship's hull and the landing craft. On this day, Cpl. Gilbert Fraser lost his grip and plunged into the waiting landing craft, the fall killing him.[1] He was the first black Marine to die. In tribute, the road leading from Camp Lejeune's mainside out to the artillery firing ranges was renamed Fraser Road.

Welcome to the War

Apart from the 51st, Montford Point Camp continued to train recruits and to churn out depot companies. The 4th Marine Depot Company was organized on June 1, 1943. The 2d and 3d Marine Depot Companies had joined the 1st Base Depot at Noumea, New Caledonia, on June 30, while the 4th Marine Depot Company arrived at Noumea near the end of July. The 5th and 6th Depot Companies formed

"U.S. troops go over the side of a Coast Guard manned combat transport to enter the landing barges at Empress Augusta Bay, Bougainville, as the invasion gets under way." Photo shows how Marines and soldiers climbed down cargo nets to LCVP landing craft. November 1943. Still Picture Branch (NNSP), National Archives, Washington, DC.

July 8 and near the end of August arrived in the Pacific and were also assigned to the 1st Base Depot at Noumea.[2]

The 1st Marine Depot Company, along with the 4th Marine Depot Company filed aboard the recently commissioned transport USS *Crescent City* (AP-40) at Noumea and sailed north across the Coral Sea for Guadalcanal, where they arrived on August 12. The men were welcomed to the war when a Japanese airplane that had just finished attacking the island flew over them. With little time to spare for sightseeing on the first Pacific island re-captured from the Japanese, the black Marines transferred to smaller transport ships. They sailed to Banika in the Russells Group to become the first depot company Marines to join the 4th Base Depot, which had moved from Guadalcanal during Operation TOENAILS.

Their arrival at Banika on August 13 occurred during a period of nightly air raids by the Japanese. They ran for their bunkers for the first time on the night of the 14th but on 15th were hard at work on the Banika docks. Marking another milestone event, the men of these noncombatant labor units were the first black Marines in World War II to see Japanese bombers overhead.[3]

The men of the earlier depot companies had quickly proven their worth, but there were not enough of them. HQMC approved a revision to the depot company T/O on July 19. The new T/O increased the number of Marine officers from three to four and Marine enlisted men from 110 to 159. Three navy medical corpsmen were added after the T/O was approved. Both the 5th and the 6th Depot Companies were disbanded soon after arriving in the Pacific, and the men were reassigned to 1st, 2d, 3d, and 4th Depot Companies to bring them up to strength under the new T/O.

During the summer months, an unnamed combat correspondent came to Banika and produced a short, upbeat "booster" article about the black Marines of the depot companies. Morale was good, even under the trying conditions in the Russell Islands. Of note, the men jokingly referred to themselves as "material maneuverers."[4]

More Racism at the Highest Levels

In the South Pacific Maj. Gen. Price requested that five depot companies be sent to his Samoan Defense Command. This seemingly innocuous request would soon prove that the odd notions about blacks that existed in the Corps prior to the start of the war were not confined to Marine Corps headquarters.

Back at Montford Point Camp, the 7th and 8th Marine Depot Companies were organized on August 16, 1943, and as soon as they were ready the men loaded on a train and traveled to Davisville, Rhode Island. From there they boarded a transport ship at Narragansett Bay. Sailing southward, the ship passed through the Panama Canal and continued on to Pago Pago, American Samoa, where the companies were to join the 700-man strong Base Depot, FMF.[5] However, a serious problem arose. When the two companies arrived at Samoa on October 13, 1943, the commanding general seems to have been surprised to discover that most of the men in the companies were *black*.

With the possibility of three additional depot companies coming to his command, almost *500 more blacks*, Maj. Gen. Price had second thoughts and immediately protested. The deployment of black units to Samoa was out of the question, he decided. Samoan women were "primitively romantic," he said. Sexual union with the white race produced "a very high-class half-caste," with the Chinese a "very desirable type," but union with blacks "produces a very undesirable citizen." Price suggested that the Marine Corps had a "moral obligation" to protect the American Samoans from sexual intimacy with blacks. He strongly urged that any black units deployed to the Pacific go instead to Micronesia where they "can do no racial harm." A Marine major general had weighed in on the problem, so the matter made its way into the hands of the Director, Division of Plans and Policies at HQMC. As a result, the assignment of the 7th and 8th Depot Companies to Samoa proved short-lived. Both companies were redeployed to the Ellice Islands in the Micronesia group where they joined the FMF Base Depot at Funafuti.[6]

The Camp Expands

The black Marines at Montford Point Camp lived and worked in the same type of buildings as the white Marines located on the main part of Camp Lejeune. By the end of the summer, additional buildings of tile block and stucco in the Marines' typical regimental post style were under construction along Montford Landing Road, the main road into the camp from Highway 24. These included a larger headquarters building, an infirmary, a guesthouse, a brig, a camp theater, classroom buildings, and gun sheds. Some of the galvanized metal buildings, insufferably hot in the summer and freezing in winter would still be in use fifty years later. To provide swim training the camp added an indoor pool late in the year.

Meanwhile, Marine Depot Companies continued to form as quickly as the men could graduate. The 9th and 10th activated on September 15, 1943, and as with others, prepared to ship out within two weeks. Private Eugene Smith, after graduating from boot camp, joined the 10th Marine Depot Company. He also bought a dress blue uniform and proudly sat for a photograph.

September brought more change. The 51st Defense Battalion moved out of the Montford Point Camp proper across Scales Creek to Camp Knox, a camp left over from the pre-war Civilian Conservation Corps days (see map 1, Montford Point 1943–1945). The men of the 51st moved into three barracks blocks while a fourth housed the War Dog Training Center. The barracks, mess hall, and offices were old wooden structures badly in need of repair. Surprisingly, most of the men were glad to move away from the main camp, and morale soared even higher as a period of intensive field work followed the move.[7]

All Marines who have ever trained at Camp Lejeune have had to deal with a significant, non-tactical impediment to their progress ashore — a big ditch with few bridge crossings. Congress had authorized an extension of the Atlantic Intra-coastal Waterway from Beaufort, North Carolina, through to the Cape Fear River below

Wilmington, North Carolina, in 1927, and the Corps of Engineers completed the work five years later. The waterway passes from Beaufort through Bogue Sound to Swansboro, and from there through the sounds and salt marshes to the south, cutting through the eastern reaches of Camp Lejeune and intercepting the Cape Fear River about 16 miles below Wilmington. The channel is 12 feet deep at mean low water with bottom widths varying from 90 feet through land cuts to 300 feet in open waters.[8] Amphibious landings on Onslow Beach itself could be carried out under realistic tactical conditions. However, after the men and equipment came onshore, tactical play ground to a halt for an administrative crossing of the waterway by barge, ferry, or temporary bridges. Once across, tactical play resumed. As every other Marine unit at Camp Lejeune did before and has done since, the 51st worked around the obstacle.

The Seacoast Group took its 155mm guns to Onslow Beach for live fire training, and the Antiaircraft and Special Weapons Groups soon followed. Frequent rains, salt spray and wind-blown sand in the air combined with sand underfoot took their toll on equipment. Inexplicably, in the last half of 1943 the firing batteries of the 51st received many men who had completed only a few days of recruit training and others with no training at all! As could be expected, the overall readiness of the battalion suffered.[9]

From day to day junior officers recently graduated from the Base Defense Course, or the army's antiaircraft courses at Camp Davis on the coast a few miles south of Camp Lejeune, were learning about black Marines. Black NCOs, many not long out of boot camp themselves, struggled to school the men on the basics of being Marines as well as learning the sophisticated electronic and ordnance equipment in the battalion. No white Marines received orders to FMF units within days after arriving at boot camp. If they ever existed at all, background documents are no longer available, so today we can only wonder about the logic of the decision to order so many untrained men to the 51st.

One possible explanation recalls the fact that, in the Marines' way of doing things, the 51st was *the* pool to be tapped when experienced blacks were needed to form other units. Headquarters Marine Corps plans called for the activation of a second black defense battalion, the 52d, early in 1944. So, the 51st was being filled in anticipation of the coming loss. Nevertheless, on a more positive note, the "veterans" on the gun crews would soon have their opportunity to prove that they could shoot with deadly accuracy.

15

Change Comes Slowly

A Routine Process

By October 1943, recruit training for blacks had become a smoothly operating routine. A reporter from the *Richmond Afro-American* (a weekly regional edition of the daily *Afro-American Newspaper* published in Baltimore, Maryland) visited the Montford Point Camp and met with the men there. The reporter listened to several complaints alleging that blacks were not receiving the same training as white Marines, and that what training they were getting was inadequate. Their discontent stemmed from the fact that relatively few blacks served in the combat unit, the 51st Defense Battalion, while the rest were "shunted into the steward's branch or depot or ammunition companies, described as 'oversized working parties.'" Also, for the first time, the complaint was heard that the men were "denied the opportunity to qualify for commissions."[1] Little was made of the complaints at the time, but the issues would simmer, resurfacing in the coming year.

Turner G. Blount, an eighteen-year-old from Keyesville, Georgia, got his draft notice the month after he registered with the Selective Service. During the induction process, a friend suggested they ask for assignment to the Marine Corps instead of the army or navy. "It's the best outfit going," his friend said.

Blount and his friend got what they wanted and on a government voucher traveled from Macon, Georgia, to Jacksonville, North Carolina. A Marine with a truck met them at the bus depot and drove them to the Montford Point Camp. Black Marines would conduct all of their training, and Platoon 232's DIs told their new charges that they had to "cut the mustard" because "eyes" were on them. Larsen's comments at the smoker were fresh in the minds of the DIs, who knew they still had to prove themselves and their trainees. "Everything was laid out straight on the line," Blount said. "There was no pity or no mercy for anyone. You was really talked to and you was in a position you could not say anything ... you just listened and had to do what you were told." Not intimidated by boot camp, Blount said, "By me being so young and unafraid I thought I could do anything. If it was running or exercising, I thought I could do just about as much as anyone could do. I really didn't see anything too hard."[2]

Two black Marine NCOs, Johnson and Huff, both members of the first group of blacks to be trained as DIs, impressed Blount because they were always to be seen, always supervising the training, always among the recruits, vocal so that "you couldn't miss them."[3] Johnson wore his three service stripes, "hashmarks," proudly on the sleeves of his green uniform, the only black Marine to rate wearing them at that time. The men soon nicknamed him "Hashmark" Johnson. He was in his thirties, older than his charges, and he was a demanding leader.

Johnson rose through the ranks quickly, was promoted to corporal (Cpl.) in April and to sergeant (Sgt.) in July. Sgt. Johnson was placed in charge of field training for all black recruits and remained so until he was transferred overseas.[4] Sgt. Huff, promoted at the same time as Johnson, was also older than most recruits, and his maturity and confidence coupled with his nearly six feet six inches height made him an imposing figure on the drill field.[5]

During his training, Blount lived in one of the "little green huts" with no heat and no running water, and the heads were located in separate buildings at one end of the long rows of huts. Cool autumn days and cooler nights came, so a trip to the head in the middle of the night could be chilly. The training days started in the pre-dawn darkness when the men fell out in formation and after roll call marched to the drill field for calisthenics. Breakfast followed. "The food was good," he said, "but recruits got only one trip through the serving line." Healthy young men involved in a physically demanding training regimen, they developed ravenous appetites. "After morning chow came drill, classes, and more drill."

Turner Blount heard of Maj. Gen. Larsen's comments while at boot camp, and recalls, "From the top coming down, it wasn't good for them to treat you like that, because the top, the whites, didn't want you. We had people like Huff and Johnson who said, 'You can't give up,' so I just fell into that, you're going to make it." Blount goes on to describe life at segregated Montford Point in a Jim Crow part of the country: "You wasn't allowed to go to mainside [where white Marines were billeted]. That's off limits. You go downtown Jacksonville, there's the railroad tracks, blacks over there and whites here, and police and MPs there to keep whites from going over there and keep blacks from coming on that side." Blount reports what was apparently a change in policy that occurred in the very short time between Herb Brewer's rifle range experience in November 1942 and his own near the end of 1943. Brewer rode in a truck out to the range, but Blount said, "In my time you had to catch a boat, a barge, down here [at the Montford Point Camp boat landing] and ride the river around to the rifle range. You couldn't follow the highway with weapons because the civilians out there was afraid of blacks with weapons on trucks."[6]

That was not the only change going on at Montford Point. Some of the black DIs were resorting to hazing recruits. It could happen to you, Blount said, "You'd be booted, you know, with the foot and nobody said anything."[7] Discipline was strict but only months earlier in Brewer's time there was no corporal punishment and little profanity at the hands of his white DIs.

Black DIs were roughing up black recruits. Such problems arose when rapidly promoted corporals and privates first class with only a few months time in service were assigned as DIs to train and indoctrinate the new recruits. The quality of recruit training suffered because some of the inexperienced DIs failed to follow the training methods they were taught. A few of the men found it difficult to assert authority over men their own age without resorting to hazing, using their fists and profanity on recruits who could not hit back.[8] Under the Rocks and Shoals, striking a superior NCO had serious consequences, so the recruits accepted the treatment as normal. After all, the Corps was reputed to be tough, wasn't it?

Another Opportunity for Black Marines

On September 29, 1943, the 9th Marine Depot Company along with Eugene Smith's 10th Marine Depot Company left Montford Point for their new home in the Pacific. Meanwhile, black draftees continued to pour into the Montford Point Camp. Along with them came expanded opportunity for the black Marines, something beyond duty with a defense battalion, a depot company, or in the stewards branch. There would be a new company-sized unit within the supply system yet different from the depot companies.

Supplies are grouped into ten classes in order to facilitate management and planning:

I. Rations and health and comfort items
II. Clothing, individual equipment, tentage, toolsets, and administrative supplies and equipment
III. Petroleum, fuel, oils, and lubricants
IV. Construction materials
V. Ammunition
VI. Personal demand items
VII. Major end items, including tanks, aircraft, and radios
VIII. Medical
IX. Repair parts and components for equipment maintenance
X. Nonstandard items

The depot company Marines received no special training; they were stevedores, strong men who could handle *most* types of general supplies. Nevertheless, amphibious assaults by reinforced Marine Divisions each involving more than 20,000 men lasting days and even weeks required many tons of supply Class V, ammunition and explosives. The men to manage ammunition required special training and handling precautions because of the danger in handling explosives, and until now this was the job of ordnance companies manned by white Marines.

In order to increase the Class V handling capacity of the base and field depots and in the FMF units, the first of a new type of unit was formed, the Marine Ammunition Company. These companies of blacks would be "built around a rock hard core of 'old Marines,' a cadre of seasoned staff noncommissioned officers, some veterans of the old 'banana wars,' China, and the Solomons."[9]

The men of this new organization trained in *safely* loading, unloading, sorting, stacking and guarding all types of ammunition. They then went to field depots supporting amphibious forces. The men would then be responsible for moving ammunition from the ships to the shore, to dumps, and then hauling it forward to Marine riflemen and artillerymen. The ammunition company performed the same functions as the white ordnance company of the Marine Divisions, including the hard labor of muscling heavy pallets and boxes of ammunition into ships holds during combat loading. It was then segregated by caliber and type in accordance with units of fire specified in operations orders and as directed by the Transport Quartermaster, a Marine officer who is a combat loading specialist assigned to each navy assault transport.

During a D-Day assault, ammunition companies would go ashore soon after the first waves. Some of the men were assigned to unloading details aboard transport ships, others worked aboard landing craft and floating dumps, and the rest of the company hit the beach.

Finally, after the fighting stopped, ammunition from scattered dumps had to be consolidated into permanent dumps for the island garrison forces. Details would be sent out to "police the brass" on the battlefield, collecting ammunition for salvage. These same details cleared Japanese ammunition dumps and disposed of most of the explosives, often at sea.[10]

In accordance with T/O E-703 (appendix E, Depot and Ammunition Companies 1943–1946), the 1st Marine Ammunition Company's three Marine officers, five Marine Warrant Officers, and 255 Marine and navy enlisted men were organized into a company headquarters and four Ammunition Platoons on October 1, 1943.[11] Unlike the depot company men who were issued only M1 rifles, some of the Ammo Company Marines received carbines. (When the depot company Marines reached the forward areas in the Pacific, they armed themselves with a variety of pistols, carbines, even .50-caliber machine guns as well.)

Most depot companies shipped out two weeks after they formed, but Ammo Company Marines usually spent about two months at Montford Point before heading out to the Pacific. The men took courses in the different types of ammunition and explosives they would be handling. Because of the technical nature of the duty, only white ordnance sergeants held the staff NCO billets in the company. That policy, which overrode any possibility for upward mobility for black NCOs, would continue throughout the war.

A white platoon sergeant in one of the ammunition companies described his experience: "The first weeks were rife with tension. There were many moments with a lot of shouting, a lot of threatening and tremendous amount of explanation, cajoling, persuading and other techniques. Many mistakes were made on both sides of the color line before the black Marines came to understand that the white staff was their ally. Open and honest communication between the two colors resulted in coordinated, cooperative, responsible results, which made what was a hell of a life at Montford Point a little easier for all."[12]

A week after the 1st Ammunition Company was activated, the 11th and 12th Marine Depot Companies stood up at Montford Point. While being organized at Montford Point, both companies were slated to become part of the 1st Base Depot on New Caledonia, but when they went overseas in December the companies were sent instead to join the 4th Base Depot on Banika in the Russells Group.

On November 1, 1943, the 13th and 14th Marine Depot Companies were activated, as was the 2d Marine Ammunition Company. The two depot companies quickly shipped out while the ammo company trained at Montford Point before being sent to Guadalcanal to join the 5th Field Depot. December saw the activation of two more depot companies and the 3d Marine Ammunition Company, but then the pace slackened. Fewer blacks were available for assignment because the monthly draft calls were never completely filled. By December 1943, only 9,916 of the 15,400 expected black inductions had been completed.[13]

Looking for a Home

Eugene Smith describes the journey of the 9th and 10th Marine Depot Companies in some detail. They traveled by train through South Carolina, Georgia, Alabama, and Mississippi and arrived at New Orleans, Louisiana, on October 1, 1943. There they waited for the convoy of troop transports and escort vessels that would take them to war.[14]

While at New Orleans, they attended a dance on October 16 given at Algiers Naval Station for the Marines. Like the men of the other depot companies, they excelled at close order drill. In a competition against sailors on October 23, 1943, the Marines won. Both Companies boarded the ship that would take them to the war, USS *LST-123*, on October 27, 1943, and the ship got under way the following day.

USS LST-123

She was a good example of America's industrial might and the speed with which ships were built. The Missouri Valley Bridge & Iron Company on the Ohio River, a principal tributary of the Mississippi River, laid down *LST-123*'s keel on June 5, 1943, at Evansville, Indiana. She was launched on August 14, 1943, and commissioned on September 7 under command of Lt. Francis P. Rossiter, USNR.[15]

After the commissioning, the crewmembers became familiar with their new home and their duties. Stores were loaded and the ship made ready for sea duty and the "shake-down" cruise. It was a time to test her power plants and guns and to train her crew, some from small towns who had never seen the ocean, in their routine duties as well as their assignment and training for general quarters stations in preparation for combat.

Watch bills assigned crewmembers to their watch stations and their general quarters stations. While under way, the crew stood watches at their assigned stations for four hours with eight hours off during which time they performed the regular duties of their rate, took care of their personal hygiene or slept. The first morning under way, they heard for the first of hundreds of times the irritating klaxon sound of the call to General Quarters for dawn. As with any green crew it took a few tries before they learned to go forward on the starboard ladders and deck and aft on the port side. Soon they were as ready as most green crews.

The 9th and 10th Marine Depot Companies Embark

The men filed aboard the ship. "There were no white Marines ever on the same ships with us, we were all black, but what the Marines did have among us were the dark Mexicans and plenty of guys from Puerto Rico."[16] There were separate heads, berthing and mess facilities, for the white crew remained segregated from the embarked black Marines. *LST 123* (the 1,152 LSTs ordered by the navy in World War II were numbered rather than named) was a flat-bottomed ship, 327 feet in length with a 50-foot beam, designed for amphibious operations. Her normal crew was seven navy officers and 104 navy enlisted. With a full load of cargo (2,100 tons), she displaced just over 4,000 tons. Two diesel engines powered twin screws for a top speed of 10.8 knots but she cruised at nine knots. Her draft was eight feet forward and 14 feet four inches aft when loaded. She carried smaller craft topside, while her tunnel-like hold carried tanks, vehicles, cargo, or guns. She was only lightly armed, with one 3"/50 caliber dual-purpose gun, one twin-barreled 40mm gun mount, and six 20mm guns.[17] Designed to ram her bow onto a beach, open the clamshell doors in the high bow and off-load men and equipment from her cavernous hold directly onto the beach, she rolled and pitched in the slightest swell.

Berthing spaces for the embarked Marines were narrow, cramped and poorly ventilated. The sooner the Marines got their "sea legs" the better, for when she rolled, in any kind of sea, the motion below decks seemed greatly exaggerated. She was slow, and the protective zigzag course increased transit times on all legs of the journey.

The ships sailed down the Mississippi through the delta, out into the Gulf of Mexico, and took up their positions in convoy. The convoy zigzagged through the Florida Strait and around the eastern tip of Cuba through the Windward Passage. In *LST-123*'s hold were LVTs (Landing Vehicle, Tracked), amphibious tractors also

"Aboard a U.S. Coast Guard-manned transport somewhere in the Pacific, a group of Negro Marines presents a cheerful front." Many of the men are wearing "fore and aft" garrison caps instead of the dungaree cap available for issue late in 1943. They are also wearing belt-type life preservers. No date. Still Picture Branch (NNSP), National Archives, Washington, DC.

called Alligators. Eugene Smith's berth was mid-ships, which offered some relief when the ship's bow rose and fell in the open ocean swells, but none when she rolled.

Prowling Nazi submarines posed a very real threat, so net tender boats opened the huge anti-submarine net stretched across the narrow mouth of Guantanamo Bay, Cuba, on November 3, 1943, to permit the ships to anchor in protected waters. After a short stay, the ship departed Guantanamo Bay on November 5, 1943, and arrived at Coco Solo Naval Station, Panama, four days later.

The Depot Company Marines attended a dance given in honor of the Marine Corps's 168th birthday by the base Recreation Officer (the Continental Marines were founded on November 10, 1775, at Tun Tavern, Philadelphia, so traditionally Marines celebrate that as their birthday). While waiting to transit the canal, the Marines had liberty each night in the city of Colon. Years later Gene Smith remembered that the men had a "swell" time. To keep the men in shape, the company hiked through the jungles of Panama, and on November 14, the company com-

"Aboard a Coast Guard-manned transport somewhere in the Pacific, these Negro Marines prepare to face the fire of Jap[anese] gunners." The men in ranks are armed with .30 caliber M-1 rifles except for the white man at left rear, who is armed with an M-1 carbine, so these Marines are most likely members of a depot company. Ca. February 1944. Still Picture Branch (NNSP), National Archives, Washington, DC.

mander killed a huge iguana. Most iguanas grow to a length of about six feet, but this one, a true monster, measured twelve and a half feet nose to tail!

With the company, Gene Smith watched an exhibition of Marine Corps war dog training on November 15, and followed that on November 18 with a gas chamber exercise with gas masks. The tear gas was very powerful and many of the men had serious burns on their exposed skin.

Their turn came finally when USS *LST-123* entered the locks at 0800 on November 21 and sailed through the Panama Canal, completing the trip in 2½ hours. While waiting for all ships of the convoy to pass through the canal, the men had liberty and a chance to tour Balboa and Panama City. The convoy got under way November 23, 1943, and sailed six days before crossing the Equator. Seeking relief from the stifling atmosphere in the troop spaces in the tropical heat, Gene Smith and his fellow Marines spent most of their time, day and night, on deck. They sought shelter from the sun and cooling breezes in the shade of the landing craft lashed to the main deck.

Navy tradition calls for a ceremony to mark the occasion of crossing the Equator. Those sailors who have already crossed the Equator are known as "Shellbacks," and claim to be the Sons of Neptune. Those making their first crossing are dubbed "Pollywogs." The Shellbacks select several of their fellow old salts as "King Neptune and his court" to officiate at the initiation ceremony, during which the Pollywogs prove their worthiness to become Shellbacks through various rituals which include wearing mismatched clothing, eating disgusting things while blindfolded, being hosed down with sea water, and sometimes even kissing fat old King Neptune's belly. The ships of the convoy continued to zigzag across the Pacific, escorts racing along on both sides, during the festivities in which the Pollywogs of the two depot companies as well as the Pollywogs among the ship's crew became "Sons of Neptune."

The ship next dropped anchor at the spectacularly beautiful Polynesian island of Bora-Bora, Tahiti, on December 18, 1943, where the men were once again given liberty. They left two days later and sailed to American Samoa, arriving at Pago Pago on Christmas Eve. After spending Christmas there they left on December 30, 1943, changing the time back an hour for the sixth time since leaving the United States.

The world travelers crossed the International Date Line on December 31 and arrived at the Fiji Islands the first day of 1944. The men got liberty the same night, attended a dance and had another "swell" time. The last leg of that journey began when they departed Fiji on January 3 and arrived at Noumea, New Caledonia, two days later.[18] Both companies were assigned to the 1st Base Depot, Supply Service, IMAC.

Certainly not every depot company went to war visiting such outstanding liberty ports as did the 9th and 10th. Most of their peers traveled a much more direct route intended to get them into the war as quickly as possible. Could the 9th and 10th have been routed in such a leisurely manner while HQMC searched for a place to assign them in accommodation of Maj. Gen. Price's wishes? No, not likely, for the navy would never have stood still for such a Marine "boondoggle" while there were other troop transport ships and escorting warships in that convoy.

Northern Solomons — Bougainville: A Lesson Relearned

While the 9th and 10th Marine Depot Companies made their way to the Pacific in the closing months of 1943, the struggle for an effective supply system continued. The 3d Marine Division, inexperienced in combat, was stationed on Guadalcanal undergoing training and rehearsals. As part of Lt. Gen. A. A. Vandegrift's I Marine Amphibious Corps (IMAC), the division would take part in the Bougainville operation in the Northern Solomons. On November 1, 1943, the division landed at Empress Augusta Bay, Bougainville. No one in the chain of command, from HQMC on down, had fully learned one of the principal lessons of Guadalcanal.

The division lacked a "competent" shore party. Vandegrift, who had taken command of IMAC less than three weeks prior to the landing, had no choice but to use combat Marines to do the hard "mundane labor of logistics," thus reducing his combat power.[19] He wanted no repeat of the Guadalcanal supply fiasco of August 1942. The only Marine Depot Companies were back with the 1st and 4th Base Depot's receiving and pushing supplies forward from there. Soon senior Marine officers besides Vandegrift would recognize the need to put Depot Company Marines forward, to include them in the early waves of landing craft during an amphibious assault.

16

A Time of Turmoil

Into the Central Pacific

In the Pacific Theatre, Japanese army and naval forces occupied hundreds of islands both large and small, many heavily fortified and defended, separated by vast distances. Airfields on key islands, defended by ground forces, combined with strong naval forces built around aircraft carriers guaranteed the Japanese control of sea lines of communication while denying them to the Allies. However, the success of Allied operations at Midway, in the Solomons, New Britain, and New Guinea and the continuing destruction of Japanese naval and air power around Rabaul meant a loss of Japanese control over increasingly larger areas, many of them key to a mutually supporting defense. These successes offered new opportunities and led the Allies to develop an "island hopping" strategy. The increasing Allied control of the seas proved costly to the Japanese by denying their strongholds of supplies, replacement men, ships, and aircraft.

Rabaul's 90,000 troops, more than 300 antiaircraft guns and 6,500 artillery pieces posed no offensive threat, so the decision to isolate and by-pass Rabaul rather than invade was made as early as August 1943. Capitalizing on lessons learned in operations to date, the Joint Chiefs ordered the capture, development, and defense of bases in the Gilbert Islands group slightly north of the Equator and west of the International Date Line, the 180th meridian. The seizure of Betio Island at Tarawa Atoll by the 2d Marine Division would open the road across the Central Pacific to Kwajalein Atoll and the Marshall Islands. The FMF Base Depot, with the 7th and 8th Marine Depot Companies on Funafuti in the Ellice Islands, provided some of the logistical support for Operation GALVANIC at Tarawa, although none of the black Marines took part in the assault. The old problem of supplies piling up on the beach would resurface in this latest assault, but this time significant factors other than available manpower came into play.

Navy and Marine officers who planned Operation GALVANIC fully understood that the shallow coral reef that spread offshore like a long wide apron in all directions from Betio Island was a major hazard. Records indicated that from the period two hours before to two hours after high tide water *normally* covered the lagoon barrier reef at Betio to a depth of from three to four feet. The risk of having enough water for the shallow draft landing craft to negotiate the reef was accepted.

On November 20, 1943, the risk-takers were wrong, for the tides at Tarawa Atoll did not run as predicted. On that day, a waning gibbous moon was approaching its third quarter and the landing occurred during a bi-monthly neap tide (a tide that shows the least range between high and low water). At a *high water* time in a neap tide the reef was covered by only one to two feet of water, but even that tidal flow did not correspond to what was predicted.[1] Water at the outer edge of the reef was too shallow for the boats.

Combat loaded LCVPs drew about three feet six inches of water. It quickly became obvious that the LCVPs loaded with supplies were grounding on the reef, 800 yards offshore and under heavy fire from the defending Japanese. They could only act as shuttlecraft from the transport and cargo ships to the reef, a distance of six and a half miles. A tremendous transfer operation went into action as sailors and Marines manhandled supplies from the LCVPs idling outside the reef and loaded them into LVTs atop the reef, all of which very measurably slowed supply support.

Overzealous ships' crews added to the confusion. The Marines wanted things landed in order of their importance, but the navy just wanted to unload everything quickly regardless of importance to the men ashore. The Marine commander ashore said, "They did not load what I wanted, they just loaded. By the time they got a message from me requesting certain items the boats were already filled with other material."[2] Once supplies made it to the narrow beaches and the seawall, Marines had to contend with the problem of stacking and sorting and distributing them.

In this assault, the 2d Marine Division's pioneer battalion was not equal to the task of handling supplies at the extremely narrow beachhead. Plans called for Marines from some of the rifle companies to sort and move supplies at the waterline, but because of the intensity of the Japanese resistance and the high number of casualties among the assault forces, the riflemen *cum* pioneers joined in the fighting. Shore Party personnel had to rely on anyone they could find to do the work. After the battle, the V Amphibious Corps (VAC) determined that the shore party was in need of overhaul. The pioneer battalion alone was simply not large enough to do the work. Its T/O needed to be redrawn, but until then, Marines to reinforce the pioneers and help move supplies would be drawn from service units rather than combat units.[3]

It was the same painful lesson learned by Lt. Gen. Vandegrift at Guadalcanal and Bougainville. Fortunately, the importance of the lesson was not lost, for in Hawaii men at the headquarters of the Fleet Marine Force, Pacific, were aware of the urgency of the problem. They studied how Marine units and their navy counterparts dealt with supply issues and they were working hard to get the solutions documented and a remedy sent out for everyone to study and put to good use.

Recruits Pour into the Camp

Back in the States, in December 1943, the Selective Service sent a total of 11,253 whites as well as blacks into the Corps while an additional 2,191 of both races volunteered to become Marines.[4] Enrolled in the Institute of Military Studies at Chicago University, eighteen-year-old John R. Griffin was one of those volunteers for the Marine Corps. Griffin swore the enlistment oath on December 18 and after an enjoyable journey by rail to Washington DC, the young man found himself with an eight-hour layover. He had always wanted to see the Lincoln Memorial, the White House, and Howard University so he used the time for sightseeing around the Capital.

The southbound train left at 6:30 p.m., and Griffin found the second leg of his journey was not so enjoyable because of "the 'Jim Crow' car" he had to ride in as he crossed the Mason-Dixon Line for the first time in his life. "It was hot, dirty, crowded, with babies crying, old men drinking, and Marines discussing the fun they had on leave."[5]

His first days as a recruit left an indelible memory. The recruit receiving barracks were "little square huts with rows of double deck bunks on both sides of the hut. Twenty-six men live in one hut." The crowded huts where Griffin lived were the same that Herb Brewer had lived in with only nine other men when he arrived in September 1942; gone was the luxury of space for single bunks. "At 6 a.m. we were called out in formation to march to breakfast. This I didn't like at first, for I was accustomed to having breakfast at 8 a.m.; however, I got used to the idea of getting up on time. After breakfast, we went back to our little green huts, where we waited for further orders of the day. About eight o'clock one of the sergeants of the receiving area called all the newcomers out and gave us a brief talk on 'The Marine Corps as Compared to the Army.' He talked about one and a half hours, and all the time we were standing up. After this we went to the Sick Bay (name given to the hospital) where we were given a vaccination, a blood type, and a shot in both arms," tetanus and typhoid.

After a morning at Sick Bay, the men were marched to noon chow. "The menu for this meal," Griffin continues, "went something like this: mashed potatoes, something they call roast beef, peas and carrots, two slices of bread, a cup of black coffee, and a piece of sweet bread (often referred to as cake)." Following chow, the men walked to a uniform issue shed. Each man drew "2 utility pants, 2 utility jackets, 2 belts, 8 undershirts, 8 pairs of drawers, 1 dress uniform (green), 6 pairs of khaki pants, 6 khaki shirts, 6 field scarves (neckties), khaki caps, 2 green caps, 1 pair of dress shoes, 2 pairs of field shoes, 1 dress overcoat (green), and 1 O.D. jacket." The men were then loaded down with still more: work and dress socks, belt buckles, a fair leather belt for wear with the dress uniform, a barracks (frame) cap and cover, gloves, and a seabag to carry everything.

Later the men marched to another equipment shed and received "1 first aid kit, 1 rifle, 1 bayonet, 1 rifle belt, 1 poncho, and mess gear." There was more field gear: belt suspender straps, blanket roll straps, a knapsack, haversack, helmet with camouflage cover, canteen with cup and cover, 2 wool blankets, shelter half with tent pole, guy line and stakes, and an entrenching tool. The men got new M-1 rifles, routine issue replacing the old '03 Springfields. Next came a visit to the "Ship's Store" where they received "toothpaste, washing soap, face soap, stationery, two bath towels," and other health and comfort items.[6] During the receiving process, the men underwent interviews and tests and heard advice about dependency allotments and government insurance.

The men were organized into 36-man training platoons with two DIs per platoon, and four platoons making a training company. John Griffin was assigned to Platoon 410 in Company F. He described an ordinary day of recruit training at Montford Point Camp

> a very strenuous schedule. For example:
> 5:15 a.m. reveille
> 5:30 clean up the barracks
> 5:35 roll call
> 5:35–5:40 drill to the parade ground
> 5:40–6:00 exercise
> 6:05 breakfast
> 6:30–7:30 police the area (clean up the area around the barracks for inspection)
> 7:30–8:00 sick call
> 8:00–11:00 military training
> 11:10 return to quarters awaiting lunch
> 11:15–12:15 lunch
> 12:20–3:30 military training
> 3:30–5:00 dinner
> 5:05–10:00 p.m. washing clothes, cleaning rifle, writing letters, and studying the Marine Corps handbook
> 10:00 p.m. taps.[7]

On Sunday, the schedule was a little different. The men could sleep until 6:30 a.m. with breakfast at 7:00. Church was mandatory, unless a man was ill at Sick Bay.

Many of the men ate better than they ever had in their lives. For example, breakfast was often creamed beef on toast (the infamous SOS, "Shit on a Shingle"), or eggs and hash browns, coffee, and sometimes rolls or pastries.[8] Griffin recalls, "Every time we went to the Mess Hall or the laundry we went running. They refer to this as 'double time.' I lived about eight city blocks from the Mess Hall, and by the time I ran from there to the barracks I was hungry again."[9]

The men hiked through the swamps and forests and attended classes on Marine Corps customs, courtesies, rank structure and traditions. When not in classes, they fell out for close order drill to learn instant and willing obedience to orders when working together as a unit. At first, the men learned the basics of close order drill but soon advanced to drill under arms, carrying rifles. The M-1 was, as recruits would memorize, a gas operated, clip-fed, air-cooled, semi-automatic shoulder weapon. "We learned how to detail strip the rifle for cleaning, the various parts, the weight, length, and firing power, how many rounds of ammunition it used ... and the serial number of the rifle," Griffin said. At one rifle inspection, Griffin's weapon was not as clean as the inspecting sergeant demanded. "For thirty minutes I had to 'duck walk,' with my rifle extended above my head, around the platoon."[10]

Griffin's next challenge was hand-to-hand combat training. "This particular course was very dangerous because one could easily get an arm or leg broken in the process of learning if one were not careful. Many a day I wished that I could get my arm or leg broken, or maybe one of my eyes put out so that I could end my military training once and for all."[11]

Field Skills

The training cycle continued, with emphasis on living in the field. The men learned the three steps for saving the life of a wounded or injured Marine: stop the bleeding, protect the wound from infection, and treat for shock. They attended classes on how to put together the various types of packs; the lighter combat pack with a short blanket roll was used when in the field or during actual fighting. It consisted of "one complete change of clothing, shoes, and mess gear. The long blanket roll was made by a shelter half (one half of a two-man tent) rolled around a wool blanket, tent guy line, five tent pins, a three-section tent pole, rolled tightly and attached to the pack by blanket roll straps and used with the field pack or field transport pack. The men used these on hikes, when moving from one camp to another, or when going overseas. This pack consisted of "just about all the clothing and equipment" a man had.

John Griffin used a long blanket roll pack for the first time on a two-day hike through the woods surrounding the camp. After the first day, the men pitched their two-man tents, sleeping on the ground with their packs for pillows. "During the two days we didn't have any cooked food. Each man had a issue of six boxes of 'K's' and each box had a different meal. You had one for breakfast, one for lunch and one for supper. Each box contained a complete meal along with a stick of gum, two cigarettes, and a bar of candy." The five-mile hike back to camp at the end of the second day was the worst part of the experience. "I was dead on my feet," Griffin said.[12]

After recruit training, the men would be assigned to FMF units, one of the Defense Battalions, Depot Companies, or Ammunition Companies. There they would receive any specialized weapons training they needed. In the boot camp training syllabus of 1943, the men did not train on the variety of infantry weapons they would find in the Pacific, such as hand and rifle grenades, machine guns, flamethrowers, and rocket launchers.

Boot Camp Recreation

Recruits had little time for play while training to become Marines. A platoon was lucky if the men saw a movie, even if it was nothing more than a training film.

Weekly visits to the Ship's Store for more cigarettes, soap, or other personal items served as recreation of sorts because it meant a change from the routine of drill and classroom work. Recruits might get an occasional cold soda, but no candy. The only time recruits could have sweets was if someone received a box of goodies from home, but the DIs insisted that it be shared among one's hut-mates, so there was little enough to go around.[13]

Live Fire Demonstration

The 51st trained for war, and the men were eager to go. The men saw depot companies formed and shipped out to the Pacific on a regular basis yet they had more training before them. Herb Brewer said of the depot companies, "They were formed after us but they went overseas before we did. I guess the Marine Corps felt the need for them was more critical, and so they were the first to go overseas. We started wondering why we hadn't gone overseas. Later on we found there was still some concern in Washington, and in the Marine Corps, as to whether or not a unit of our type would do well out in the Pacific."

The 90mm antiaircraft gun batteries of the 51st were at Onslow Beach for live fire training in November. Brewer recalls that someone said, "Look. There's the Secretary of the Navy." Secretary Knox and Lt. Gen. Holcomb had come out, escorted by Lt. Col. Stephenson, the battalion commanding officer, to observe the training and see for themselves if the battalion was ready to go to war. "A few minutes after he stepped out of his car," the 90mm guns opened fire on a target towed behind an airplane scoring hits within 60 seconds and destroying the target. Brewer said, "We blew the target out of the air."[14] Holcomb commented to Knox that the 51st was ready.

En Route to War

Stephenson had proposed a certain length for his pre-deployment training schedule and HQMC approved it. However, for unknown reasons, that training schedule had been cut short by five weeks. The men may well have never received their advanced gunnery training.[15] At the conclusion of the field training, the battalion returned to Camp Knox in early December. The men who had transferred in without ever completing recruit training, mere warm bodies to fill out unit rosters, needed to go to the rifle range to qualify. Some of the "old hands" applied for Christmas leaves. However, before the holiday routine could take effect, the battalion commander learned that HQMC had moved up the battalion's West Coast departure date. To add to the confusion, the activation date of the 52d Defense Battalion was moved up as well. As a result, over 400 experienced officers and men found themselves pulled from the 51st to become the nucleus of the 52d.[16] White

NCOs moved over to the new battalion and their black understudies "fleeted up" to replace them.

The 51st Packs Up

All hands turned to and began the time-consuming "mount out" process of inventorying and packing the battalion's equipment in wooden boxes and crates. Morale was high, even through the Christmas season. The first black Marine combat unit was on the move! Guns were cleaned, tampions strapped over muzzles, and protective canvas covers lashed down tight. The early January weather turned foul with rain, sleet, and snow. Allocated 175 railroad freight cars, the men loaded them at a rate of 25 a day. Troop trains marshaled and the battalion made ready to depart in increments. By January 19, most of the battalion had left the camp. A small rear echelon, scheduled to depart on the 20th, remained at Camp Knox. Unfortunately, an alcohol-fueled incident occurred late in the afternoon of the 19th, which clouded the reputation of the battalion. Major D.A. Routh, Provost Marshal of the Montford Point Camp, described the incident in a report to Col. Woods.

According to Routh, some men from the 51st went for a few beers at the Montford Point slop chute and soon were ordering beer by the case. A white military police corporal arrived for duty at the slop chute at 1645. Black Marines pelted the MP with paper wads, and despite his pleas, the men refused to behave. A sergeant from the 51st, saying "they were going to tear the place down," started pushing and shoving the MP while the other men, yelling, began climbing on the tables. The MP corporal retreated to the camp brig, armed himself with a pistol and gathered more MPs to help him quiet the disturbance. The MPs returned and closed the slop chute. Once outside, the men got rowdier, breaking windows and throwing rocks and bottles at the MPs. An MP sergeant fired three rounds from his carbine into the air. The crowd scattered. Some of the men ran into the theatre, so the MPs closed the movie house as well. The camp Officer of the Day (OD) arrived and ordered the area cleared. By 1930, full darkness had come, and things had quieted down; the men dispersed.

Around 2000 some 15 or 20 shots, ball and tracer rounds, were fired from the direction of Camp Knox across Scales Creek toward the Montford Point Camp.[17] One of the bullets struck a drill instructor at Montford Point Camp, Corporal (Cpl.) Rolland J. Curtiss, in the shoulder but he was not seriously wounded and was taken to Sick Bay. Lt. Col. Stephenson and several of his officers arrived. They made their way to Camp Knox to investigate; the officers inspected all rifles at Camp Knox. They found one rifle had been fired recently and another freshly cleaned with hair oil in a likely attempt to make it appear that it had not been fired.

Col. Woods conducted his own investigation and reported the results to the commanding general of Camp Lejeune.[18] Every Marine memorizes the serial number of the rifle issued to him, but the investigators found men in possession of rifles other than their own. Armory records were in disarray and of no help in determining ownership of the fired rifle. The camp commander, Col. Woods, personally walked through the barracks vacated by the 51st. Col. Woods raised questions in his report on the incident. Weapons and personal equipment accountability in the battalion was sloppy. The officers and men of the rear party left by the 51st failed to ensure the barracks at Camp Knox were cleaned.[19]

Oddly, the Camp Provost Marshal made no comment on the fact that none of his MPs took the names of the men who started the disturbance at the slop chute. Further, MPs placed no one under military restraint for later release to a responsible officer or NCO from the 51st.

The 51st had many young and inexperienced men in positions of leadership who were either unschooled or unaccustomed to their responsibilities, and some of these were members of the rear party. Marine leaders learn that after giving orders, the final troop-leading step is always SUPERVISE. Statements taken by the investigators reveal a pattern best described as "I told so-and-so to do this or that," and "He said/I said," but little in the way of actual supervision by responsible NCOs and officers. Given the foregoing, it would have been surprising if there had been no incident.

Most of the men in the battalion, already on troop trains heading west, were unaware of the incident. Herbert Brewer had not seen his parents since he left San Antonio for Montford Point in September 1942. His troop train "happened to come through San Antonio, my hometown. We couldn't get off the trains, and I looked out the window and saw one of my old high school instructors standing on the platform, so I called to him, and he called my parents — we didn't live too far from the station — and they came down so I got a chance to say goodbye to them."[20]

Expansion Demands Manpower

The number of black Marines grew from 790 in December 1942 to 12,400 by December 1943.[21] Blacks served at Montford Point Camp schools and units, in security guard detachments at Naval Ammunition Depot McAlester, Oklahoma, at the Philadelphia Depot of Supplies, and in Marine Depot Companies in the Pacific.[22]

Nineteen defense battalions had been formed, the 1st through the 18th and the 51st and 52d Defense Battalions (the 5th Defense Battalion became the 14th, so that the 19 units accounted for 20 numbers). The Marine Corps had already formed five 19,000-man divisions and planned for a sixth, and its three air wings accounted for almost 47,000 men with a fourth wing soon to be activated. The commandant directed that men for the new units come from currently authorized manpower levels. Brigadier General (Brig. Gen.) Gerald C. Thomas, Director of Plans and Policies at HQMC, recommended eliminating special units, including the defense battalions. The 26,685 Marines and sailors in those battalions were a lucrative pool

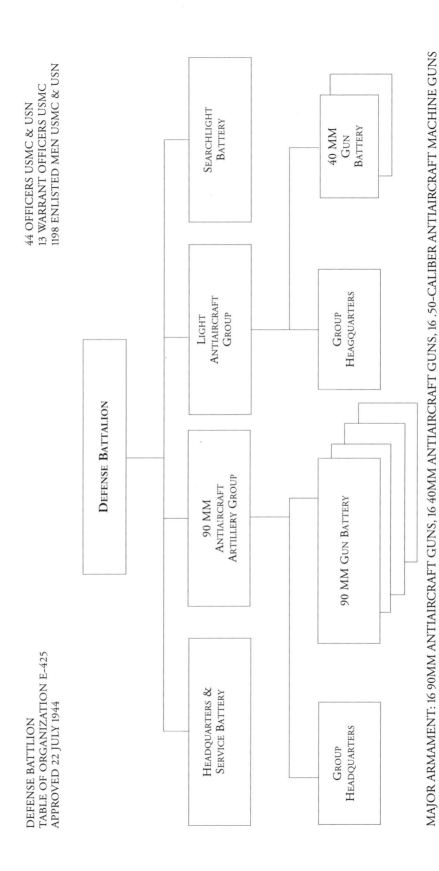

DEFENSE BATTLION
TABLE OF ORGANIZATION E-425
APPROVED 22 JULY 1944

44 OFFICERS USMC & USN
13 WARRANT OFFICERS USMC
1198 ENLISTED MEN USMC & USN

DEFENSE BATTALION

90 MM ANTIAIRCRAFT ARTILLERY GROUP

LIGHT ANTIAIRCRAFT GROUP

SEARCHLIGHT BATTERY

HEADQUARTERS & SERVICE BATTERY

90 MM GUN BATTERY

GROUP HEADQUARTERS

GROUP HEADQUARTERS

40 MM GUN BATTERY

MAJOR ARMAMENT: 16 90MM ANTIAIRCRAFT GUNS, 16 40MM ANTIAIRCRAFT GUNS, 16 .50-CALIBER ANTIAIRCRAFT MACHINE GUNS

Figure 4: The final Table of Organization for the black defense battalions.

that headquarters looked to for filling out new units. The Navy Department balked at the plan. Their position was that, not only should no defense battalions be eliminated, but 10 additional defense battalions were needed to defend advance bases!

Vandegrift argued that as the war progressed, the Japanese Navy had lost many capital ships while the United States Navy grew stronger and more capable of denying Japanese ships access to waters around our own advanced bases with each passing day. Japanese aircraft, Vandegrift said, posed the most significant threat to advanced naval bases rather than bombardment from Japanese surface ships. Therefore, he intended to reorganize Marine Defense Battalions with an increased heavy antiaircraft capability.

A defense battalion commanding officer said of that time, "We had good Navy action that kept those [Japanese] ships away from us. Our people broke their radio [codes] in the war. We knew what they were doing as well as they did. They [the Japanese] did get to me a few times — mostly at night" with bombing raids.[23] That battalion commander's opinion mirrored Vandegrift's: On a day-to-day basis, the most serious threat they faced in the Pacific was Japanese aircraft.

Japanese tactics changed as the war dragged on, and far too many Japanese underground defenses were not being found, hit and destroyed by battleships, cruisers, destroyers, or airplanes. Evidence for that was Marine casualty lists, increasing with each assault. Navy acceptance of Vandegrift's argument meant an opportunity for the Marines to shift the 155mm guns from the seacoast artillery groups to general support artillery units of amphibious corps to shell Japanese troops and gun positions in support of Marine ground attacks — Marine gunners putting Marine shells on Marine targets when Marines needed them. Vandegrift managed to bring the Navy around to his point of view. Plans went forward to deactivate two of the existing 19 defense battalions and reconfigure the remaining 17 to meet the evolving threat. The new defense battalion (actually, antiaircraft artillery battalion) T/O, E-425, approved July 22, 1944, is shown in Figure 4.[24]

SECTION IV

1944

17

Activating the 52d Defense Battalion

A Smoother Evolution

If experience is a good teacher, then the 52d Defense Battalion had all the advantages. The 51st Defense Battalion was born during the darkest days of the war at a time of frantic reaction to Japanese advances in the Pacific. The fact that blacks were in the Corps was still a novel and not widely known concept. Mistakes had been made, men learned from them, found better ways, learned that the principles of leadership applied regardless of a man's race. Over time, the whole process of enlisting and training black Marines, forming them in newly activated units and sending them off to the Pacific had become a little smoother.

The 52d's first battalion commander, Lt. Col. Augustus W. Cockrell, like Col. Woods, Lt. Col. Stephenson, and Lt. Col. LeGette, was a Southerner, hailing from Florida (it seems that in the early days of their existence, either Southern commanders were the black battalions' destiny or else many Marine officers hailed from Dixie and pure chance decided their assignments). Cockrell had previously served as executive officer of the 2d Defense Battalion, and he had commanded the 8th Defense Battalion overseas.[1]

Cockrell had a much easier beginning with the 52d than did Col. Woods with the 51st. The 400-odd men, officers and enlisted, pulled from the 51st brought *experience* as Marines seasoned by time in service and time in grade as NCOs. The cadre of black NCOs in the 52d would supervise black Marines fresh from boot camp or from technical schools, unencumbered by friendships with men from their own boot camp days. That nucleus was experienced as well with the myriad of guns and technical equipment common to a defense battalion and knew how to operate and maintain the gear.

125

Griffin's Great Day

"This day I shall never forget," John Griffin said when his boot camp graduation finally arrived. "It was the day I was appointed to the Marine Corps Administration School." Most of his friends marched off to Depot or Ammunition Companies. After the graduation ceremony, he gathered up his gear and reported to Headquarters Battalion at Montford Point for his school. Griffin's welcome aboard was to stand a uniform and equipment inspection. This was not harassment; it was expected, a routine way to ensure that when a Marine joined a new unit he had all the uniforms and gear he was supposed to have, and that it was clean and serviceable. Then he was assigned to his barracks and granted *base liberty!* "I hadn't been to a movie in thirteen weeks," so he went to the camp theater, which could seat 1500 men and showed all the latest movies. After the show he walked to the Enlisted Men's Recreation Center, the "Slop Chute," and got loaded with cold beer and listened to the jukebox. The following Sunday he slept in until 11:30 a.m. and said, "I felt very strange not having to get up before day as I did in boot camp." He recalls that, like so many other recruits, both white and black, during nights in boot camp, "we used to say what we were going to do to the [drill] instructors when we completed boot camp, but this never happened, for once you leave" the recruit area "you don't want to see it again."[2]

His administration course lasted five weeks, after which Griffin was assigned to Headquarters Battalion for a short time before being given eight days leave to visit his home, which he had not seen for almost six months. Family and friends found the young Marine more grown up, more serious about life. His mother was pleased to find that her once picky-eater son "could eat any kind of food." His new creed was, "If you can't find a dinner to suit your taste, find a taste to suit your dinner." However, thanks to the Marine Corps, there was one exception — he refused to eat a potato.[3] Returning to Montford Point, Griffin learned that his new unit was the 52d Defense Battalion at Camp Knox.

The Marshall Islands

Meanwhile, overseas the march into the Central Pacific continued with Operation FLINTLOCK. The 276 ships of the Joint Expeditionary Force carrying 53,400 Marines and soldiers of the assault forces and 31,000 troops in the Reserve and Garrison Forces steamed toward the Marshall Islands in January 1944.[4] The low-lying, coral limestone and sand Marshall Islands include the atolls of Bikini, Eniwetok, Kwajalein. Also included are the large islands of Roi and Namur, Majuro, Rongelap, and Utirik. The Marshalls are located in the Central Pacific Ocean, about one-half of the way from Hawaii to Australia.

Sixteen black Marine Depot Companies had been activated and sent to the Pacific (two, the 5th and 6th, had been disbanded and the men reassigned to the

1st, 2d, 3d, and 4th Marine Depot Companies); two black Marine Ammunition Companies were also in the Pacific. These men were not a part of the forces that assaulted the Marshalls, but they worked as part of the Base and Field Depots that supplied the operation. The 15th Marine Depot Company, activated December 1, 1943, reached Allen Island at Kwajalein in the Marshall Islands on March 7, 1944, and was later reassigned to Roi-Namur as part of the garrison force.

The hard-fought landings at Kwajalein Atoll saw the first use of DUKWs, a U.S. Army amphibious development. The "duck" was properly known as a Truck, Amphibious, Cargo, 2 1/2 ton, 6x6 DUKW. Made by General Motors Corporation, it used their nomenclature: "D" for 1942 (the year of manufacture), "U" for Utility Vehicle, "K" for all-wheel drive, and "W" for rear tandem axles. The DUKW, based on GMC's two-and-a-half-ton cargo truck, was fitted with a watertight hull and propeller. It could travel 6.4 miles per hour in water and about 50 miles per hour on land with five tons of cargo. Capacity was increased by the addition of a "Trailer, Amphibious, Cargo." This 20-foot long trailer could carry up to three tons of supplies or equipment within a 210 cubic foot bay.[5]

The lessons of Operation GALVANIC at Tarawa, where the flow of supplies to the assault units had been slow and uncertain, were painfully fresh. In an effort to prevent a recurrence in the several amphibious assaults that would take place in the upcoming Operation FLINTLOCK, U.S. Navy Rear Admiral (R. Adm.) Richmond Kelly Turner, commanding the Joint Expeditionary Force, directed that the navy's beach party and the Marines' shore party should sail in the same transport ships, prepare joint plans, and land quickly. Elements of both were assigned to the fourth wave of boats to land on each assault beach.[6] A navy officer explained, "Without adequate organization on the beach, with excess personnel to meet emergencies, the whole operation is imperiled. Needed supplies do not reach the front, are not removed from the beach, may not even be landed, because of congestion and disorder."[7]

The command-level attention and the planning paid off in well-executed movement of supplies ashore on the islands taken during the operation. A recommendation went up the chain of command urging the organization of a permanent shore party, a well-trained nucleus that could be reinforced with labor and garrison units when needed (a concept later known as task organizing). When such a change became SOP, there would never again be a need to take riflemen from the assault battalions and use them to unload supplies, sort them and place them in dumps and move them to the front lines.

DIs Haze Recruits

By the early months of 1944, more black Marines earned promotions and took the field as DIs. The rapid advancement had its drawbacks because the men lacked experience in handling recruits. The physical hazing (an occasional boot to the rear) Turner Blount received from his black DIs in the previous October and November had by January 1944 manifested itself in other forms that actually had nothing at all to do with proper discipline. One recruit who answered a question with "yes" instead of "yes sir" was told to use his toothbrush to scrub the entire barracks floor. Moreover, later that night, a half hour after taps had sounded, the entire platoon fell out for "locker box parade." Clad only in their skivvies, the men stood in platoon formation in the chill night air with their footlockers. At the DI's command, they performed close order drill under arms with twenty-pound locker boxes instead of rifles. Two men fainted during the hour and a half of pointless drill.[8] That kind of petty harassment was not limited to black recruits nor was it limited in time to the World War II era. It was one of many forms of hazing that continued in the Marine Corps into the 1960s.

The 52d Trains in the Field

By February, the 52d Defense Battalion moved from Montford Point Camp across Scales Creek to Camp Knox as training intensified. Morale was high, and the men proudly sewed the distinctive new unit patch onto the left shoulder of their uniforms. The 52d's patch emphasized the Marine Corps's colors, scarlet and gold. There was a red shield featuring a blue diagonal bar with four white stars. A scarlet "52" inside a gold shell burst was in the upper left corner while the lower right corner showed a gold 90mm gun and mount with scarlet letters "U.S.M.C." on the mount.[9]

As the 51st had done when it moved to Camp Knox, the 52d continued to receive men from boot camp and schools, and started through the training phases from the basics up, including crossing the Atlantic Waterway and setting up on Onslow Beach where it conducted live fire training. In June, the reorganization ordered by Lt. Gen. Vandegrift came to the 52d. The 155mm guns were turned in, and the Seacoast Artillery Group disbanded. The artillerymen joined the 90mm Antiaircraft Artillery Group, to form a fourth 90mm gun battery. At the same time, the Special Weapons Group reorganized as the Light Antiaircraft Group; the 20mm guns were replaced by 40mm guns, and of course, the crews had to be retrained.[10]

In addition, the Montford Point Camp's 7th Separate Pack Howitzer Battery, a "step-child" holdover from the early days of the old 51st Composite Defense Battalion, was disbanded; the men, experienced artillerymen, reported to the new defense battalion. Every enlisted man in the 52d was black, including the Navy corpsmen.[11]

18

South Pacific

First Impressions

Gene Smith recalls his welcome at Noumea on January 5, 1944. "When we arrived on New Caledonia a tent city type of thing was already set up for us, about a mile from the rest of the camp — everything was separated." That tent city would be Smith's home for the next nine months. "The one good thing about New Caledonia, it was a French Island and under their control. We could go down into the city of Noumea and be accepted by the French people, served in all of the restaurant and bars and be treated with dignity."[1] In fact, novelist James Michener's *Tales of the South Pacific*, later made into the stage musical and movie *South Pacific*, were based on his experiences with sailors, Marines, French planters and Tonkinese citizens of the islands in this war theatre.

Although the French accepted the black Marines, some of the Americans on the island brought their Jim Crow attitudes with them from the States. "Of course many of our white comrades did all that they could to create problems. Don't get me wrong there were many whites on our side and in our corner." Smith said, "Our company commander, a captain, tried very hard to make things easier, but he only had so much authority." Clearly, that officer had the respect of his men. "We would have followed him anywhere." Smith continues, "There were more than just American military on New Caledonia; groups of course came from France, New Zealand, Canada and Australia. The Canadians had some blacks among them and they were not segregated like we in the American military were. They seemed like one happy family. Seeing that really made one think."[2] The integrated Canadian unit made quite an impression on the young man from Birmingham, Alabama.

Segregation Rears its Head

The men of the 51st Defense Battalion came together at Camp Elliot near San Diego to await transportation to the Pacific. There they drew unit shoulder patches to sew on their uniforms. Marine uniforms are generally spartan when it comes to pinning or sewing on devices, ribbons and badges. Probably the most well known embellishment of the uniform is the green and scarlet French *fourragère* (called a "pogey-rope") awarded to the men of the 5th and 6th Marine Regiments during World War I. For a short period during World War II Marines were authorized to sew unit identification patches on their uniforms. The patches were not considered decorations or service awards, and they were not to be worn in forward areas where the enemy could see them. The unit patches were sewn on the left shoulder of over coats, field coats, uniform blouses, and on shirts when the blouse was not worn. Only one unit patch could be worn.

The 51st Defense Battalion's identification patches were a red cloth oval with the large white numerals "51" in the center above the letters USMC in smaller white letters. Superimposed in front of the 51 was the blue silhouette of a 90mm antiaircraft gun.[3] The patches added to the men's general feeling of pride. Some of the men attended an open-air movie at the camp's amphitheatre. When white Marines told them that blacks had to sit in the rear, the men of the 51st disrupted the movie — after all, they were Marines going to war, segregation be damned.

At Camp Elliot, the men were surprised when word came down for the 51st to turn in to the quartermaster all the ordnance and motor transport equipment they had brought from Camp Lejeune. The 51st took another blow on January 27 when a new battalion commander, Lt. Col. Curtis W. LeGettte, a South Carolinian and a Marine since 1910, took over the battalion. LeGette, the former commanding officer of the 7th Defense Battalion in the Ellice Islands, had recently returned to the United States and met with Lt. Col. Gould P. Groves, the battalion XO. "I asked him [Groves], 'Where is the commanding officer?' He said that he had orders to so-and-so, somewhere. I believe he showed me a copy of the orders." There was no meeting, no turnover between the outgoing and incoming commanders.[4]

LeGette addressed the men at a battalion formation soon after he took over and his comments included a verbal reprimand of the entire battalion for their discipline and behavior. Today we are left to ponder whether LeGette based his remarks on what he observed around the battalion while taking over or if he had been briefed beforehand that the battalion had problems. Whatever the case, one of the basic principles of leadership holds that an officer "praises in public, admonishes in private." While publicly admonishing the men, LeGette chose to address them in such a way as to almost guarantee offense to blacks. Rather than call them Marines he called them "you people." It was reminiscent of the Larsen speech many of the men heard the previous summer back at Montford Point.

Was this a routine replacement of the commanding officer? No. The incident at the Montford Point slop chute, with shots fired and a Marine wounded, problems with weapons accountability, and the poor condition of the barracks and property at Camp Knox most likely led to the change of command. A full report had reached the Lieutenant General Commandant and shortly thereafter LeGette took over while the battalion was on the move.

When the men turned in the guns and equipment they had trained on, become familiar with and packed at Camp Lejeune, no one explained to them that this was a common practice in the Corps when a unit relieved another unit of the same type in a routine rotation of units. The men of the relieving unit simply took over equipment already in place. There was no need to load and ship the more than 9,000 tons of equipment belonging to the 51st to the Ellice Islands, offload it, load the equipment of the 7th Defense Battalion and ship it somewhere else.[5] The process represented a saving of more than 84,000 cubic feet of shipping space that could be used for other essential material. Therefore, the men kept only their personal gear and some battalion property, and at San Diego on February 11 they filed aboard a troopship, the SS *Meteor*.[6]

Troopships

The SS *Meteor* was a U.S. Merchant Marine ship. She came from the fleet of ships that import and export goods during peacetime but deliver troops and war materiel as a naval auxiliary during war.[7] The *Meteor* was not a converted passenger liner and neither was it configured for troop comfort, for the men of the 51st were crowded into their berthing spaces in a time before troops rated the comfort of air conditioning. While she lacked amenities, the *Meteor* did have an armed naval guard aboard, that is, U.S. Navy sailors who manned defensive guns mounted aboard the ship.

The United States employed a wide variety of troopships during World War II, including passenger liners such as SS *America*, type C2, C3, and C4 cargo ships, Liberty and Victory ships, and foreign ships taken over by the United States. The Army Transportation Service operated some troopships, some with civilian crews, some crewed by men of the Merchant Marine, as did the U.S. Navy and the War Shipping Administration. Black Marines would sail on several of these in the course of the war.

19

Leaving the States

First Time at Sea

After graduation, Turner Blount received orders to the 19th Marine Depot Company, organized on February 1, 1944. After the usual short period of assembly, the company loaded onto a train for Norfolk, Virginia, on February 22, and with their sister unit, the 20th Marine Depot Company, boarded the USS *James O'Hara* (APA-90). They joined a convoy, sailed for Panama on February 26, transited the canal and made for Hawaii.[1] Blount remembers that was his "First time aboard ship. First time out in the world. Never been so sick in all the days of my life. That was the sickest I've ever been, riding on deck, watching the water and the waves out there. It just made me sick to my stomach."[2]

When they arrived in Hawaii, both depot companies and the 3d Marine Ammunition Company became part of the 6th Base Depot, V Amphibious Corps (VAC), where they were immediately put to work moving supplies at Camp Catlin on the island of Oahu. On April 20 they transferred to the newly formed 7th Field Depot. The 7th Field Depot, commanded by Lt. Col. Edwin D. Partridge, would soon become part of the Corps Troops, VAC, preparing for Operation FORAGER, the June assault on the Mariana Islands.

During the last week of April, the company commander, Captain W.C. Adams, addressed the men at a company formation. "You men have been asking when you would operate under actual combat. Well, you asked for it and you're going to get it! Start getting your gear packed for we're going to move out very soon. You men have a job to do and, damn it, you're going to do it — come hell, high water and little fishes!"[3]

Also working as part of the build up for FORAGER, the 2d and 4th Marine Ammunition Companies, with the 5th Field Depot on Guadalcanal, helped load supplies on cargo and transport ships of the assault forces. The 20th moved to the island of Maui and worked 12-hour shifts loading ships for the coming operation. They learned they would be attached to the 4th Marine Division Shore Party for the assault.[4]

132

Destination: Ellice Islands

The Gilbert and Ellice Islands Group were part of a British Protectorate. Earlier in the war, the Japanese intended to occupy the Funafuti in the Ellice Islands, about ten degrees south of the Equator (see map 4, Guadalcanal Supply Lines), but losses at Midway in June 1942 caused a change of plans. This enabled the Americans to move eleven ships forward and to occupy Funafuti on October 2, 1942. When American forces arrived, the islanders relocated to the small island of Lakena. The Japanese did not learn of the occupation of Funafuti until March 1943, when a reconnaissance airplane flew over the islands. A U.S. Navy Construction Battalion (C.B. or Seabees) in a very short time constructed an airstrip on Funafuti. The new airfield was operational before the end of 1942 and began sending reconnaissance aircraft against the Japanese-held islands of Tarawa, Mili, and Jaluit. Twenty-two army air force B-24 bombers launched the first offensive operation from the Ellice Islands on April 20, 1943, with a raid on Nauru. The Seabees also built a seaplane ramp on the lagoon side of Funafuti for operations by both short and long-range seaplanes.

At various times in the war, large numbers of ships anchored in Funafuti lagoon. In October 1943, forty-three ships entered the harbor as part of the buildup for Operation GALVANIC, the amphibious assault at Tarawa, some 700 miles to the north. In January 1944, shortly before the 51st Defense Battalion arrived, there were 174 ships at anchor in the lagoon.[5]

The island of Nanomea, also part of the Ellice Islands, has a large lagoon in the northwest corner and borders two smaller islands inside a barrier coral reef that extends about 1500 feet from the islands. Nanomea, 295 miles northwest from Funafuti, was accessible only by sea. Seabees began building an airfield on Nanomea, and the Marine Corps's 7th Defense Battalion, then commanded by Lt. Col. Curtis W. LeGette, landed on the island in August 1943 to provide much needed protection for the base. Several Japanese air raids targeted Nanomea wounding several of LeGette's men, and in August the ship *John Williams* came under air attack while it was unloading supplies.[6]

The airfield, completed in October, took up one sixth of the island's land area and included a mile long bomber runway and a service force of 2,300 men. That airfield was important because it was the closest American-held island to the Marshalls.[7] Reconnaissance and bombing missions into the Gilberts and Marshall Islands launched from the airfield. By late 1943 the Ellice Islands were home to over 6,000 American soldiers, sailors and Marines.[8] A bombing raid by Japanese aircraft on the night of November 10, 1943, killed one soldier and caused some minor equipment damage.[9] It was the last Japanese offensive action against the Ellice Islands.

The *Meteor* sailed for the Ellice Islands where the men of the 51st would replace the 7th Defense Battalion, Lt. Col. LeGette's former command. Ironically, the lightly armed transport ship was destined to see more combat than the Marines' 51st Defense Battalion. After stopping in the Ellice Islands, the *Meteor* went on to

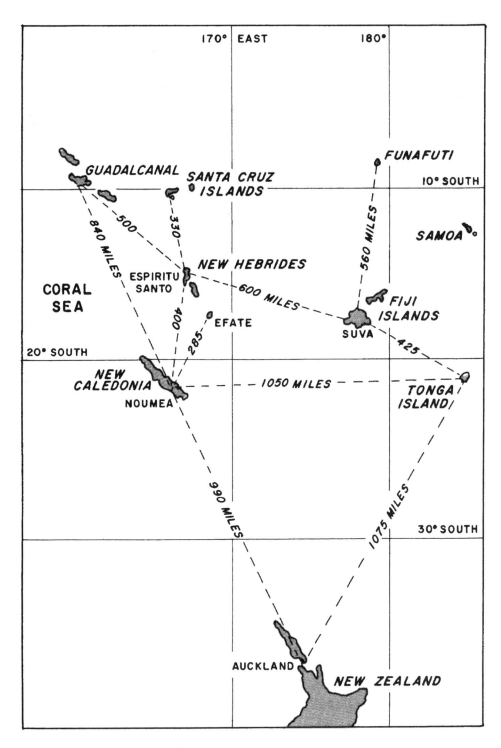

Guadalcanal supply lines.

Source: Dyer, *The Amphibians*, Vol. I, 418

participate in several amphibious operations, and her armed naval guard earned two battle stars in combat.[10]

The 51st Divides Itself

While in route to the Ellice Islands, plans were made for the 51st Defense Battalion to divide into two components to take over the 7th Defense Battalion's dispersed locations. Lt. Col. Groves, the battalion's executive officer, would take a part of the battalion designated as Detachment A to garrison Nanomea Island. The rest of the battalion, under Lt. Col. LeGette, would take over the defenses of Funafuti and Nukufetau. The entire unit unloaded at Funafuti and Detachment A transferred to two smaller ships and reached Nanomea on February 25. By February 27, the 51st had finished taking over the departing 7th Defense Battalion's weapons and equipment. A black Marine suggested that the men of the 7th "were never so glad to see black people in their lives." In the war's backwaters the men settled into the daily routine of a Marine's life — gun drills, practice firing and then cleaning the corrosive powder residue from the gun tubes, and cleaning ever-present coral dust and salt spray from the guns and optical equipment.[11]

Herbert Brewer said:

> It was rather quiet at that time after Tarawa. As I remember our only activity was an occasional false alarm, maybe a plane would come by and we were hoping we could shoot at it. The island of Funafuti was our battalion headquarters; our battery was on the smaller island called Nanomea. You could almost throw a rock across it, but it did have an airstrip. We were stationed around the airstrip. The natives stayed on an adjacent smaller island, and during the day they'd come and wash clothes. At night they'd be taken back to their island. There were cocoanut trees. It was nice, but boring at times. You could fish if you were interested and enjoyed it. We got a can of beer and a bottle of coke every week. I didn't drink, so I'd trade my beer for somebody's coke. So I ended up with two cokes.

The splitting of battalion resources between the islands included the medical staff. "I lost my first tooth there on Nanomea. We didn't have a dentist on our island; he was on the main island. So I put up with it, put Vicks [salve] on it and tolerated the pain until I was able to get to the dentist. Just our [90mm antiaircraft gun] battery and a 155mm battery were there on Nanomea. It was sort of boring. We kept waiting and hoping. Maybe the Japs heard we were there and decided, 'No, we don't want to go there.'"

There was one brief moment of excitement for the detachment at Nanomea on the night of March 28. An unidentified blip appeared on radar — a suspected Japanese submarine — and the 155mm guns fired eleven rounds before the target disappeared. "Other than that," Brewer said, "it was just very routine."[12] By the middle of 1944, the war moved further to the north and American forces began withdrawing from the islands to follow the war.

An OCS Applicant

At battalion headquarters on Funafuti, Fred Branch, now a corporal, mailed a letter to HQMC in Washington containing his application for OCS. However, in his rush to apply, Branch had not gotten the required commanding officer's endorsement so his application came back, denied. Branch needed to make a favorable impression on Lt. Col. LeGette, so a senior NCO decided Branch should deliver the morning mail to LeGette. That night Branch washed, starched, and ironed his service khaki uniform, polished his shoes and brass, and assumed his new duties. Branch resubmitted his OCS application and LeGette gave him a positive endorsement. A response from HQMC was not long in coming.[13]

The Blame Game

Questions about Lt. Col. Stephenson's handling of the 51st had not ended with the change of command back at Camp Elliot but carried on into mid–1944 with a series of charges and countercharges revolving around the combat efficiency of the 51st Defense Battalion.[14] Unknown to the men, in June 1944, Lt. Col. LeGette received a letter from the commandant stating that some of the big guns and vehicles the 51st turned in at San Diego had not been properly maintained. "They had let some of the motors freeze" for lack of oil. Lt. Col. LeGette investigated and concluded in a response to the commandant that the equipment maintenance problems were his predecessor's fault, and even recommend that Lt. Col. Stephenson be court-martialed![15]

LeGette soon followed up with another report blaming Lt. Col. Stephenson for the lack of combat efficiency in the battalion. "I remember one case," LeGette said later, "in which they blew off the end of a 40mm gun." The crewman "who was supposed to remove the tampion [a plug or muzzle cover to keep out moisture, sand, or dust when a weapon is not in use] ... didn't do it." LeGette called the man over and asked him why he did that. "I forgot," the man answered. LeGette pointed out that the crewman had been correctly removing the tampion for several weeks, and supposed that the man lacked sufficient advanced gunnery training and drills.[16]

After his relief, Lt. Col. Stephenson deployed in the Pacific and became the commanding officer of Headquarters and Service Battalion, Corps Troops, III Amphibious Corps, at Guadalcanal. There he was busy with planning for the coming assault on Guam and with writing letters strongly defending his actions, calling the 51st the "finest organization in the whole Negro program in the Marine Corps."[17]

In a July 20, 1944, report to the commandant, LeGette wrote, "Every attempt has been made to prepare this unit for combat. This includes firing of all organic weapons, daily drills ... rifle and carbine firing (which, I might mention, was never completed before the 51st left the states) and essential schools and close order drills."[18] It was true that the 51st suffered because of a shortened training period, but LeGette set out to fix that.

Responsibility Cannot Be Delegated

A unit leader must delegate his authority to subordinates to get things done. However, while *authority* may be delegated, *responsibility* cannot. The commanding officer is always responsible for what his unit does or fails to do. A unit's subordinate leaders — from the vehicle operator or gunner all the way up to the battery or group commander and ultimately the battalion commander — are at fault if equipment maintenance is not done. An inspecting NCO or officer need only look at a piece of equipment and compare it to the equipment records, and if the record says maintenance was performed but the gear appears dirty or will not work, something is amiss. When equipment is not cleaned and checked by the operators, but the records are doctored to show the work was in fact completed, then the records disagree with visual inspection, and this is called "gun decking." Such a state is evidence of irresponsible operators and of a failure of leaders to supervise. Supervision begins with good, experienced junior NCOs who ensure equipment is properly handled. Because of segregation and the fact that prior to 1942 there were no black Marines, a solid core of experienced black NCOs did not exist.

A Harsh Taskmaster

Nevertheless, the Corps is unforgiving of failure. A commanding officer is always responsible for what his unit does or fails to do. It is a simple matter: either get the job done right or be replaced by someone who can, and in the Marine Corps, there is *always* someone who wants to command a unit in war. Ideally, after the new commander is in place, especially when several months have passed, any problems in the unit should have already been identified by the new commanding officer and once that is done, remedial action to fix them should be ongoing. But things sometimes do not happen that way.

LeGette had a plan to remedy the ills of the 51st, but parts of it were more ambitious than practical. He wanted all the black enlisted men in the 51st who scored in Classes IV and V on the GCT transferred out and replaced by men who scored in Classes I, II, or III.[19] However, there was the problem of finding nearby black units willing to give up men in exchange. The only such units in the Ellice Islands were the 7th and 8th Marine Depot Companies, assigned to the FMF Base Depot at Funafuti after being re-routed from Samoa the previous year. However, even as LeGette was looking for men to exchange, both Depot Companies were in the process of moving to the 6th Base Depot on the Hawaiian island of Oahu in July. Furthermore, some of LeGette's officers were not happy to be serving with a black unit far in the rear area, so LeGette wanted those officers reassigned and replaced by other officers. Unfortunately, in mid–1944 few officers were asking for assignment to *any* defense battalion in the rear areas.

Gung-ho

It turns out that during the previous year, men in some of the defense battalions, including LeGette's 7th in the Ellice Islands, felt they had been left behind in the backwash of war. Their lot was boredom yet they were "gung-ho" (aggressive, eager to get into the war), and they would much prefer to be fighting the Japanese than waiting and watching someone else do it.

Major General Alexander A. Vandegrift, who in 1943 was serving as the commanding general of I Marine Amphibious Corps (IMAC), noticed the low morale in some of the defense battalions while on an inspection tour with his chief of staff, Colonel Gerald C. Thomas. "The war had gone beyond them," recalled Thomas. Some of the officers were "pleading just to get into the war," and as a result, thirty-five officers received transfers out of the rear area defense battalions.[20] Lt. Col. LeGette had no recourse but to make do with the officers and men he had.

An Organizational Maze

The tactical and administrative functions of the various corps-level amphibious commands operating in the Pacific earlier in the war were evolutionary in nature as amphibious warfare doctrine continued to be refined. By early 1944, the forces were cobbled together to form an organizational maze in which many administrative functions overlapped with resulting duplication of effort. March 1944 brought the first steps toward a significant reorganization of Marine forces in the Pacific that would later culminate in the formal establishment of Fleet Marine Force Pacific (FMFPac) on September 17, 1944.[21]

Major elements comprising FMFPac included six Marine Divisions and four Marine Aircraft Wings as well as the new antiaircraft artillery battalions created from the old defense battalions. Interestingly, the 51st Defense Battalion's two detachments were omitted from the list. The Supply Service, IMAC and Supply Service, VAC, consolidated to become Supply Service, FMFPac. Under the new organization came the Field and Base Depots and the 1st through 4th Service and Supply Battalions. Marine Supply Service reorganization was ongoing throughout the next year.[22]

20

The Marianas

Operation FORAGER

The loss of Kwajalein, Majuro and Eniwetok in the Marshalls revealed to the Japanese the vulnerability of their Pacific island bases to American attack. Only months earlier the Japanese fleet had been "at least as strong as our own."[1] Newly won bases in the Marshalls brought protected lagoon anchorages for the fleet and for the assembly of large amphibious forces, as well as land area for advanced supply dumps and airstrips that could accommodate all types of aircraft. In a series of carrier strikes, U.S. Navy aircraft had littered the bottom of Truk Atoll in the Carolines with the blasted hulks of Japanese ships, leaving about 8,000 Japanese soldiers isolated. The strategic situation in the Pacific Ocean Areas shifted in favor of the Americans.

The United States was refining its strategy of neutralizing and bypassing enemy strongholds. Further American advances into the Central Pacific would seriously threaten the inner defense line surrounding the Japanese home islands. The stage was set for the next major operation that would firmly establish advanced bases in the inner perimeter of Japan's defense. Operation FORAGER was to be a three-phased assault against the Marianas Islands.

The Marianas Islands lie in the North Pacific Ocean on a direct northwest line 1,850 miles from Tarawa in the Gilbert Islands and passing through the Marshalls (see map 5, Japan to the Gilberts). The Marianas were a vital link in an almost unbroken chain of islands extending 1,350 miles southward from Tokyo. Many of the islands were militarily valueless, but others, like stepping-stones, became bases to protect lines of air and sea communications from the Japanese home islands to other island fortresses.

Capture of the Marianas by American forces would cut a vital link in the chain of Japanese bases along the lines of communication. The Marianas would then provide bases from which Americans could control sea areas farther west in the Pacific. Finally, from the Marianas, the army air corps's new land based long-range B-29 bombers could reach Tokyo.

139

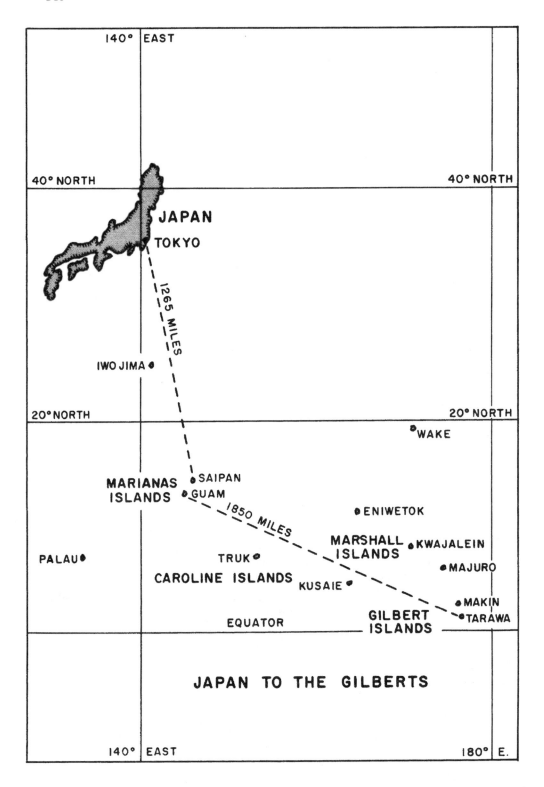

140° EAST

40° NORTH   40° NORTH

JAPAN

TOKYO

1265 MILES

IWO JIMA

20° NORTH   20° NORTH

WAKE

SAIPAN
MARIANAS
ISLANDS   GUAM

1850 MILES   ENIWETOK

MARSHALL   KWAJALEIN
ISLANDS

PALAU   TRUK   MAJURO

CAROLINE ISLANDS   KUSAIE

MAKIN

GILBERT   TARAWA
EQUATOR   ISLANDS

JAPAN TO THE GILBERTS

140° EAST   180° E.

The group's islands are volcanic and rise from the sea to form precipitous, conical peaks. Of the 14 islands comprising the group, only Saipan, Tinian, and Guam, all in the southern Marianas (see map 6, Lower Marianas), were military objectives in Operation FORAGER. In the southern islands, the temperature of the warm, damp air averages 87 degrees Fahrenheit, and they are frequently called "the white man's tropics." Rain soaks the islands almost every day between July and December. Saipan, fourteen miles long and five miles wide, is the northern-most of the three islands. An extinct volcano, 1,500 feet high, Mt. Topatchau, dominates the middle of Saipan. The terrain is rugged with steep cliffs and deep ravines.[2]

The Marianas operation would eventually involve amphibious assaults on three fortified islands: Saipan, Tinian, and Guam. These islands were 1,200 miles from the nearest American bases in the Marshalls, and the troops would come from areas from 4,000 to 7,000 miles distant. The largest fleet ever assembled in the Pacific, involving more than 800 ships, would transport, land, cover, and support the landing and garrison forces.

The V Amphibious Corps (VAC), located in the Hawaiian Islands and commanded by Lt. Gen. Holland M. "Howlin' Mad" Smith, had the task of seizing Saipan and Tinian. His forces consisted of the 2d and 4th Marine Divisions reinforced by the U.S. Army's 27th Infantry Division. D-Day was set for June 15, 1944, with H-Hour to take place at 0830.[3]

Army Versus Marine Terminology

Both the service organizations include ground combat units called divisions, each numbered and similarly built around regiments and battalions. While the army designates its divisions as, for example, the 27th *Infantry* Division (to differentiate from an *Airborne* division), the Marines have only one type of division, so they are simply called by number, that is, 1st (2d, 3d, 4th, 5th, or 6th) Marine Division.

An army regiment, the 106th Infantry Regiment, is referred to as "the 106th" or "the 106th Infantry." The 1st Battalion of the 106th Infantry Regiment is written as 1/106 and referred to as the "first of the 106th." A Marine regiment, the 5th Marine Regiment, is referred to as "the 5th Marines." The 1st Battalion of the 5th Marine Regiment is written as 1/5 and referred to as "one five."

To show military time, the army and the air corps say, for example, "oh eight hundred hours" and write, "0800 hours." The navy and Marines say, "zero eight hundred" and write "0800," omitting the word "hours."

Opposite: "Japan to the Gilberts." Source: George Carroll Dyer, Vice Admiral, USN (Ret.). *The Amphibians Came to Conquer*, Vol. II (Washington, D.C.: U.S. Department of the Navy), 735. (Hereafter Dyer, *The Amphibians*, Vol. II).

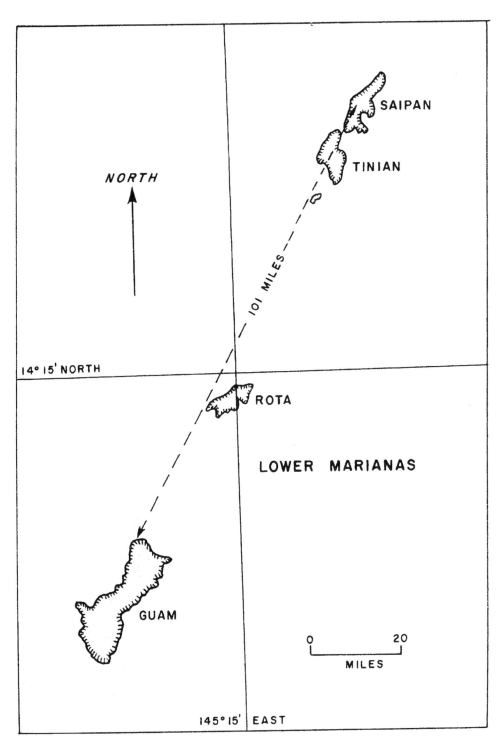

Source: Dyer, *The Amphibians*, Vol. I, 231.

Supply at Saipan

Logistics is that branch of military art that comprises everything relating to the movement and supply of troops. Most fighting men shorten that to "beans, bullets and bandages." Few men who made the landing realized the scope of the supply effort at Saipan. Embarked in the assault shipping was a ratio of over a ton of equipment and supplies to *each man* of the landing force. The tonnage carried by individual ships at Saipan was greater than in previous operations. Initial supplies landing with the assault forces were:

Class I (Rations)	32 days*
Class II (Organizational and Individual Equipment)	20 days
Class III (Fuels and Lubricants)	20 days
Class IV (Miscellaneous supplies)	20 days (except medical supplies, which were 30 days)
Class V (Ammunition)	7 units of fire for ground weapons**

This unusual load of supplies carried by the assaulting units may account for the decision to supplement the divisions' Pioneer Battalions with the extra manpower provided by Marine Depot Companies.

Earlier in the war, when air supremacy over target areas was questionable, transports were lightly loaded with the aim of quick unloading and fast transit to a rear area out of harm's way. Control of the air around Saipan allowed for increased tonnage. In general, throughout the operation, supply would function without critical hitches.[6]

The Marine Supply Service formed the 7th Field Depot to support VAC units of the Northern Landing Force at Saipan initially and in the following garrison phase. Because of the amount of supplies to be carried, plans called for detachments of the 7th Field Depot, including the 18th, Turner Blount's 19th, and the 20th Marine Depot Companies, along with the 3d Marine Ammunition Company, to embark in assault shipping (LSTs) to augment the divisions' shore parties. Other echelons of the field depots were due to arrive later in garrison shipping.

"We stayed in Hawaii until June," Turner Blount said. "We formed up with a task force and were put aboard ship on Memorial Day, May 30. We set sail, didn't know where we were going; they didn't say until about ten days at sea." Aboard

---

*The usual components of standard rations were: D, an emergency individual ration consisting of a special chocolate bar; C, the individual combat ration of canned hash, stew, or meat and beans, canned biscuits, packets of sugar, powdered coffee, and candy; K, another emergency or combat ration with breakfast, dinner, and supper units each consisting of canned luncheon meat, canned biscuits, a sugar packet, and gum; and B, a rear-area unit ration of canned meats, dried or canned fruit and vegetables, canned bread or biscuits.[4]

**A unit of fire is a planning tool to estimate the amounts of ammunition needed for one weapon for one day during an operation. It was established by the Commander-in-Chief, Pacific Operating Area (CinCPOA). For example, a unit of fire for a rifleman's .30-caliber M-1 rifle was 100 rounds. T/O F-100 for a Marine division in 1944 lists a total of 5,436 M-1 rifles. So, for the first day at Saipan the 2d Marine Division went ashore with 7 units of fire for each rifle, almost 4 million rounds of ammunition for the rifles alone! The same T/O lists 962 officers and 16,503 enlisted men in a division. Considering that the total cube and weight of all classes of supplies coming across the beach to sustain them had to be muscled into dumps and distributed to the users, this is an almost mind-boggling feat.[5] (For a listing of the ammunition requirements for landing force weapons see Appendix F: Pacific Ocean Area Units of Fire for Ground Weapons.)

ship, Blount and his fellow black Marines "got acquainted" with many of the white Marines they would serve with in the coming battle. "They weren't too bad," he said. "We maybe played a few cards and things like that. But the ship had ropes across it where they separated whites and blacks.... of course," he laughs. "Down below we used to play cards under the ropes! Then they told us we were going to take part in an operation on the island of Saipan, in the Mariana Islands. That was the first stop," he said. "We took part in the invasion of Saipan. The 15th of June was D-Day for that operation, in 1944."[7]

Neither Marine division planned to use combat troops to help in the beachhead supply effort. For the first time the depot companies and one black ammunition company were going in with the assault forces[8]:

4th Marine Division
  18th Marine Depot Company — scheduled to land on D-Day
  20th Marine Depot Company — scheduled to land on D-Day
1st Battalion, 25th Marines, 4th Marine Division
  20th Marine Depot Company — scheduled to land in the 4th wave on D-Day
3d Battalion, 23d Marines, 4th Marine Division
  One platoon of the 18th Marine Depot Company attached — scheduled to land about H+2½
2d Marine Division
  19th Marine Depot Company — scheduled to come ashore D+7 (June 22)
  The 3d Marine Ammunition Company was in general support of both divisions.

Saipan: The First Phase of FORAGER

The assault required simultaneous landings on the beaches of the southwestern coast of the island. The northern (left) flank of the assault beaches began at a point midway between Mutcho Point in the north and extended south about 8,000 yards to Agingan Point. The town of Charan Kanoa and an airstrip were close to the beaches. The assault by two divisions of Marines would cross a coral reef 250 to 700 yards wide and then a lagoon in some places up to 600 yards wide (see map 7, Saipan).[9]

The battalion landing teams of the 2d Marine Division's 6th Marines would come ashore on the north or left flank beaches, Red 1, 2, and 3. The 8th Marines would land to their right on Green Beaches 1, 2, and 3. The 4th Marine Division's 23d Marines would come in on their right on Blue Beaches 1 and 2 while the 25th Marines would land at the extreme right or southern flank on Yellow Beaches 1, 2, and 3.

"I did not get ashore the first day," Blount said. "I watched others go ashore ... we were that close aboard ship. I saw all the bombing and strafing of the island, softening up before the landings of course. All the larger ships, the destroyers and battlewagons and whatnot were all ahead of the taskforce we were in."[10]

The LSTs that brought the assault forces and their attachments, including Turner Blount, along with the attack transports were between 6,000 and 12,000

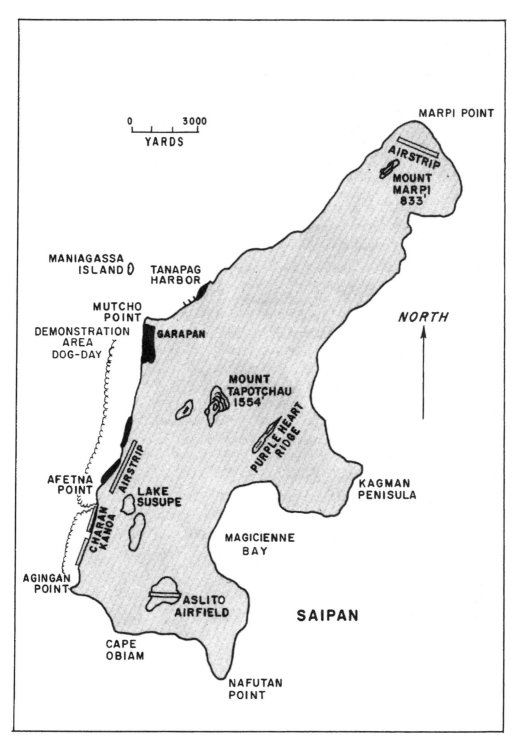

Saipan.

Source: Dyer, *The Amphibians*, Vol. II, 871.

yards from shore. The naval gunfire support ships (NGF), in order to bring more accurate fire on Japanese positions, were for the first time *anchored or steamed inside* the line of departure less than 4,000 yards off the beaches.

The weather for D-Day was partly cloudy with a few scattered squalls getting up around midday. Winds were southeasterly 10 to 15 knots, with light to moderate southeast swells. A 0830 H-Hour slipped to 0840 in order to get some control personnel in place.[11]

One Can Almost Picture It

What was it like on Dog-Day morning? Those who have never done such things can only imagine today what Marines feel as they prepare to make an amphibious assault.... Aircraft began bombing and strafing Saipan on June 11. Naval gunfire took turns with the aircraft blasting the island beginning the morning of June 13.

The LSTs carrying the Marines nosed toward the transport area off Saipan in the evening darkness of June 14. The night of June 14, *LST-272*'s war diary shows the entry, "At 2010 sighted glow on horizon (port bow) and this developed to be battle action on Saipan. Star shells and other evidence of battle were seen all night."[12] As the LSTs near the anchorage, the irregular cracking thunder of naval gunfire pounding the Japanese rolls across the water. The southeasterly winds carry the smell of burned black powder from the twelve 14-inch/50-caliber and fourteen 5-inch/38-caliber guns of the battleship *Tennessee*, upwind of the transports. Note: 5 inches is the size of the gun's bore; 38 caliber indicates the length of the barrel, or 38 times the bore size, 190 inches, for a barrel length of 15.83 feet.

There is much to be done; reveille sounds early for the embarked troops, sometimes as early as 0130 for those few who manage a restless sleep. After breakfast, the pre-assault standard of steak and eggs, the men have time to make last minute adjustments to their gear, draw ammunition. Some think and solemnly prepare for what lies ahead while others laugh, joke, and engage in what NCOs call "grab-ass," or horseplay. In the dim light of early morning, a few make their way to the weather decks to get a first look at Saipan. Shortly before 0700 the LST Flotilla anchors in Areas A, B, C, and D, the first two closer to shore, about 1,250 yards seaward from the line of departure, which itself is 4,000 yards off the beach. Between the LSTs and the island is a line of LCI (G) gunboats that will precede the first wave of landing craft at H-Hour. Closer inshore lie the naval gunfire support ships, still pounding the island.

Near the line of departure there is a bustling confusion of control vessels, guide boats, and the 24 light gunboats jockeying into position. The gunboats, firing salvos of 4.5-inch rockets and 20 and 40mm guns directly onto the beach, will turn away at the reef. Armored amphibians, mounting 75mm guns and constituting the first wave, will provide fire support for troop-carrying LVTs of the follow-on waves from the reef to the beach and then execute fire missions as required. Farther out, hundreds of landing craft and vehicles plod patient circles in their assembly areas as the assault waves carrying Marine riflemen gather.

On some of the LSTs the ships' 1MC loudspeakers come alive booming the call, "Now embarked Marines report to your debarkation stations." The black Marines, loaded down with their combat gear, each controlling fear in his own way, make their way below to the dimly lighted tunnel of the tank deck and the waiting forest green amphibious tractors, LVT(4) Alligators. Bluejackets scuttle among the vehicles making last-minute checks. There are jokes and catcalls, men whistling past a graveyard, while they clamber into their assigned LVTs — 26 feet long and almost 11 feet wide — and the rear ramps are winched closed. The ship's blowers roar as the bow doors grind open to the sea, and on each LVT a 200-horsepower Continental air-cooled seven-cylinder radial engine roars into life and the air reeks with exhaust fumes. Men shout to be heard above the noise.

With a lurch the first LVT rumbles toward the light of the opened bow, crawls upslope, levels briefly, and then angles down the ramp to splash into the waiting sea. The Marines, relieved and always surprised when the tractor floats, fill their lungs with fresh air and look back at the safety of the receding ship, still disgorging LVTs. A few exchange nervous grins as the track flanges throw up spray and they move toward the assembly area. In the open LVTs, the sounds of gunfire are louder, even above the roar of the engines. There is an almost universal urge to urinate. The seas are not rough, but somebody vomits. Not seasick, for the men have their sea-legs now. Fear. The bold ones — they are always to be found in any group of Marines — laugh and joke, some skylarking to relieve their tension. Other men, full of youthful invincibility, almost dare the Japanese to try and kill them.

When all the LVTs of the wave complete the circle, the wave leader pulls out of line and all the other tractors follow in trail, running parallel to the line of departure where they will head toward the beach behind the unit they will support. It will take about 27 minutes to make the 4,000-yard run to reach the shore after they cross the line of departure. As one, the LVTs turn toward the beach into a line abreast formation — the wave forms — and engines howl at full-throttle, pushing the craft up to about five knots. A few curiously crane their necks, trying to see what lies ahead. Others are cotton-mouthed with anxiety. A tractor crewman commands the men to get down; they're crossing the line of departure. The wave passes the line of warships, firing now at targets inland from the beaches. Approaching the reef, shells from the ships rustle and roar overhead. The tractors slow, lurch as the tracks bite into coral, and then climb into the shallow water over the reef. The Japanese fire at them. For the first time the men, eyes dilated and glittering excitedly with the realization that somebody is shooting at them, trying to *kill* them, hear the sharp "crack" and hiss of bullets passing near over their heads. There are shrieks and roars of approaching shells, explosions, and the whirr of shrapnel cutting the air. Dirty black smoke drifts from shell bursts. The amtracs are over the reef, splashing across the lagoon. The crew calls out three hundred yards and the command comes, "Lock and load!" Men fumble eight-round clips from cloth bandoliers draped across their chests into the magazines of their M-1 rifles and bolts slam home. Unheard in the noise, safeties click. Sergeants check the men. LVT crewmen jump to the .50- and .30-caliber machine guns, chamber rounds, duck for safety. Mouths dry, men try to swallow. Sphincters tighten, the tractor grounds and crawls up out of the sea into incredible noise, smoke and violence.

Fighting Men, Strong and Fit for War

The naval gunfire had shifted to targets further inland and the 719 amtracs of the assault waves experienced little difficulty proceeding as far as the reef. However, beginning at the coral shallows, the Japanese defenders took the approaching LVTs under a deluge of heavy automatic weapons, artillery and mortar fire. The fire grew in intensity as the 2d, 3d, and 4th waves hit the beaches. The sound of shells from direct fire flat trajectory guns bursting around the amtracs was terrifying, but worse were the high-angle shells that screamed ominously as they dropped toward the bobbing, slow-moving LVTs.

In the first hour, 8,000 men in LVTs land on a beach frontage of about 8,000 yards. When they reach the water's edge, the amtracs cross a sandy beach lined by fire trenches, some sections of anti-tank trench under fire from numerous machine gun emplacements and some dual-purpose antiaircraft and coastal defense weapons.[13] At Yellow Beach 2 in the south, the 20th Marine Depot Company, commanded by Captain William C. Adams, was attached to 1st Battalion 25th Marines (1/25), which was brought ashore in amtracs of the U.S. Army 773d Amphibian Tractor Battalion.

Captain Adams told the men of his 20th Marine Depot Company soon before the landing, "You are the first Negro troops ever to go into action in the Marine Corps. What you do with the situation that confronts you, and how you perform, will be the basis on which you, and your race, will be judged."[14]

Met by an intense and accurate fusillade of frontal and enfilade fire, the Marines of 1/25 were forced to debark from their tractors at the water's edge. Fortunately the men landed in newer tractors, the LVT(4)s. Similar to the LVT(2), the newer model had its engine moved forward to install a hand winch-operated stern ramp so men could scramble out the back rather than expose themselves to Japanese fire by climbing over the sides and dropping almost seven feet to the ground. It could carry up to 30 men and their field gear or as much as 6,500 pounds of cargo.[15]

At the end of the first hour, the riflemen had clawed out a beachhead only 12 yards deep. Japanese artillery and mortar fire hammering the congested beach areas caused the hasty departure of the LVTs, many of which backed off the beach and fled before unloading anything but the riflemen, thus leaving the battalion critically short of radios for three days. Worse, some mortars and machine guns, together with ammunition for them, were still aboard when the LVTs pulled out.

Heavy resistance from Agingan Point on their right flank and from the sparsely

"Negro assault troops await orders D-day to attack enemy shortly after they had come ashore at Saipan in the Marianas." June 1944. T/Sgt. [sic] William Fitch, U.S. Coast Guard. Still Picture Branch (NNSP), National Archives, Washington, DC.

wooded beach area to the south, coupled with fighting on their direct front caused extremely heavy casualties. Agingan Point was a honeycomb of Japanese positions, originally constructed to fire out to sea but capable of traversing to bear against troops on shore. At 0930, the enemy counterattacked from the direction of Agingan Point, and small groups of Japanese moved across the ridge on the right front. The battalion commander immediately called for an air strike on these targets. Within five minutes, navy planes attacked the area although it was impossible to judge results (the only Marine airplanes at Saipan were little OY observation planes used for artillery spotting and intelligence gathering). Fires of the battleship *Tennessee*, anchored just off Agingan Point, were invaluable in keeping the Japanese off balance in their efforts to push the 1st Battalion into the water.

The battalion commander called for tank support as well as an additional rifle company from the reserve battalion. Fire from at least four direct fire artillery pieces (about 75mm) emplaced on the high ground 800 yards inland beat upon the beachhead. The gunners made the most of their excellent observation, firing whenever groups of three or four Marines were visible.[16]

First Black Marine KIA

Into that maelstrom of fire LVTs carrying 75 men of the 20th Marine Depot Company hit the beach in the third wave at about H+5 and ½, around 1400 (the rest of the men remained on LSTs unloading supplies as part of the ship's platoon). Their arrival coincided with the peak intensity of Japanese fire. Captain Adams said, "All hell was breaking when we came in. It was still touch and go when we hit shore, and it took some time to establish a foothold." Private Kenneth J. Tibbs was hit and later that day died of his wounds, earning the distinction nobody wanted — he was the only casualty the 20th suffered at Saipan, and the first black Marine killed in combat during the war.[17]

PFC James W. Williams rode LVTs up to the front lines to deliver supplies and ammunition. "Often on those trips the men were under Japanese rifle and machine gun fire," Adams said. Williams was hit by a Japanese bullet, which fortunately was deflected by his helmet. He kept it for a souvenir. "They did a swell job," the company commander said of his men.[18]

Adams went on to describe the men's prowess at what Marines politely called scrounging or moonlight requisitioning, euphemisms for begging, borrowing, trading for, or when nothing else worked, stealing equipment they needed. "They were very provident, and by the second day had all types of arms they had never been issued, such as ... machine guns, and even .50 (caliber) machine guns."[19] Every Marine unit had its expert scrounger.

At about H+2 1/2 (H-hour plus two-and-one-half hours) a platoon of Captain William M. Barr's 18th Marine Depot Company that was attached to 3/23 hit Blue Beach One under fire. "Everybody was happy — it seemed kind of like a big football game," PFC Augustus Witcher said of the men in his LVT off Blue Beach One, adding, "When we were near shore a Jap mortar shell landed in a nearby 'alligator.' The singing and joking stopped."[20] Ashore, a mortar round burst about 25 feet from the platoon and wounded four of the black Marines (PFC Charles F. Smith and Privates Albert W. Sims, Jeff Smith, and Hayse Stewart).[21] "We dug foxholes and then started unloading ammunition," Witcher said. "When the explosions got too close, we'd dive into the holes until it slackened up. My foxhole was only about two feet deep to start with, but it was double that depth before the first night was over."[22]

During World War II every fighting man carried a first aid pouch containing a packet of sulfa powder and a battle dressing (bandage) attached to the cartridge belt around his waist. Marines were taught in first aid classes to immediately call for a corpsman (a navy Hospital Corpsman assigned to Marine units; the Marines have no medical branch) and then open a wounded man's aid pouch, take out his packet of sulfa powder, tear it open and sprinkle sulfa powder on any open wound to prevent infection. Next he would take the battle dressing from the wounded man's pouch to cover the wound. After the wounded Depot Company Marines were given first aid under fire they were loaded into an LVT and evacuated to an LST anchored offshore. That ship was configured as an aid station for 100 casualties (three were so configured, one off the 4th Marine Division's beaches and another off the 2d Marine Division's beaches, with the third standing by to replace the ship that first took on its full complement of wounded). That was SOP for all wounded men; on the LST, navy doctors treated the wounds and the men were later moved to one of the larger hospital configured ships.

One squad from the platoon of black Marines joined white Marines in a hasty defensive perimeter about 100 yards in from the beach.[23] The remainder of the platoon moved further inland. Increasing swells slowed the number of boats and LVTs bringing supplies; several sank with the loss of their crews. By the time the remainder of the 18th Depot Company came ashore, Japanese artillery and mortar fire was frequent but no longer continuous.[24] The black Marines turned to their normal duties, unloading the supplies from LVTs, sorting and stacking it in dumps. Captain William M. Barr said the black Marines "set up 'security' to keep out snipers" while others "helped load casualties" for evacuation to hospital ships. "They stood waist-deep in surf unloading boats as vital supplies of food and water were brought in."[25]

By nightfall on Dog-Day the advanced elements of 3/23 took up positions about 800 yards inland from the beach. The weather deteriorated with heavy swells beginning about dusk and lasting the night. Rough seas prevented delivery of supplies across the reef at Red, Green, and Yellow beaches, forcing all supplies to come in across the Blue Beaches.

In the early evening hours a navy fighter intercepted a Japanese plane above the island and sent it crashing into Blue Beach One, about 50 yards away from a foxhole occupied by 19-year-old Pvt. Edward H. Seals. "I prayed night and day after that," the shaken young man said.[26]

Sgt. Leo Mann, former professional boxer who won 24 of his 27 bouts, was directing one of the unloading groups when he had a similar experience. "I jumped into my foxhole when the mortar shells began moving in, for about the 10th time," he said. "One thudded down right beside me. I covered my head. When I looked up I was lying outside the foxhole. Guess I was blown out."[27]

During the night, a gap developed between 3/23 at Blue Beach One and the 2d Marine Division's 8th Marines at Green Beach Three on their left. Approximately 200 Japanese entered the gap and attempted to overrun 3/23. In the ensuing mêlée of rifle and machine gun fire and exploding grenades, a black Marine killed a Japanese infiltrator who crept into a nearby foxhole.[28] The battalion, aided by black and white Marine shore party troops and their army counterparts, held firm.[29]

The following morning, D+One, the black Marines joined white Marines in hunting down and killing Japanese soldiers who had infiltrated the gap, and Private Willie J. Atkinson was wounded and evacuated.[30]

Later on D+One the flow of supplies ashore was increased when a causeway pier was constructed off Blue Beach One. However, here occurred one of the worst supply jams on the beaches when the Army's 165th Infantry was landed across the Blue Beach causeway in the rear of the 23d Marines. All supply traffic to the Marines ground to a temporary halt as the supply area behind the beach deteriorated into a hopelessly confused jumble of mixed army and Marine supplies. That aside, there was no serious shortcoming in the shore parties' performance.[31] Later on D+One, LSTs were able to beach directly on the reef off Yellow Beach One. By Dog plus Three there were nearly 50,000 men ashore.

"They moved us up to the front to help halt a counter-attack," PFC John M. Jenkins said. "This gun opened on me from close range. It must have thrown 20 shells as I jumped into a ditch. I could see three Japs moving about the gun. After pulling the pin on a grenade, I got to thinking they'd have time to throw it back, so I held it a few seconds and let it go. It landed right on the gun. Guess it got 'em all." The Marine correspondent that wrote the news release said those were "the first Japs sent to their ancestors by Negro Marines in this war."[32] This may be the same Jenkins whose expertise with a grenade *Time* correspondent Robert Sherrod would describe in a July issue of the magazine. The black Marines remained with 3/23 through the fighting until the operation ended.

Ammunition Company Comes Ashore

On Dog-Day, sixteen men of the 3d Marine Ammunition Company were assigned to the ships' platoons, muscling ammunition from ships into landing craft. Another twenty-five worked aboard "floating dumps" (pontoon barges moored on the ocean side of the reef; these had been lashed to the sides of LSTs during the voyage from Hawaii and now served as lighters, floating way points for the movement of supplies). The men on the barges would transfer the ammunition to DUKWs or LVTs for delivery on shore. "At 0600 it was bright enough to see an island dead," and like Turner Blount, Sergeant (Sgt.) Ernest W. Coney of the 3d Ammo Company watched the softening up process. "Smoke was pouring up from the earth as our planes was bombing and strafing. We went over the side at 0700 and into the waiting landing boat (an LCVP)."[33]

The boats pulled into a marshalling area and began circling. When the open boats started for the island they came under Japanese artillery fire. They turned away and waited until amphibious alligators used in the early assault waves became available. About 1,500 yards off the reef the flat-bottomed craft bobbed and tossed as the swells built, and the boats, unable to cross the reef, pulled alongside idling LVTs, which could crawl across the barrier with ease. Timing their leaps between swells — if a man fell he would either be crushed between the tractor and the boat or be dragged to the bottom of the sea by the weight of his gear — men made a hazardous "cross-deck" transfer into the Alligators. They reached the shore at about H+5 and 1/2, that is, around 1400, the men "immediately started diggin' in because it seemed as though the Japs had gotten the range." At the water's edge, one Alli-

"Negro Marines, attached to the Third Ammunition Company, take time out from supplying ammunittion to the front line on Saipan. Riding captured ... bicycle is Pfc. Horace Boykin; and left to right, Cpl. Willis T. Anthony, Pfc. Emmitt Shackelford, and Pfc. Eugene Purdy." June 1944. Still Picture Branch (NNSP), National Archives, Washington, DC.

gator was hit and destroyed by Japanese fire, but none of the men were hurt. As the afternoon wore on, Private First Class Leroy Seals of Brooklyn, New York, was wounded. He died the following day, the second black Marine killed by the Japanese in the war.[34]

Captain Louis P. Shine, company commander of the 3d Marine Ammunition Company, had won a "spot" promotion to captain on Guadalcanal in December 1942. Shine said of the Japanese shells bursting on the beaches, "Sometimes the men were almost completely buried in showers of sand. Then I'd start back to the boats. They came right after me. They worked around the clock and did a swell job" unloading tons of ammunition.[35] The men found some Japanese saki, so they took a short break to try the drink. After sampling the wine, they concluded that it was probably made of rice and TNT.[36]

That night, the Japanese launched several counterattacks at different points along the lines. Illumination was called for, and intensely burning star shells soon hung in the night sky, their stark, eerie light revealing the advancing enemy. Naval gunfire thundered in from offshore and the massed fires of Marine riflemen and machine gunners, including those brought to bear by the black Marines of the 3d Marine Ammunition Company, cut down the Japanese. The next day, D+One, a shell burst near PFC Robert L. Neal sending him to a hospital ship suffering from concussion.

A Close Call

Near midnight on D+5, a 14-man working party on an LST knocked off and lay on the deck, trying to get some sleep. A Japanese bomber passed high overhead and released a bomb that exploded 30 to 40 feet from the ship. Shrapnel from the bomb wounded PFC Roy North, Sr., of the 20th Marine Depot Company, along with two sailors. North was lucky, for his head wound was not serious. After getting it dressed by a corpsman, he returned to duty. The Beach Aid Station never verified his wound, so he never received a Purple Heart.[37]

Turner Blount Comes Ashore

"Of course it was a few days later before I got ashore," Blount explained of his D+7 arrival, "but some of the other companies were with us here, black Marines." For five days after landing, the 19th Marine Depot Company worked as part of the 2d Marine Division shore party. Blount said their duties were to ensure "supplies and ammunition got to the front lines. I remember one night being a guard aboard a truck with supplies on it moving to the front lines. I was on top of the supplies and guarding the truck next to it so the driver did not get ambushed at two or three o'clock in the morning, going to the front," he laughed with the memory, "in the dark." There were no guides. "You just followed the trail."[38]

The army had landed several antiaircraft batteries, and the ships offshore could bring a significant number of antiaircraft guns to bear on any Japanese raiders who ventured over the island. Blount went through several night attacks by Japanese aircraft, and recalled his reaction. "I used to get, I don't know, a lot of joy out of seeing them at night over us, with the white lights [searchlights] and they'd cross up like this [gestures with his hands to show light beams coning a target] and they'd keep the plane in that cross as it moves and you'd see it shot down, or explode in the air, that was sort of exciting!" His reaction, satisfaction and pleasure watching the enemy die, was not uncommon among men under the stress of combat. However, the young man from Georgia often asked himself, "What am I doing here?"[39] Thus he saw men die in a war up close, became a veteran. Turner Blount learned what to expect in the next island invasion.

Control of the 19th reverted to the 7th Field Depot for the remainder of the operation. On June 25, Col. Earl H. Phillips took command of the 7th Field Depot; the colonel was impressed by the performance of the black units under fire and would not forget to credit the men.

Stewards Earn Purple Hearts

The 3d Ammunition Company's PFC William B. Townsend was wounded on D+Two, June 17, and on D+Three PFC Lawrence Pellerin, Jr., of the 20th Marine Depot Company was wounded. As the fighting continued into early July, casualties continued. Corporal (Cpl.) John S. Newsome of the 18th and Private (Pvt.) Willie S. King of the 20th were wounded on July 4, 1944. Pvt. John S. Novy of the ammunition company was wounded on July 9, and the last black Marine wounded during the battle, Pvt. Willie Travis, Jr. of the 18th, was hit on July 13.[40]

The Depot and Ammunition Company Marines were not the only black Marines on Saipan, for the Stewards Branch was well represented in the 2d Marine Division's headquarters. There, on June 20, Japanese artillery hit the compound, wounding Cook 3d Class Timerlate E. Kirvin and Steward's Assistant 2d Class Samuel J. Love, Jr., giving them the distinction of becoming the first Steward's Branch combat casualties of the war.[41]

Spam and Corned Beef

Shortly before the island was secured, the 20th Marine Depot Company bivouac was set up about 200 yards in front of a heavy artillery group. The guns were firing at Japanese positions on the northern tip of the island. The men quickly adapted to the noise of shells passing overhead — outgoing sounds different from incoming — so they learned to ignore the shooting. They spent off work hours improving foxholes, cleaning their rifles and trying to keep them dry, and looking for souvenirs. Almost everyone had collected a rifle, pistol, helmet, flag, or some Japanese currency.

When Japanese resistance ended, the men went to work in 12-hour shifts putting supply dumps in order. They were impressed with how much Spam and corned beef had been stockpiled on the island. By December, their monotonous diet of Spam earned the meat a solid lead in a "Most Hated Food" contest. PFC Paul D. Rountree got a package from home — food! When he opened the package he found, of course, a can of Spam.[42] What he did with the can is not recorded.

Marines Never Retreat

On July 9, organized resistance ended and the island was declared secure. However, mopping up action against Japanese soldiers holding out in caves and pillboxes would continue for several weeks more. On July 17, a short distance north of the town of Garapan, a group of Japanese soldiers, by-passed holdouts, stormed out of a cave and attacked an army working party. Corporal Joseph Gogins joined a volunteer group of Marines and sailors, some armed only with rocks, and set out

"First Negro Marines decorated by the famed Second Marine Division somewhere in the Pacific (L-R) Staff Sgt Timerlate Kirven [sic] ... and Cpl. Samuel J. Love, Sr... They received Purple Hearts for wounds received in the Battle of Saipan..." At the 2d Marine Division's headquarters on Saipan on June 20, Japanese artillery hit the compound wounding Cook 3d Class Timerlate E. Kirvin and Steward's Assistant 2d Class Samuel J. Love, Jr., giving them the distinction of becoming the first Steward's Branch combat casualties of the war. 1944. Still Picture Branch (NNSP), National Archives, Washington, DC.

to rescue the beleaguered G.I.s. After one Marine was wounded in the arm by Japanese rifle fire, the unarmed members of the rescue party decided to withdraw. Gogins, himself unarmed, shouted, "You come back here! Don't you know the Marines never retreat?" The soldiers, sailors and Marines stood their ground, killing 18 Japanese and capturing two before running out of ammunition and withdrawing.[43]

What Did the Capture of Saipan Mean?

Turner Blount, the young man from Keyesville, Georgia, and a few of his fellow Montford Point Marines had proven their mettle wading through fire-swept surf and across deadly beaches. They saw blacks hit by Japanese fire, yet they were Marines and they did not falter. They did their jobs in the largest amphibious operation in the Pacific up to June 1944.

At Guadalcanal in 1942, Americans broke though the Japanese outer defense ring; at Saipan Americans broke through the Japanese inner defense ring. Saipan may have been *the* key turning point in the war. In 1945, Marquis Koichi Kido, Lord Keeper of the Privy Seal of the Imperial Japanese government, said, "The fall of Saipan meant the intensification of American air attacks upon the Japanese home islands." When the island fell, Prime Minister Hideki Tojo's cabinet resigned.[44] Vice Admiral Shigeyoshi Miwa said, "Our war was lost with the loss of Saipan."[45]

Presidential Unit Citation (PUC)

After the battle of Saipan, the Lieutenant General Commandant of the Marine Corps, Lt. Gen. Alexander A. Vandegrift, said, "The Negro Marines are no longer on trial. They are Marines, period."[46] Unfortunately, the commandant's words went unheard or unheeded, for black Marines were still targets of racism.

The men earned further recognition when the Detachment, 7th Field Depot (the 18th, 19th, and 20th Marine Depot Companies and the 3d Marine Ammunition Company) was included in the citation, given below, for the Presidential Unit Citation awarded to the 4th Marine Division, Reinforced.

> For outstanding performance in combat during the seizure of the Japanese-held islands of Saipan and Tinian in the Marianas from June 15 to August 1, 1944. Valiantly storming the mighty fortifications of Saipan on June 15, the Fourth Division, Reinforced, blasted the stubborn defenses of the enemy in and undeviating advance over the perilously rugged terrain. Unflinching despite heavy casualties, this gallant group pursued the Japanese relentlessly across the entire length of the island, pressing on against bitter opposition for twenty-five days to crush all resistance in their zone of action. With but a brief rest period in which to reorganize and re-equip, the Division hurled its full fighting power against the dangerously narrow beaches of Tinian on July 24 and rapidly expanded the beachheads for the continued landing of troops, supplies and artillery. Unchecked by either natural obstacles or hostile fire, these

indomitable men spearheaded a merciless attack which swept Japanese forces before it and ravaged all opposition within eight days to add Tinian to our record of conquests in these strategically vital islands.

　　For the President.

JAMES FORRESTAL,
Secretary of the Navy47

Today, the citation reminds us of the courage of those Marines, both white and black.

21

Operation FORAGER Continues

Saipan to Tinian

After the battle of Saipan, the 2d and 4th Marine Divisions prepared to stage a shore-to-shore amphibious assault on the narrow beaches (usable width was only 200 yards) of the nearby island of Tinian, three and a half miles from Saipan. During the planning process, the day of the assault, July 24, was called Jig-Day to avoid confusion with Saipan's Dog-Day. Initial supplies of water, rations, and ammunition sufficient for the entire attack force for the first three and a half days were top loaded on 30 LSTs and two LSDs.

The men of the 18th, 19th, and 20th Marine Depot Companies and the 3d Marine Ammunition Company on Saipan helped load follow-on supplies into trucks and trailers. These were then put aboard amphibious vehicles and landing craft that then, in a departure from normal shore party SOP, shuttled back and forth from Saipan to each division's supply dumps on Tinian. A few men from the 3d Marine Ammunition Company accompanied the assault forces on Tinian, but the depot company Marines remained on Saipan as part of the garrison forces.[1] During the battle, the edges of a typhoon passed close by the island raising heavy seas from July 28 until August 1, but the supply plan was a success. After the island was secured, VAC's G-4 said, "A reinforced corps was landed over less than 200 yards of beach and over a difficult reef, and was supplied throughout nine days of heavy combat without handling so much as one pound of supplies in the usual shore party manner. Everything rolled in on wheels.... The troops never lacked what they required at the time it was required."[2] Marines learned another valuable lesson — preload supplies on vehicles to reduce handling at the waterline.

Guam: The Final Phase of FORAGER

Guam had been a United States possession since the Spanish-American War in 1898, but the Japanese seized it in December 1941. For purely emotional reasons,

159

recapturing the island was a point of national honor. However, militarily, it was important as an advanced naval base and for basing B-29 bombers within range of the home islands.

Plans for the recapture of Guam were concurrent with those for Saipan and Tinian, and the battle would open while the fighting for Tinian was still going on. To avoid confusion during planning, the date of the assault on Guam was called William-Day, and was eventually set for July 21, with H-Hour at 0830. Almost 56,000 Marines and soldiers would take part in the assault and recapture of Guam.

The Marine Supply Service formed the 5th Field Depot on Guadalcanal in the Solomon Islands to support the III Amphibious Corps (IIIAC) initially and in the following garrison phase. IIIAC, consisting mainly of the 3d Marine Division and the 1st Provisional Marine Brigade, would become the Southern Landing Force at Guam. The landing beaches chosen were on the mid-western and southwestern coast of the island, separated by a peninsula. Once the island was back in American hands, the commanding general of the Island Command would be an officer notorious among black Marines, Maj. Gen. Henry L. Larsen.[3] Plans called for detachments of the 5th Field Depot to embark in assault shipping (LSTs). Over 500 Marines of the 2d and 4th Marine Ammunition Companies, activated at Montford Point in December 1943 and January 1944, respectively, and with only a few months experience in theatre were among those detachments.

Three platoons of the 2d Marine Ammunition Company were in direct support of the 3d Marine Division landing on Red Beaches One and Two, Green Beach, and Blue Beach at Asan, north of the Orote Peninsula (see map 8, Guam). The 4th Marine Ammunition Company and the 4th platoon of the 2d Marine Ammunition Company were in direct support of the 1st Provisional Marine Brigade on Yellow Beaches One and Two and White Beaches One and Two at Agat, Guam. In direct support, they would augment the shore parties and push supplies ashore. There would be no depot company Marines in the assault forces; they would arrive later in the garrison phase.

By the end of May, IIIAC forces had boarded ships at Guadalcanal and set sail for the Marianas, and while waiting to land, sailed around under the hot sun. The ships were crowded and heavily loaded — LST 278, for example, had 339 men aboard in addition to her crew of 117. She also had 100 drums of gasoline and 70 tons of ammunition deck-loaded.[4] One LST Group Commander logged this: "The days underway were very hot and filled with uncertainty, bogies, snoopers, shadowers, one enemy torpedo plane attack on our group and on one adjacent group."[5] By William-Day the men would be more than ready to leave the ships and stretch their legs ashore.

W-Day at Guam

Three regiments of the 3d Marine Division, with the 2d Marine Ammunition Company in direct support, landed across beaches that fronted a natural amphithe-

"Invasion of Cape Gloucester, New Britain, 24 Dec. 1943. Crammed with men and material for the invasion, this Coast Guard-manned LST nears the Japanese held shore. Troops shown in the picture are Marines." No cargo space was wasted during amphibious assaults in the Pacific. PhoM1c. Don C. Hansen. Still Picture Branch (NNSP), National Archives, Washington, DC.

atre, and the Japanese held the high ground with excellent observation of the beaches. The Marines moved inland, and across the beaches, equipment and supplies came ashore smoothly. LVTs and DUKWs loaded with ammunition and supplies arrived on the beach where dumps were quickly established. Shore party personnel routed the vehicles from the follow-on waves directly to the dumps.

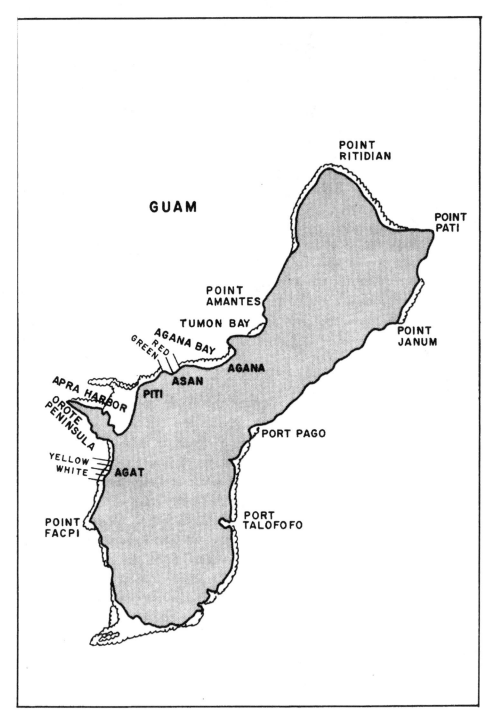

Guam.

Source: Dyer, *The Amphibians*, Vol. II, 926.

Heavy mortar fire continued to strike the beach areas throughout the day. While this interfered with the progress of the working parties on the beach, things kept moving.

The supply flow across the Agat beaches to the 1st Provisional Marine Brigade was a different story. There the 4th Marine Ammunition Company was reinforced by one additional platoon to support the Brigade. There was a problem with the transshipment of supplies from landing boats to LVTs. Landing craft moved supplies from 12 LSTs standing off the reef to the transfer area on schedule, but a lack of sufficient amphibious vehicles developed. Accurate Japanese mortar and artillery fire exacted a heavy toll on LVTs on W-Day, resulting in a serious supply backlog afloat that caused shortages ashore.[6] Expedients, such as rubber boat causeways, rafts, and floating fuel drums manhandled across the shallows by wading Marines, were only somewhat helpful in making up the shortfalls.

In addition, the inner edges of the coral reefs were deeply silted, which made it difficult to locate suitable places to beach landing vehicles. The brigade commanding general requested that ammunition and water be placed on a priority list, adding to a message he sent at 1830, "Own casualties about 350. Enemy unknown. Critical shortages fuel and ammunition all types. Think we can handle it. Will continue as planned tomorrow."[7] The navy continued unloading throughout the night in an effort to get more gear ashore.

The night of W-Day saw a series of Japanese counterattacks at different places along the Marine beachheads. While the enemy managed to penetrate the Marine lines in several locations, they were not successful in holding. At 0515 in the predawn darkness of W+One, a platoon of the 4th Marine Ammunition Company was guarding the brigade ammunition dump. A Japanese demolition group headed for the dump. The Marines were ready, and after a brief but intense firefight, the Japanese withdrew, leaving behind 14 dead.[8] None of the black Marines were hit. Later on W+One (July 22), PFC Henry L. Jones of the 2d Ammunition Company was wounded and evacuated. Then on W+Three, Japanese fire coming from the Orote Peninsula struck three more black Marines: PFC Wilbert J. Webb and Privates Darnell Hayes and Jim W. Jones.[9] There were no further casualties among the black Marines at Guam, even though the two companies continued in direct support until August 22, when they reverted to the control of the 5th Field Depot.

Brig. Gen. Lemuel C. Shepherd, Jr., commanding general of the 1st Provisional Marine Brigade at Guam and later the 20th Commandant of the Marine Corps, wrote a letter to the company commander of the 4th Marine Ammunition Company. In it, he commended First Lieutenant (1st Lt.) Russell S. LaPointe for the "splendid and expeditious manner in which supplies and equipment were unloaded from the LSTs and LCTs of our Attack Group. Working long hours, frequently during nights, and in a least two instances under enemy fire ... [you] so coordinated your unloading efforts as to keep supplies flowing to the beach. You have contributed in large measure to the successful and rapid movement of combat supplies in this amphibious operation."[10]

Shepherd's 1st Provisional Marine Brigade was awarded the Navy Unit Commendation for its actions on Guam. The citation reads:

> For outstanding heroism in action against enemy Japanese forces during the invasion of Guam, Marianas Islands, from July 21 to August 10, 1944. Functioning as a combat unit for the first time, the First Provisional Marine Brigade forced a landing against strong hostile defenses and well-camouflaged positions, steadily advancing inland under the relentless fury of the enemy's heavy artillery, mortar, and small arms fire to secure a firm beachhead by nightfall. Executing a difficult turning movement to the north, this daring and courageous unit fought its way ahead yard by yard through mangrove swamps, dense jungles and over cliffs and, although terrifically reduced in strength under the enemy's fanatical counterattacks, hunted the Japanese in caves, pillboxes and foxholes and exterminated them. By their individual acts of gallantry and their indomitable fighting teamwork throughout this bitter and costly struggle, the men of the First Provisional Marine Brigade aided immeasurably in the restoration of Guam to our sovereignty.

Secretary of the Navy James Forrestal signed the citation. The list of units that comprised the brigade and were authorized to receive the award include the 4th platoon of the 2d Marine Ammunition Company. The 4th Marine Ammunition Company is not named.[11]

The Fighting Continues on Guam

Guam was secured on August 10, but that did not mean the fighting was over. On September 27, Japanese soldiers who had been bypassed wounded two men from the 4th Marine Ammunition Company, PFCs George F. Gaines and Lawrence H. Hill. In December 1944 while guarding an ammunition dump on Guam, PFC Luther Woodard of the same company discovered footprints that made him suspicious. He followed them into the thick brush and came to a clearing where he encountered six Japanese soldiers. Woodard opened fire, killing one of the Japanese, but the others got away. Woodard returned to his camp for help. With five other black Marines, he returned to hunt down the remaining Japanese. Woodard killed one more Japanese, while his pick-up team killed yet another.

A few days later, Woodard and a fellow Marine chased two Japanese into a cave. Woodard threw a grenade and one of the enemy soldiers ran out. Woodard shot that one, handed his rifle to his friend, and went into the cave to get the other Japanese armed only with his K-bar knife.[12]

PFC Woodard was awarded the Bronze Star on January 11, 1945. He became the only black Marine to earn the Bronze Star in World War II. His Bronze Star was later upgraded to a Silver Star.[13]

Encounters with Japanese soldiers hiding in the backcountry would continue for years to come. The last Japanese survivor of the battle for Guam, Sergeant Shoichi Yokoi, was captured on January 24, 1972. "We Japanese soldiers were told to prefer death to the disgrace of getting captured alive," Yokoi said.[14]

Awards

Early in the eighteenth century, commanders recognized the value that fighting men placed on distinctive bits of colored ribbon awarded in recognition of their bravery or wounds. Today, ribbons, badges, and medals are worn on uniforms, usually above breast pockets, in order of precedence. The Medal of Honor, the senior medal awarded, recognizes courage above and beyond the call of duty. Much of a Marine's military experience — what, where, and when — can be read in the colorful ribbons he or she wears. The old barracks axiom that "Marines shake hands with their chests" is more truthful than many will admit.

In the Marine Corps, awards fall into four categories: personal and unit award decorations; commemorative, campaign, and service medals; rifle and pistol marksmanship awards;

"Pfc. Luther Woodward [sic]..., a member of the Fourth Ammunition Company, admires the Bronze Star awarded to him for 'his bravery, initiative and battle-cunning....'" On Guam, PFC Woodard opened fire on six Japanese soldiers, killing one, but the others got away. With five other black Marines he hunted down the remaining Japanese. Woodard killed one more Japanese, while his pickup team killed still another. Later, Woodard and a fellow Marine chased two Japanese into a cave. Woodard threw a grenade and one of the enemy soldiers ran out. Woodard shot that one, handed his rifle to his friend, and went into the cave to get the other Japanese with just his K-bar combat knife. The award was later upgraded to the Silver Star. April 17, 1945. Cpl. Irving Deutch. Still Picture Branch (NNSP), National Archives, Washington, DC.

and badges such as parachutists wings and scuba pins. The Marine Corps is notoriously stingy with personal and unit awards.

Marine officers are responsible for seeing that their men are promptly recommended for awards they have earned. In most cases, the recommendation is written and forwarded up the chain of command, usually beginning at the company or battalion level. If the battalion commanding officer concurs that an award is merited, the recommendation will go forward with an endorsement recommending approval. An awards board at the division level has final authority in most cases to approve, downgrade, or deny the award.

As often happens, when a recommendation makes its way through higher echelons of command (and further to the rear away from danger, ever more removed in time and distance from the place where the Marine's actions were noted) the more likely the award will be downgraded to a lesser medal or even denied. Several of the men interviewed for this book remember with pride that they were recommended for an award or a promotion and that was the end of it; they heard nothing more of the matter. Understandably, the memory galls, even today.

A few black Marines at Saipan and Guam earned the Purple Heart, a medal awarded in the name of the President of the United States to any service man or woman wounded or killed, or who died after being wounded in action against an enemy of the United States. As stated earlier, all members of several black Marine units on those islands earned the Presidential Unit Citation or the Navy Unit Commendation. In the coming battles, more black Marines would earn personal and unit awards, and a few would die doing so.

All black Marines in the Pacific were eligible for the Asiatic-Pacific Campaign Medal, awarded for service within the Asiatic-Pacific Theater between December 7, 1941 and March 2, 1946, and for the World War II Victory Medal for military service between December 7, 1941, and December 31, 1946.

22

Moving Out

Defense Battalions Reorganize

In July 1944, the new AAA battalion table of organization reflected the emphasis on 90mm and 40mm antiaircraft weapons (the 20mm was considered too light against Japanese aircraft). The new T/O called for a battalion of 57 officers and 1,198 enlisted men, little changed from the earlier table. As before, it was organized into a headquarters and service battery, but the real changes came in the type and number of guns. Four 90mm guns were added to form a heavy antiaircraft group with a total of sixteen 90mm guns. The light antiaircraft group added four guns for a total of sixteen 40mm guns and sixteen .50 caliber machine guns (no change from the earlier T/O). There was also no change in the searchlight battery.[1]

By September 1944, all the defense battalions had turned in their 155mm seacoast artillery pieces as well as the 20mm guns to become purely antiaircraft artillery (AAA) battalions. The 6th, 51st and 52d Defense Battalions retained their unit designations, while the other battalions became Antiaircraft Artillery Battalions but kept their old numerical designations.

The 52d Prepares for the Pacific

John Griffin reported to his new unit, and after a welcome aboard from the battalion sergeant major, went to work as a file clerk and mimeograph operator. Griffin noted that the officers and men seemed to get along well, and he settled into his new unit.[2]

It was a time of rapid change for the black defense battalions. On July 15, 1944, the 51st followed the 52d's lead. The Seacoast Artillery Group disbanded and the men were reassigned in the battalion as the emphasis for the 51st shifted over to that of an antiaircraft unit. The war was moving north, and alert orders came down to the 51st Defense Battalion: prepare to move to a new location.

The 52d Heads West

Meanwhile, the first step in the process that would see the 52d move from North Carolina to California for further transfer to the Pacific came on July 12, 1944, when Lt. Col. Joseph W. Earnshaw took command of the 52d. The reorganized battalion turned in its guns and heavy equipment and split into two nearly equal elements, one designated as 52d Defense Battalion (less Detachment "A") and the other as Detachment "A" 52d Defense Battalion. Earnshaw commanded one and entrusted the other to his executive officer, Lieutenant Colonel Thomas C. Moore, Jr., (who hailed from Georgia!). An experienced officer, Moore had commanded the 3d Defense Battalion on Guadalcanal in the Solomon Islands. The two contingents entrained at Camp Lejeune on August 19, bound for Camp Pendleton, California, to make final preparations for deployment to the islands of the Pacific.[3]

John Griffin described the trip across the southern part of the country as a very enjoyable one. At a two-hour stop at Yuma, Arizona, Red Cross workers passed out magazines, candy, ice cream, fruit, and Bibles. It seemed to the men that "the entire city, including Mexicans and Indians," turned out to see such an extraordinary sight — a battalion of black Marines.[4]

Arriving at Camp Pendleton on August 24, the men lived in a transient area, in dirt-floored tents; meals were prepared in a field mess tent, but the food was good. Only two outdoor showers were set up for units using the transient area, and there was no hot water. The cool air and foggy coastal California skies ensured that the men did not linger when using the showers. However, officers divided the men into port and starboard liberty sections, and Duty NCOs were generous with 3-day passes. Along with many of the men, John Griffin got his first look at Los Angeles.

The 51st Displaces Forward

In mid–July, the 51st Defense Battalion's Detachment A disbanded and all the scattered elements of the 51st came together at Funafuti prior to moving forward to a new island base, Eniwetok, north of the Equator in the Marshalls. In a now familiar process, they turned in all guns and equipment to quartermasters — no defense battalion was coming in to replace them because the fighting was moving far to the north and west. The men boarded a U.S. Army transport ship, the *Kota Agoeng*, and on September 8, the ship sailed, arriving at Eniwetok six days later.[5]

The 51st relieved the 10th Antiaircraft Battalion and followed the standing procedure of taking over the guns and equipment of the departing unit scattered across Eniwetok, Engebi, Parry, and Porky Islands. The Marshalls were much closer to the war than the Ellice Islands and had played a significant role during the recently concluded operations in the Marianas. The 51st launched an intensive training program. Japanese holdouts lurked on some of the smaller nearby islands. Eniwetok

Atoll's lagoon bustled with the coming and going of warships, and the chances for action brightened the men's spirits and morale. However quick the radar operators were to locate inbound aircraft or how accurately the gunners worked their pieces, there would be no combat for the Marine Corps's first black combat unit.[6]

Departure from San Diego

Too soon for the liberty hounds among the battalion, the 52d got the word to move out and officers cancelled all passes. Bussed on September 21 to pier #18 at San Diego, the men filed aboard a relatively new amphibious cargo ship, the USS *Winged Arrow* (AP-170), and got a memorable sendoff. The Marine band from MCRD San Diego stood on the pier and played "Sentimental Journey" as lines were taken in and the ship got under way. Girlfriends of recent acquaintance came to see the men off and lined the pier, many crying and waving. For however short the time the men and women may have had, wartime romances were just as intensely sweet as those of the old, prewar days, if not more so. The band struck up "The Star Spangled Banner," and it was a grand experience. The girls on the pier may not have been the only ones wiping away a tear.

After two days at sea every member of the battalion had succumbed to seasickness. By the fifth day, arriving at Honolulu, Territory of Hawaii, liberty beckoned, and the seasickness was forgotten.[7] Even in 1944, Honolulu was an expensive town, and while they had liberty every day, the young Marines were not sad to leave.

The Marshall Islands are located a few degrees north of the Equator a distance of about 1,950 miles from Hawaii, but because the ship sailed a zig-zag course to avoid Japanese submarines, the distance was a bit greater. "While in route to the Marshall Islands [see map 5, Japan to the Gilberts, and map 9, The Marshall Islands], we crossed the 180th Meridian at 2330 one night, and all the men that hadn't crossed before were made members of the 'Secret Order of the Golden Dragon,'" John Griffin mused, but "The significance of this I never knew."[8]

Rumblings from the Black Press

An editorial writer for the *Richmond Afro-American* had pointed out to his readers as early as October 1943 that black Marines aspiring to become commissioned officers and warrant officers were "Denied [a] Chance to Qualify."[9] For the Marine Corps, commissioning blacks was beyond the pale. Headquarters had no intention of allowing any blacks to become officers. An April 1944 study of the "problem of colored officers in the Marine Corps" recommended that no black officers be procured. "But, in the event of necessity of such program, colored officers should ... be appointed from the ranks only."[10] The rumblings grew louder.

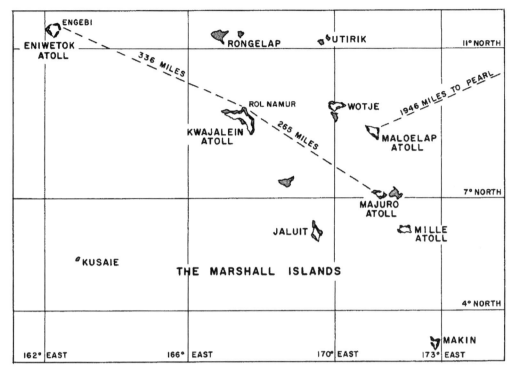

The Marshall Islands.

Source: Dyer, *The Amphibians*, Vol. I, 231.

The Honeymoon Is Over

In a "Marines Combat Report," *Time* magazine noted in July 1944 that the Corps had not experienced any of the "public race troubles" such as the U.S. Army had seen, but pointed out that "The Corps still has no Negro officers." Citing a report by combat correspondent Robert Sherrod, the article gave a very positive view of the conduct of black Marines under fire during the battle of Saipan. However, Sherrod's description of a black Marine named Jenkins sharing a foxhole under fire with a wounded white Marine aroused the ire of the black press. According to the article, the white Marine handed a hand grenade to the black Marine who said, "I don't know how to use this thing." After quick instruction, he threw the grenade, killing three Japanese and knocking out a machine gun.[11] Black newspapers hammered the Corps for putting "service and supply" men in battle with inadequate training on one of the basic tools of war, a hand grenade.

"*Not One Officer in Marines ... Refused Commissions ... Saipan Battle Proves Training Inadequate*," the editor of the *Richmond Afro-American* wrote in an article that was picked up by another regional *Afro-American* newspaper, this one in Philadelphia. The Richmond editor recalled his reporter's visit to Montford Point

"Marines receiving instruction in the Demolition Course at Montford Point Camp (NC), during intensive combat training in preparation for action in the Pacific." Note that one of the white Marines is holding a satchel charge. It is a canvas bag of explosives with a friction fuse. In the Pacific fighting, Marines threw one or two of these into a cave or bunker to clear it of the enemy. Black recruits began receiving instruction in flame throwers, rocket launchers, satchel charges, hand grenades and other infantry weapons after press reports of a black Marine on Saipan who had never been instructed in how to use a hand grenade. February 1945. Sgt. L. A. Wilson. Still Picture Branch (NNSP), National Archives, Washington, DC.

the previous October and stated flatly that "*Most Charges Still Stand.*" Almost a year had passed, there were "18,000" black Marines (in September HQMC counted 15,700), yet there were no black commissioned officers.[12] The *Baltimore Afro-American* joined in with a similar editorial, including a damning cartoon challenge to President Roosevelt to take up the issue in his next fireside radio chat.[13]

"Black Marines with transport packs (note the camouflage shelter half making up the blanket roll) study a map prior to a field problem at Montford Point Camp." No date, but pos-
sibly early 1945. Used with permission of the Montford Point Marine Museum, Camp
Lejeune, NC.

The public chastening was not lost on Marine officers in Washington. The
expedient of shipping Depot and Ammunition Company Marines with no combat
training to places where they would have to know how to fight or die was uncon-
scionable. Within months, the training syllabus at Montford Point expanded to
include training for all black recruits in firing flamethrowers, rocket launchers, hand
grenades, using satchel charges, and other infantry weapons commonly used by
Marines in the Pacific. Added also was training in how individual Marines advanced
under fire, crawling through an infiltration course while machine guns fired overhead and explosive charges were detonated in pits near the men. It was another step
forward.

The V-12 Program

During World War II, the United States Navy commissioned over 5,500 ships
and operated thousands of airplanes. Most of the planes were flown by officers
(although Enlisted Naval Aviation Pilots — NAPs — flew some). The Marine Corps
activated six ground combat divisions and five air wings, the 1st through 4th and
the 9th. The latter was a training wing in North Carolina (again, some of the planes

were flown by enlisted Marine NAPs).[14] Hundreds of naval shore installations and Marine posts and stations were built around the world, all requiring enlisted men and competent officers to command and operate them.

Prior to the war, most navy and Marine officers came from the Naval Academy at Annapolis, Maryland, and the small Naval ROTC Program, established in 1926. A few obtained direct commissions from private life or transferred from the army, but with the war came various programs to school enlisted men and commission them as officers. These could not graduate enough officers to meet the demands of the Fleet and Fleet Marine Force.

Millions of men caught in the draft or volunteering for military service had caused a drop in student enrollment at colleges and universities with a corresponding loss in tuition funds. It came down to this: The navy and Marines needed college-educated leaders and had the men and the money to pay for their schooling; the colleges needed students and money. Agreements were forged, and the navy's V-12 program came into being. The services got what they needed as did the colleges. The first students reported to colleges on July 1, 1943. A massive officer candidate program, V-12 would become one of the most important producers of Marine officers.[15]

High school seniors who passed screening exams, enlisted sailors and Marines recommended by their commanding officers and Navy and Marine Corps ROTC members were eligible for the program. The federal government paid tuition to participating colleges and universities for courses taught to the men, and paid for books and supplies the men needed. The students in V-12 wore uniforms, drilled, did physical fitness training and, as officer candidates, were paid $50 per month, almost as much as a corporal (Fifth Pay Grade).

Although the length of each student's stay depended on past college work completed, the men usually studied for three terms of four months each. Sailors then went on to four months at a Naval Reserve midshipmen's school. Those students who chose to enter the Marine Corps moved on to boot camp and following that the three-month Officer Candidate Course at Quantico, Virginia. Of course, enlisted Marines in the program had already completed boot camp so they went directly to Quantico after completing the college work. At the completion of all the training, participants received commissions as navy ensigns or Marine Corps second lieutenants.

An Opportunity Presents Itself

Changes were coming, events that would immediately affect the lives of several young black men and set them on paths that would forever alter the Marine Corps. Black U.S. Marines were on the threshold of an opportunity that would never be taken away from their race, marching for the first time in a new direction. Whatever the reason, be it mounting pressure from the black press or accepting the inevitable, the Marine Corps backed off from its April 1944 position of no black officers. HQMC adopted what today would be called its stated "fall back" position: Any black officer would have to come from the enlisted ranks.[16] For some of the men affected, it began in the routine of an ordinary summer day in the South Pacific of 1944.

As his battery turned in its guns and prepared to move to the Marshall Islands, Herbert Brewer recalls, "I was walking down the company street one day and this fellow came up to me and asked me, 'How would you like to go back to OCS (Officer Candidate School)?' I hadn't applied for anything; I said, 'Oh, I wouldn't mind at all.' He was Corporal Fred Branch. He was in the headquarters company." Branch, said Herb Brewer, "was always looking ahead; he wanted to become an officer so he had applied. At that time they had what was called the Navy V-12 Program to obtain the minimum two years of college required for a commission. Branch and I were selected to go from our battalion."[17] Brewer had never applied, but his academic record combined with his performance and demonstrated leadership potential as a Marine made him a standout in the 51st, and a logical choice for the program. Brewer and Branch were the 51st Defense Battalion's nominees for the V-12 program. Thus began a lifelong friendship.

The First Black Marine Officer Candidates

Herb Brewer described the sudden change in his life brought about by this new development. "Two other African Americans, a Master Sergeant Johnson from another unit located somewhere else, and a Corporal Davis were selected; the four of us were sent back to the states under this V-12 program. The senior member, Master Sergeant Johnson, was from Iowa, I think. We had to select the schools we wanted to go to. I selected Cornell, I think, and Colgate, and, my mother being from Boston, some of the schools in the east. This fellow Johnson, the senior NCO, had selected Purdue, and we were all sent to Purdue so we'd be together. I'm glad now it worked out that way because that's how I got into the engineering field.

"Coming back for the V-12 program, I remember when we were half way to Johnson Island; there was trouble with the plane. A little excitement," Brewer said. "To lighten the plane, we threw out everything except our personal papers."[18]

Integrated Dormitory — A First for the Corps

"When we first got to Purdue we found that all V-12 students were assigned to a dormitory. The four of us African Americans were not assigned along with the others and we wondered what the delay was. We found out that apparently up to that time there had been no African Americans in the dormitories at Purdue." Before the black V-12 students arrived on campus, black students at Purdue had "lived in housing in the community. As I understand it, the school was trying to call people in the community to see if they would take us on." University officials were unsure about placing black Marines in the same dormitories with white Marines, no matter that they were in the V-12 program. School officials "explained to the [white] captain in charge of our unit what was going on, and he said, 'Well, these men are Marines, and they're going to stay wherever the other Marines stay. We'll all stay together, we're all Marines.' So, they assigned us in one of the regular dormitories with the rest of the V-12's."[19] Even though segregation was still the rule and law in all branches of the nation's military services and black servicemen lived in separate barracks from whites, a lone white officer of Marines did exactly what people have come to expect from Marines: *He took charge and made a decision*. Clearly, here was an officer for whom the admonition, "Take care of your men," had *real* meaning. He arbitrarily integrated the V-12 dormitory at Purdue University, anticipating President Truman's decision to integrate the armed services by four years!

Brewer continues. "The program at Purdue was just the regular engineering school program, accelerated in that there was no summer vacation. We attended school continually because the idea was that after we attained two years of college (which was the requirement then in order to get a commission) we would go back to basic school and receive a commission."[20]

Integration — Again

Back in the Pacific, Detachment A, 52d Defense Battalion arrived in the Marshall Islands and disembarked at Majuro on October 16, relieving the 1st Antiaircraft Artillery Battalion. The *Winged Arrow* continued on to Roi-Namur, arriving on October 18. The remainder of the 52d went ashore and relieved the 15th Antiaircraft Artillery Battalion on October 22.

Marine Air Group 31 (MAG-31) was already located on Roi-Namur with three fighter squadrons and nearly 1,500 officers and enlisted men. A good working relationship grew between the white Marines of the air group and the black Marines of the defense battalion. The staff non-commissioned officers (SNCOs) of the two units (the senior enlisted men in the third, second and first pay grades) even got together and set up the first integrated club in the Corps.[21] The 15th Marine Depot Company had been in the Marshall Islands since March 7, 1944, and was also located on Roi-Namur as part of the garrison force, but no mention is made of including the SNCOs from the 15th in the club.

The informally declared truce in the battle between the races reflected an attitude, found in Marines of all generations, like that of the Marine captain that Herbert Brewer met at Purdue. It is an attitude that says, "Screw it. It's better to have to ask for forgiveness than to beg for permission." Added to that was the feeling expressed as, "What are they going to do, cut off all our hair and send us to (blank)?"

Here the speaker filled in the blank with an appropriate location — the Pacific, Guadalcanal, Tarawa, Bougainville, or some other undesirable place. In the author's time, the blank stood for Vietnam, the Arabian Gulf, any Middle Eastern desert, or Iraq.

When MAG-31 departed in March to participate in the Okinawa campaign, the defense battalion remained behind. Whether the informal integration continued with other units is now a matter of speculation, for no one speaks of it.

The Marshall Islands, scattered across 600 miles of Pacific Ocean (see map 9, The Marshall Islands), was to be the home of both the 51st and the 52d Defense Battalions for some months to come.[22] As the end of 1944 drew near, Lt. Col. Gould P. Groves, the former executive officer of the 51st Defense Battalion, fleeted up to replace Lt. Col. LeGette as battalion commander. Groves was destined to be the 51st's last commanding officer. For the men of both battalions, the enervating dullness of life far behind the war front set in.[23]

23

Pushing Black Marines Through

A Depot Company Forms

Since the advent of depot companies in March 1943, the 1st through the 16th Marine Depot Companies had been formed. However, of those, the 5th and 6th were disbanded within months and the men reassigned to bring the first four up to T/O strength. From November 1, 1943, the sequence of forming new black units at Montford Point became two depot companies and one ammunition company per month, and that policy remained in effect until November 1944.

First Lieutenant Miles Q. Romney penned a description in mid–1945 of the activation of one unit, the 23d Marine Depot Company. After graduating from boot camp, all men slated for assignment to depot companies were joined on the rolls of Company A, 7th Separate Infantry Battalion at Montford Point, and at the end of March 1944, three 51-man platoons stood ready to form a company. On April 1, the 23d Marine Depot Company activated, with Platoon Sergeant Fred L. Calhoun of Birmingham, Alabama, as the acting first sergeant and sole member of the company. Four days later 1st Lt. Romney reported aboard, and the platoons joined and began a brief shakedown and training period. By April 18, the company came to full strength when five commissary men joined, and the 23d boarded a train the next day for its port of embarkation en route to Oahu, Territory of Hawaii. Sergeant Ernest C. "Judo" Jones, the man who had assisted Alvin "Tony" Ghazlo as bayonet and unarmed combat instructor at Montford Point, served as the company's acting provost marshal to supervise the train's of police and security.[1]

In Hawaii, the company joined the 6th Base Depot, Supply Service, FMFPac and the men went to work. When the day's supply work ended, each platoon leader held an evening inspection and drilled and schooled his platoon. Then the men formed a "school circle" around the officer, and they talked over current events, administrative requirements of censorship (Romney himself was cautious about revealing troop movements and locations), war bond allotments, and the G.I. Bill of Rights.

Life on Oahu was comfortable, and recreation included beach parties, hikes, dances, and a range of sports including baseball, softball, basketball, swimming, and boxing. PFC Kay "V" Jackson pitched for the company softball team and led the team to the Base Depot championship pitching two no-hit-no-run victories.[2]

The company transferred to Guam and joined the 5th Field Depot on November 3, 1944, and found conditions were much different from Hawaii. The men trained and cross-trained in a variety of specialized jobs, including auto mechanics, riggers, crane operators, switchboard operators, and stock men, and, because they were definitely in a war zone, morale was high.[3]

By the end of 1944 twenty-six new depot companies and nine ammunition companies had formed. In September 1944, the 12th Marine Ammunition Company, the last of the black ammo companies, was activated at Montford Point.

In July 1944, there were 1,442 blacks in the Steward's Branch, roughly nine percent of the Marine Corps's total black strength of 15,771.[4] There were 452 stewards in FMF units and 351 at various Marine Corps shore stations. Stewards Branch Battalion at Montford Point Camp accounted for 614, while the remaining 25, unaccounted for at HQMC's M-1 branch (Personnel) were probably on leave, in transit, or in casual status.[5] The number of black Marine stewards remained at about that same level until the end of the war.[6]

The Palaus — Operation STALEMATE

After the Marianas, plans called for Marines to continue their drive into the North Pacific. U.S. Army General Douglas MacArthur had completed the capture of New Guinea and was preparing to advance into the Philippines. MacArthur insisted that it was necessary to protect his lines of communication from Japanese bases approximately 500 miles to the east in the Palau Islands. Therefore, STALEMATE had two objectives: first, to secure MacArthur's flank; and second, to secure an American base to support further operations in the southern Philippines.[7]

The Palaus, an arc of islands about 80 miles long, are the westernmost of the Caroline Islands lying southwest of the Marianas and east of Mindanao in the Philippines. The islands are only a few degrees north of the Equator with a debilitating humid, hot equatorial climate (see map 10, Peleliu). Early plans called for the capture of all of the islands in the Palaus, including heavily defended Babelthuap, but in July plans were scaled back. The 1st Marine Division, seasoned veterans of Guadalcanal fame, and the army's newly arrived 81st Infantry Division were to assault and capture Peleliu. It would be a bloody and intensive battle with high casualty rates. When the public read the casualty figures, swells of outrage broke against the Corps, an echo of those following the brief but costly battle at Tarawa. The protests were short-lived, overtaken by the greater casualties at Iwo Jima and Okinawa. After the war Peleliu was largely forgotten, remembered today only by historians and those who fought there.

Supply planning and embarkation was complicated from the beginning: After

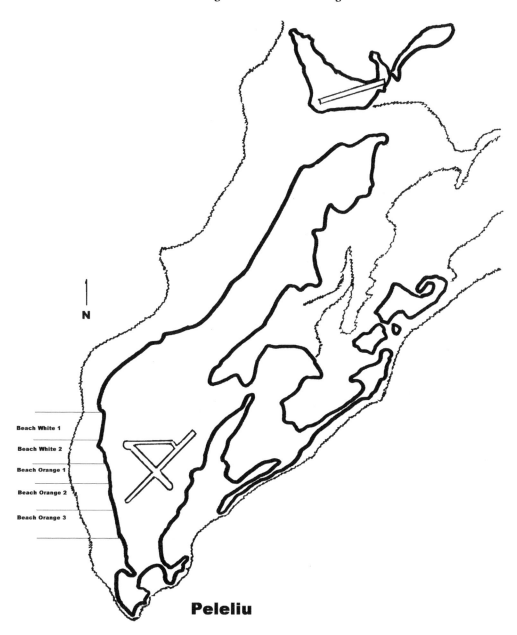

N

Beach White 1

Beach White 2

Beach Orange 1

Beach Orange 2

Beach Orange 3

Peleliu

Source: Historical Reference Branch, History Division, USMC.

the Cape Gloucester operation the units that made up the 1st Marine Division scattered across training and staging areas on the islands of Pavuvu and Banika in the Russells and Guadalcanal and Tulagi in the Solomon Islands. The 16th Field Depot at Guadalcanal, including the 11th Marine Depot Company and the 7th Marine Ammunition Company, was assigned to support the assault echelons of the 1st Marine Division at Peleliu.

Organized on October 7, 1943, the 4 officers and 173 enlisted men of the 11th Marine Depot Company came to the South Pacific Area in December 1943. While being organized at Montford Point they were slated to become part of the 1st Base Depot on New Caledonia, but the company was diverted to the 4th Base Depot on Banika. In July 1944, the company transferred to Guadalcanal to join the 16th Field Depot.

In August the 7th Marine Ammunition Company, which had formed only four months earlier at Montford Point, arrived. It too joined the 16th Field Depot while the division was in the final stages of preparing for Operation STALEMATE. The 7th Ammo launched an intensive training program, ranging from small arms repair to jungle fighting, to get the men ready for the coming battle. There were 15-mile conditioning hikes with full packs, brutal in the heat and humidity of the Solomons, and the men became stronger.[8]

Supply Planning for STALEMATE

The boldest plans carried out by the strongest, most determined men are doomed to failure without the help of the men of the service units who follow close behind them to move the beans, bullets, and bandages forward and evacuate and tend the wounded, bury the dead, and repair broken weapons and disabled vehicles. Peleliu would be no different. Operations orders required that the assault units carry 32 days of rations, five days of water (at two gallons per man per day), 30 days of medical supplies, a 20-day supply of clothing, fuel, lubricants, and miscellaneous supplies. Five units of fire would be landed for the assault phase.[9]

Peleliu posed a unique dilemma for the coral islands rose steeply from the ocean floor far below, and as a result, there were no near shore anchorages available. The landing craft had to come alongside and be loaded while the transports and cargo ships continued under way, slowly, but not swinging at anchor, as was usually the case.[10] After all the assault supplies were ashore, the beach dumps would be taken over by the 16th Field Depot. The Depot was slated to become part of the Island Command after the fighting, but it was attached to the 1st Marine Division for the assault phase. In other words, the field depot was subject to the direct orders of the division commander. Such an arrangement, in the words of the commanding officer of the 1st Service Battalion, made all the "difference between ordering and asking" when getting things done.[11]

Landing Plans

The landings would take place September 15 on the southwest coast of Peleliu on 2,600 yards of beaches. The 1st, 5th, and 7th Marine Regiments would land abreast, with the 1st on the left (northern) flank, the 5th in the center, and the 7th on the right (southern) flank. To gain the beaches the Marines would have to cross a coral fringe reef varying from 600 to 800 yards wide and then continue across a shallow lagoon. After the naval gunfire and aircraft strikes shifted prior to H-Hour (0830), 18 LCI gunboats firing 4.5-inch rockets would precede the first wave of LVT(A)s across the line of departure, while the following waves would consist of the troop-carrying LVTs.

Dog-Day, September 15

Naval gunfire began pounding Japanese defenses hidden deep beneath the honeycombed coral rock of Peleliu at about 0530. Dawn broke on a clear and calm Dog-Day at 0552. By 0715, the LSTs arrived at their launching area on schedule. The sea was calm and there was almost no surf to contend with at the reef. While the assault waves of LVTs formed, the men watched as fifty airplanes bombed and strafed the island from 0750 until 0805. The LVT(A)s crossed the line of departure at 0800. Naval gunfire continued during the air attacks with the planes flying high enough to avoid the flat-trajectory shells from the ships. When the gunboats were 1,000 yards offshore they turned away, took up new positions and continued with rocket salvos. Forty-eight navy fighters then attacked the beaches, gradually shifting their fire further inland as the assault waves approached and landed. Successive waves of LVTs crossed the beaches at five-minute intervals. Heavy mortar and gunfire struck the beaches. Above the high water mark, the Japanese had sown mines and 75-kg aerial bombs but many of these failed to explode. Intense enemy fire knocked out more than 60 LVTs and DUKWs, some at least only temporarily, on D-Day. The Marines faced a "murderous" volume of fire but continued to push inland.[12]

Early in the assault, most of the black Marines served in ship's platoons working with sailors and other Marines. When the LVTs and DUKWs returned from the beaches after disgorging men and supplies, depot company Marines pulled combat loaded supplies from cargo holds as they were called for and loaded them into the vehicles for delivery to the men ashore. When regimental dumps were established close behind the lines, small detachments of depot and ammo company Marines were landed to work the dumps.

Once ashore, the black Marines, sorting and moving supplies and ammunition into dumps or to the front lines, came under fierce Japanese fire. They did not return from the front empty handed, but worked as litter bearers to evacuate wounded Marines to the beach. One navy medical officer said, "I especially remember the bravery of the black Marines who volunteered as stretcher bearers to retrieve the casualties and bring them to our aid station for whatever we could do for them — patch them up and evacuate them as fast as possible."[13]

As the beachhead expanded, the division's shore party and attached depot company Marines worked hard to keep up a steady flow of supplies across the beaches

"Peleliu Island ... Marines move through the trenches on the beach duing the battle." Photograph taken sometime on D-Day, September 15, 1944. Fitzgerald. Still Picture Branch (NNSP), National Archives, Washington, DC.

and inland to the men on the lines. They labored under a storm of artillery, mortar, and machine gun fire, and casualties among the shore party were greater than the division had suffered in any other operation. For the first time the division made use of large numbers of amphibian trailers loaded with prepackaged artillery and machine gun ammunition. The trailers could be towed behind LCVPs to the reef and picked up by LVTs or DUKWs to be taken ashore and from there towed by trucks to supply dumps. These proved an excellent gap-filler when off-loading ceased at nightfall until it resumed at dawn on D+1.

Another innovation at Peleliu was the use of cranes mounted on a tracked chassis (crawlers) lifted from ships onto nine modified pontoon barges that were then anchored seaward of the reef.[14] Once in place, the cranes were able to lift prepackaged cargo nets full of ammunition and pallets of other bulk supplies from boats to LVTs and DUKWs at the transfer line. (Note: The pallets were an army innovation first used in the Marshalls and adopted by Marines at Saipan. These were wooden sleds, four by six feet, with runners that could be loaded to a height of about three feet with up to 3,000 pounds of supplies. Flat metal strappings secured the load.)[15]

This was a considerable saving in manpower and time, far easier than exposing hundreds of men to enemy fire while lifting one ammunition box or carton of rations or floating one fuel drum at a time across the lagoon. Other crawler cranes landed early in the assault to lift net-loads from LVTs onto trucks for further delivery forward, once again saving time and muscle.[16] Even so, the shore party, depot and ammo company men continued work exposed to Japanese fire.

Private Russell Davis was a rifleman in the 2d Battalion 1st Marines. Pvt. Davis was digging in for the night on Dog-Day just off White Beach One when he saw an odd sight. "Down along the path came a file of dark-faced men in Marine dungarees. They were tall and rugged-looking men, and their faces couldn't be distinguished in the darkness. They were the first Negro Marines I had seen in the war. They were carrying water and ammunition in from the beach, led by a huge sergeant who carried a box of ammunition on each shoulder. They dumped their supplies at the foot of the bank, and just as they did the Japanese fired a twilight salvo in on the line and everybody scattered for their holes." One of the black Marines spent the night in the front lines and shared the foxhole with Davis, taking his turn on watch. Just like his white comrades, he stood one of the watches as a full-fledged combat Marine fully entrusted to protect the lives of his newfound buddies.[17]

Bringing supplies and ammunition across the beaches proved to be a challenge. Little beach space was available to receive the huge amounts of supplies and material needed by a Marine division in close combat with a well dug in and fanatical enemy. Headquarters tents, dumps for all classes of supplies, communications centers, field messes, and bivouac areas for the men, artillery batteries, vehicle parks and repair facilities of the division "rear" area were crowded together in apparently random order. All were only a few hundred of yards behind the lines, and all made excellent targets for Japanese observers and gunners concealed in the sharp spines of the jagged coral hills.

On Dog+1 the temperature of the dead calm air at Peleliu reached 105 degrees Fahrenheit, and the following days were as hot or hotter — temperatures as high as 115 degrees Fahrenheit were recorded. In such heat, men needed water to stave off heat exhaustion or heat stroke. Anticipating this, two gallons of water per man per day was on hand. The water for the assault troops came ashore in scoured-out oil drums and five-gallon jerry cans. Unfortunately, steaming out the oil drums had left a residue of oil, sickening the men who drank water from them, which led to an increase in heat casualties among the men.[18]

The Marines of the 1st Pioneer Battalion continued their shore party function as the lines advanced and the regimental dumps displaced to positions close behind the lines. Black Marines continued to move supplies during the day. At night, any above ground movement was assumed to be Japanese and drew a grenade or a burst of fire, so black Marines took their places in the lines wherever they were needed. White Marines took note, and remembered. Word of the black Marines' performance went from Marine to Marine. They were probably not aware that anyone noticed, but however small, it was another step forward for the black men.

Accounts of the casualties among black Marines reflect the intensity of the

fighting. The 7th Ammunition Company's Pvt. Dyrel A. Shuler was wounded on
D+5; no blacks were hit on D+6, but from D+7 through D+11 the Depot Company Marines were hit hard — PFCs Kenneth R. Stevens and Earl L. Washington
were wounded on September 22. Then on September 23, four men fell in action:
Cpl. Clifford W. Stewart and PFCs Willie A. Rushton, Carleton Shanks Jr. and
Edward J. Swain. Japanese fire continued to hit the depot company men on the fol-
lowing day, when four more black Marines were wounded: PFCs Bernard L.
Warfield and Oscar A. Edmonds and Privates Joseph Williams and Predell Ham-
blin. The following day Cpl. Lawrence V. Cole and PFC Edgar T. Grace were felled
by Japanese fire. The final black casualties of the month came on the following day,
September 26, among Depot Company Marines: PFCs Irving A. Banks, Timothy
Black, and Paul B. Cook were hit by Japanese fire.[19]

On September 28 and as planned, "stevedores" of the Island Command's 16th
Field Depot (including Depot and Ammunition Company Marines) took charge
at the beaches and supply dumps while the battle still raged. On October 9 (D+24)
the 7th Ammunition Company's Cpl. Charles E. Cain was hit as was Pvt. John
Copeland, who died of his wounds the same day. Gy. Sgt. Victor B. Kee and Pvt.
Everett Seals, both of the 11th Depot Company, were wounded on October 19, and
the last black casualty of Peleliu, PFC James E. Moore, occurred on October 26
(D+41).[20] (Author's note: The HQMC Casualty Card printout dated April 9, 1948,
entitled *Negro Marine Battle Casualties*, does not include the names of Shuler, Rushton, Swain, Cole, Grace, or Copeland. I found their names in Shaw and Donnelley's *Blacks in the Marine Corps* monograph. Their wounds may have been slight,
not treated by a corpsman and so not reported. In the case of Copeland, his death
may have been non-combat related. In case the error is mine, I chose to include
their names here in recognition for their service.)

The performance of these black Marines did not go unnoticed on the beachhead. Word of their efforts traveled up the chain of command, prompting the division commander, Maj. Gen. William H. Rupertus, to write identical letters of
commendation to the commanders of both the 11th Marine Depot Company and
the 7th Marine Ammunition Company, which stated:

1. The performance of duty of the officers and men of your command has,
   throughout the landing on Peleliu and the assault phase, been such as to
   warrant the highest praise. Unit commanders have repeatedly brought to my
   attention the whole-hearted cooperation and untiring efforts exhibited by
   each individual.
2. The Negro race can well be proud of the work performed by the 7th Ammunition Company [and 11th Depot Company] as they have demonstrated in
   every respect that they appreciate the privilege of wearing a Marine uniform
   and serving with Marines in combat. Please convey to your command these
   sentiments and inform them that in the eyes of the entire Division they have
   earned a "Well Done."[21]

The 1st Marine Division (Reinforced) received a Presidential Unit Citation for the fighting during the period September 15 to 29, 1944, at Peleliu. The 16th Field Depot, which included the 11th Marine Depot Company and the 7th Marine Ammunition Company, was attached to the division as a reinforcing unit, and both black companies are part of the select group of men entitled to the wear the PUC ribbon for Peleliu.[22]

The Cost in Casualties

The 1st Marine Division (Reinforced), consisted of roughly 25,000 men (including the men of the 16th Field Depot, attached to the Division in direct support); Marine casualties numbered 6,526, including navy corpsmen and doctors: 5,274 were wounded and 1,252 killed.[23] Of those numbers, 20 of the wounded were black Marines and one of those killed was black. The black units were not limited to duties far behind the lines, safe from harm; on Peleliu there *was no* safe rear area, and the black Marines took their share of the casualties. The 11th Marine Depot Company had the highest casualty rate of any company of black Marines during the entire war.

The fighting on Peleliu would continue for months and, as on Guam, Japanese holdouts would continue to appear. The army's 81st Infantry Division took over from the Marines on October 20, but the operation was not wrapped up until November 27, 1944. Not until April 21, 1947, did the last of the enemy garrison, 33 Japanese soldiers, surrender on Peleliu.

Supply in Comparison

In terms of ships, men, and supplies and equipment, STALEMATE was only slightly larger than GALVANIC in the Gilberts in 1943 and would be dwarfed by later, multi-division operations.

Operation	Total Ships	Personnel	Measurement Tons*	Short Tons**
Gilberts	63	34,214	148,782	58,376
Marshalls	122	85,201	293,792	146,949
Marianas	210	141,519	437,653	201,256
Palaus	109	55,887	199,963	92,920

The above table shows the massive weight and volume of material that had to be moved in the major amphibious assaults leading up to and including Peleliu.[24] The black Marines in the Field Depot of the garrison force followed close behind the

*Measurement ton: 2,204.6 pounds; one measurement ton equals 40 cubic feet.
**Short ton: 2,000 pounds.

assault waves to work with the division Marines, mainly the men in the Pioneer, Service, Motor Transport, Engineer, and Medical Battalions of a division's Service Troops.

A combination of arms wins battles: infantry, armor, artillery, and aircraft. However, to sustain the battle the shooters depend on the men who push supplies and ammunition forward, the men of the combat service support units. No single group can claim to shoulder the entire burden or to take credit for supply success in that battle. It takes the combined efforts of all combat service support Marines, from the lowest ranking private lugging boxes through the surf while under fire to the generals at Headquarters, FMFPac, in Hawaii to give the fighting men the means to succeed.

Sunny Tropic Seas...

Since January 1944, Eugene Smith and the 173 "Barracuda Leathernecks" of the 10th Marine Depot Company had been assigned to the 1st Base Depot, Supply Service, IMAC, at Noumea, New Caledonia. The organization of the supply service was still evolving, and with that came new unit designations: On March 1 the 1st Base Depot, Supply Service, IMAC, became the 1st Field Depot, and on April 1 it changed names again to become 1st Base Depot, Marine Support Service, Fifth Amphibious Corps (VAC). Still another name change came on June 9: 1st Base Depot, Supply Service, FMFPac, this latter a manifestation of ongoing development of the Fleet Marine Force, Pacific, headquartered in Hawaii.[25]

The war advanced further into the central and western Pacific and ever closer to Japan, and Eugene Smith's company moved forward as well. On October 19, 1944, the 162 officers and men of the 10th Marine Depot Company filed aboard the Crater Class Liberty ship *Alderamin* (AK-116). Commissioned in 1943, she, like her sister ships of that class, was named for a star. The ship's top speed was a plodding 11 knots. Zig-zagging to avoid Japanese submarines, the 250-mile voyage north to Efate Island and, from there, another 150 miles to Espirito Santo in the New Hebrides Islands took them until October 24. They continued under way for the final 500 miles of their journey to arrive at Guadalcanal in the Solomon Islands on November 12, 1944. The company disembarked the same day they arrived. As part of the 4th Service and Supply Battalion, their new home was much different from the one they left behind on New Caledonia.[26]

Mostly volcanic in origin and lying within the world's wettest area, the Solomons are jagged, jungle-covered, and steamy with humid tropical heat. Swiftly flowing streams and rivers sharply erode the lofty peaks and ridges of the islands. Guadalcanal is some 90 miles in length and about 25 miles wide. On the north central coast, where Eugene Smith and his fellow Depot Company Marines came ashore to make their homes in tents, a coconut plantation covered much of the flat plain around an airfield. From there the land rises inland through foothills made famous in the 1942 battles to a mountainous backbone before dropping rapidly to the south coast. The annual rainfall is about 120 inches. Seasonal differences are not pronounced, but Eugene Smith's arrival coincided with the northwesterly wind shifts of November that bring more rainfall and occasional squalls or cyclones lasting through April. This, together with an average temperature in the high 80s, results in an unhealthy climate. Malaria, dengue, and other fevers, as well as fungus infections, are prevalent. Smith had missed the slightly cooler period of June through August.[27]

Guadalcanal is beautiful when approached from the sea, but once ashore, the island loses its beauty. There are stinging ants, black flies, mosquitoes, coconut crabs and such debilitating humidity that clothing was always damp and sticky, and rotted quickly. On Guadalcanal, the smallest cut refused to heal, forming sores running with pus if not treated.

"When we docked and began to unload on the island of Guadalcanal, all of the white Marines started chattering, 'Here comes the night fighters,'" Smith said.[28] Far removed in distance from the recent battles in the Marianas and on Peleliu, the white Marines at Guadalcanal either knew nothing about the black Marines who fought and died in the fierce fighting on other islands far to the north or simply chose to ignore their accomplishments.

Lt. Gen. Vandegrift had called the blacks "Marines, period." They had proven themselves to the Commandant of the Marine Corps, but it seemed that the commandant's opinion did not count for much with some of the white Marines on Guadalcanal. For Smith it was a familiar attitude, and one he would encounter again.

To the black Marines, Guadalcanal was just another island where there was still some fighting in the jungle. Gene Smith recalls, "At night Japanese holdouts would have a woman's voice broadcast over loud speakers, 'Marines, you die tonight.' Every one would laugh, no worry at all. As a depot company we were back behind the lines doing our job as usual, supplying."[29] A photograph taken on Guadalcanal about this time shows a work-worn Gene Smith holding his M-1 carbine, his boondockers caked with mud, and there is a hole in the knee of his faded dungaree trousers. A Japanese freighter, victim of the intense fighting in 1942, was beached up the coast from where the men camped and attracted the curious among the black Marines. Eugene Smith's snapshot of the hulk shows her bow high on the beach, surrounded by coconut palms.

On October 31, after three weeks on Guadalcanal, the 10th Marine Depot Company was transferred to the 4th Base Depot at Banika, in the Russells Group for three months' temporary duty. Broken into three 40 man sections, "A" departed Guadalcanal on November 1 aboard APc 26, a 103-foot long, 22-foot wide diesel powered coastal transport; "B" left on November 2 on APc 39 and the final group, 39 men and the company commander, 1st Lt. James M. Howell, boarded LCT 917 and departed on the third.[30]

24

Garrison Life

The 52d in the Marshalls

The two parts of the 52d Defense Battalion settled into a routine of training and firing drills. Men went on working parties, and John Griffin, with the battalion headquarters on Roi-Namur, was promoted to PFC. "I also played on the battalion softball team which won the 1944 island championship by beating Area Control, a navy team, 3 to 2." The battalion's basketball team went undefeated.[1]

In November, Battery G, Detachment A, on Majuro embarked a detail of 63 officers and men aboard an LCI for a reconnaissance of Erikub Atoll, but no Japanese were found. A similar reconnaissance patrol went back to Erikub in December, and after a search proceeded to Aur Atoll, once again, with negative results. The patrols continued into the early months of 1945, the chance of encountering Japanese soldiers providing the men some break from the tedium of life in a rear area.

Racism on Guam

Although declared secured on August 10, Marines on Guam continued to encounter Japanese holdouts; perhaps as many as 10,000 Japanese soldiers were still alive in the jungles of Guam. It was here that PFC Luther Woodard of the 4th Marine Ammunition Company earned his Silver Star in December.[2]

While the fighting yet raged on Peleliu, and 3d Marine Division training exercises on Guam frequently took on the tone of mopping up actions when holdouts were flushed from the jungle, conflict of a different sort festered on Guam. This time the conflict was racial. In Guam's garrison, the 2d and 4th Marine Ammunition Companies and the recently arrived 23d, 25th and 27th Marine Depot Companies, 5th Field Depot, Supply Service, FMFPac, certainly recognized racism when they saw it. Oddly, the company commander of the 23d, 1st Lt. Miles Romney, made no mention of the highly-charged racial atmosphere his men encountered on Guam.[3]

An estimate of the island's population, made soon after this time, shows 21,838 Guamanians of all ages and both sexes, 65,095 soldiers, 77,911 sailors, and 58,712 Marines.[4] If only a few of those servicemen were looking for female companionship, that was a lot of healthy young men competing for the favors of but a few local girls. Discord was inevitable. The conflict, triggered by jealousy over women, centered in the town of Agana where white Marines of the 3d Marine Division attempted to keep black sailors from the Naval Supply Depot out of the town.

The ugly situation turned deadly in December when a white sailor got into an argument over a Guamanian woman in Agana with a black Marine from the 25th Marine Depot Company. The sailor shot and killed the Marine. On the heels of this came still another incident. A black Marine from the 27th Marine Depot Company, on guard duty, shot and killed a white Marine who had been harassing him. Tried by courts-martial, both assailants were found guilty of manslaughter.

However, even before legal proceedings could be brought against the killers, rumor spread that a black sailor from the Naval Supply Depot was shot to death by a white Marine, so two truckloads of black sailors, labor troops from the island's Naval Supply Depot, confronted Marine MPs in Agana. The situation was defused, and the sailors returned to camp. Nevertheless, in what came to be called "the third battle of Guam," on Christmas Day the navy labor troops, once again out of the control of their officers and petty officers, commandeered trucks and roared out of their camp and back to Agana. This time a riot ensued. When the situation was finally brought under control, 43 black sailors had been relieved of a variety of stolen pistols, knives, and clubs and taken into custody, charged with rioting and theft of the trucks.[5] That night, someone from inside the Naval Supply Depot fired shots at Marine MPs patrolling near the camp, wounding one of the Marines. A sweep of the navy camp the following day uncovered a number of weapons stolen from the Supply Depot armory.[6]

The island garrison commander, Marine Major General Henry L. Larsen, he of the "you people" speech at Montford Point in 1943, convened a court of inquiry. Larsen appointed Colonel Samuel A. Woods Jr., the former commanding officer of the 51st Defense Battalion and Montford Point Camp, then serving on Guam, as president of the court. The convening of the court coincided with a visit by Walter White, Secretary of the National Association for the Advancement of Colored People (NAACP), then on a fact-finding tour of the Pacific theater. By request, White participated in the proceedings. The court of inquiry revealed "a pattern of pervasive racial harassment, unofficial, spontaneous, but nonetheless cruel," and based on recommendations from Col. Woods, the black sailors who rioted in Agana and several white Marines apprehended for harassing blacks were court-martialed and all convicted and sentenced under the "Rocks and Shoals."[7]

In an interesting aside, the incident revealed a significant contrast between the conduct of black Marines and that of their black sailor counterparts at the Naval

Supply Depot. Black Marines from the two ammunition companies testified as to the high state of morale in their units and about their experience on the island. The well-disciplined black Marines reported only scattered racial incidents, most of which were attributed to newly arrived white Marine replacements that came in after the fighting ended. The blacks testified that they "got along well with ... the fellows who hit the island, the ones who were here before being shipped home."[8]

First Lieutenant Romney and First Sergeant Fred Calhoun ensured the men of the 23d Marine Depot Company continued to enjoy an active recreation program, expanded now to include horseshoe pitching and even chess. Cpl. William L. Land, Jr., PFC Andrew W. Robinson, and Pvt. Robert E. McLee fought in the Island Boxing Tournament, and Cpl. Leon L. Smith organized a choir that entertained at company and camp functions, including the Depot Chapel for Sunday services. As free time increased, several of the men enrolled in correspondence courses from the Marine Corps Institute to improve their minds and help pass the time.[9]

A Jim Crow Welcome

As 1944 drew to a close, 20-year-old Orvia O. Cottman from Clairton, Pennsylvania, was drafted into the Corps. In December he traveled by train from Baltimore, Maryland, to Rocky Mount, North Carolina, and on to Jacksonville by bus. It was his first visit to the South, but "I wasn't surprised," he said. Going anywhere by bus in the Jim Crow South was not easy for a black man, and Cottman's experience, shared by Melvin Borden, serves as a reminder of what many blacks found when traveling from the North to Montford Point. "At the bus station you had to wait until all the white people got on first," Borden said. "There was a seat in the back for the black people and they [the whites] would say, 'Don't you touch me when you go back there.'"[10]

"You knew the history of the South and you knew about discrimination ... you were prepared for it," Cottman sums up his bus trip. When he got to the receiving huts at Montford Point Camp, he said, "I didn't know what the Marine Corps was about, I just took it as I found it."

The pace of training at Montford Point boot camp had not slowed, and Cottman found himself with about twenty-five other men crowded into one of the notorious little green huts. December can be very cold and damp at Montford Point, and no improvements or comforts had been added to the huts. "I don't think they were heated, and the row of heads was outside. Our day began around six in the morning. We ran before we had breakfast. The training day was composed of drills and classes ... to get you indoctrinated to become a Marine." The training was not especially difficult for the young man, and he was granted two weeks home leave after graduation. When he returned to Montford Point he was assigned to a replacement draft and sent to Hawaii where he remained until after the war.[11]

SECTION V
1945–1946

25

No End in Sight

How Did the Corps Stand?

The Corps stood poised to begin 1945, the last year of the war, with a strength of 421,605 Marines, 15,609 of whom were black.[1] Six Marine Divisions had been activated; the 1st, 2d, and 6th made up the III Amphibious Corps (IIIAC), FMF-Pac, while the 3d, 4th, and 5th came under V Amphibious Corps (VAC), FMF-Pac.[2] Other FMF units accounted for almost 75,000 additional Marines in the Pacific. The structure for supply support continued to evolve. Two provisional field service commands, one at Guam and the other at Guadalcanal, supported two amphibious corps in the Pacific. In addition, there were seven field depots and four service and supply battalions located close to the Marine divisions. The Marine Depot and Ammunition Companies were scattered across those supply units as operations demanded.

Other units were available to support the amphibious corps, such as antiaircraft battalions, amphibian tractor battalions, 155mm howitzer battalions, and others. A few of the antiaircraft battalions, including the 51st and 52d Defense Battalions, continued to carry out island defense duties.[3] Operational plans under way for early 1945 would see some Depot and Ammunition Company Marines actively engaged in combat. The two black defense battalions would train hard, but the only combat they were destined to see would consist of hunting down Japanese holdouts.

Jim Crow Is Alive and Well

Glenn J. White, a tall, lean eighteen-year-old, got his draft notice in the early days of July 1945. Born in South Carolina, White had left the worst Jim Crow treatment behind when he moved to Baltimore, Maryland. At the induction center, he was given a choice of service branches. If he chose the army he would leave for a training center in one week; if he wanted to go into the navy he would have to wait two weeks. "If I had 21 days I would go to the Marine Corps. I didn't know nothing about the Marines." He chose the Corps.[4]

Train and bus tickets to Montford Point meant a return to the South. White joined many of his fellow black Marines in the common experience of changing to a Jim Crow car before crossing the Mason-Dixon Line. He left the train at Rocky Mount to find a seat at the back of a bus bound for Jacksonville. From the bus station in Jacksonville, White made his way to the main gate at Montford Point Camp. The gate guard greeted him with a genial, "How you doin,' son? Have you come to see your father or to shine shoes?" White replied, "No, sir. I came to be in the service." He was directed to Hut One for the receiving process, "And they suited me out." White was assigned to a platoon in one of the newer barracks with open squad bays instead of the little green huts. The platoon went through the routine of medial exams, tests, filling out insurance and allotment forms and uniform and equipment issue. White says of the food, "It was okay. Not my mama's cooking, but it was okay. You could live with it." White's DIs pushed the young men hard, starting at about 0430 (in August, coastal North Carolina can be hot, which would account for an earlier start in the training day). "The hardest part for me was the cussing all day long," White said. It took some getting used to, but he adjusted; "The quicker you caught on, the quicker you got along."[5]

Even though the war ended during White's training at Montford Point, nothing changed. When it came time to qualify with the M-1 rifle, White's platoon traveled by boat from the Montford Point Landing downriver to Stone Bay. "They said we might want to take off," if recruits rode in trucks off-base. "I can't tell you why they thought that and I don't agree with it." His platoon stayed in barracks at the range (segregated facilities had been completed), and White fired well, "Pretty good for a rookie."[6] Like thousands of other men he learned about "M-1 thumb," that is, when pushing an eight-round clip of cartridges into the rifle, a man must quickly raise that thumb out of the way of the spring operated bolt. Otherwise, the thumb gets smashed between the face of the bolt and the rifle's chamber. It is a painful rite of passage among riflemen. After graduation and boot leave, White returned to Montford Point Camp and was assigned 30-days mess duty, peeling potatoes while waiting for the 4th Colored Replacement Draft to form and be filled.

Operation DETACHMENT

On the final, direct approach to Japan, war planners had to decide which island to attack first: the island of Okinawa in the Ryukus, only 350 miles south of the Japanese Home Island of Kyushu, or Iwo Jima. While not so close to the homeland, Iwo Jima had real importance to the Japanese. One Japanese officer wrote, "Iwo Jima is the doorkeeper to the Imperial capital."[7]

In mid–1944, American plans called for up to twelve groups of massive long-range B-29 bombers, based in the recently captured Marianas, to carry the war of sustained aerial bombardment to the Japanese home islands. A base from which fighters could escort and protect the bombers, midway between the two locations, assumed major strategic importance. Such a base offered an added benefit: Bombers crippled in the skies over Japan and unable to make the long flight back to the Marianas might use the fighter base for emergency landings.

As a steppingstone to the home islands, the Americans decided on Iwo Jima, one of the islands in the Volcano Group about 670 miles south of Tokyo and about 700 miles north of the B-29 bomber bases on Guam in the Marianas. In the Volcano Group, Iwo Jima was the only island suitable for the construction of airfields capable of handling B-29's.[8] Iwo Jima (the name means Sulphur Island in Japanese), with an area of less than eight square miles, consisted of sulphur deposits, black volcanic ash and hard, sharp-edged igneous rock. By October, detailed studies for Operation DETACHMENT moved forward.

If the war had gone badly for the Japanese in 1944, then 1945 would prove to be disastrous, the empire's death knell, for the Americans were preparing to launch what historians would call "the classical amphibious assault of recorded history."[9] A detailed description and analysis of the Iwo Jima operation is beyond the scope of this work; however, readers who want to know more may wish to begin with a study of Bill D. Ross's excellent 1986 work, *Iwo Jima: Legacy of Valor.*

The V Amphibious Corps (VAC) scheme of maneuver for the operation was relatively simple. The 4th and 5th Marine Divisions were to land abreast on the eastern beaches (see map 11, Iwo Jima) with the 3d Marine Division in reserve. In the area of supply support, the VAC G-4 prescribed levels for Class I supply of two days' rations for the assault troops plus a 30-day backup supply and water at two gallons per man per day for five days. Class II and IV supplies were to be stockpiled for 30 days. Ammunition (Class V) for ground forces was to be provided in quantities of seven units of fire for artillery, mortars, and antiaircraft guns, and five units of fire for all other types of weapons. For an operation calling for three reinforced Marine divisions, the numbers were staggering: 174 ships, 86,516 men, 280,447 measurement tons of supplies and equipment.[10]

Thirty-eight LSTs were preloaded with balanced amounts of fuel, ammunition, and rations, and these were to be available on D-Day and D+1. There were no reefs at Iwo Jima, which meant that LSTs would be able to nose directly into the beaches when called, unload, and retract to allow other ships to do the same. When beached, the Large Slow Target appellative became Large Stationary Target.

Additionally, 42 DUKWs were preloaded with ammunition and medical supplies for use on D-Day. VAC organized the 8th Field Depot for the Iwo Jima operation.[11] The depot was task organized to serve as the nucleus of the shore party, and included the 8th Marine Ammunition Company, the 33d, 34th and 36th Marine Depot Companies. The 8th Field Depot commander was given the dual designation ("dual-hatted") as Shore Party Commander of the Landing Force.

The 8th Marine Ammunition Company and the 36th Marine Depot Com-

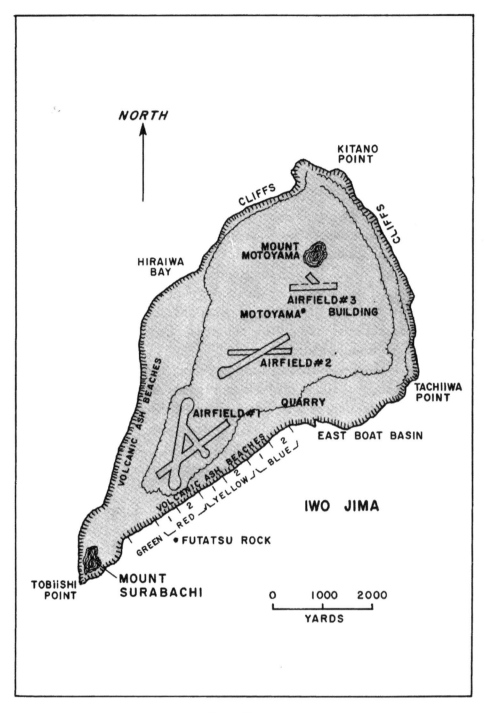

Iwo Jima.

Source: Dyer, *The Amphibians*, Vol. II, 990.

pany would land on Dog-Day, while the 33d and 34th Marine Depot Companies would initially work as part of ships' platoons in the LST area until called ashore on February 25, D+5.[12]

Seen from the air, Iwo Jima is shaped like a pork chop. Mt. Suribachi, a 550-foot high extinct volcano, dominates the southwestern tip of the island. The narrowest as well as the lowest part of the island, an isthmus less than 1,000 yards across, lies at the foot of Suribachi. From there the terrain soon rises to a height of about 300 feet, while further in the northeast along the Motoyama Plateau the elevation nears 380 feet. From the high ground, Japanese gunners had excellent observation of the 3,500-yard-wide landing beaches on the southeast shore.[13]

Dog-Day at Iwo Jima

On February 19, 1945, morning twilight began at 0549, with sunrise at 0707. The weather was clear, with a ten-knot trade wind blowing, pushing southeasterly swells into the beaches. How-Hour was set for 0900. The transport area was about 15,000 yards off the beaches, and the line of departure was 4,000 yards off the designated beaches. The LST area was between the two, about 8,000 yards off the beaches. When the first wave of LVT (A)s crossed the line of departure, the run in was expected to take about 30 minutes at the amtracs' normal speed of four knots. The plan called for 9,000 men to be ashore in the first 45 minutes after H-Hour.[14]

When the assault began, good news came early with the report that, "No anti-boat gunfire was reported by the initial waves."[15] However, the first men ashore discovered that there was neither hard-packed sand nor a mere four-foot high beach terrace. The beaches, and even the entire isthmus, consisted of coarse black volcanic ash. The terrace rose in places at an angle of 45 degrees to a height of fifteen feet. A walking man sank into the ash above the tops of his shoes, and tracked vehicles moved up the slopes only with great difficulty, if at all. Wheeled vehicles bogged down. The first waves dumped men and supplies between the waterline and the first terrace.[16] Uncomfortable to the men and damaging to equipment as the ash was, it at least absorbed much of the concussion and shrapnel of Japanese artillery and mortar fire. Shore party men would greatly benefit from that characteristic of the beaches and terraces. Follow on waves piled onto the beaches at five-minute intervals, adding to the jumble of men and equipment.

Following the waves of amtracs came the landing craft, LCVPs and LCMs carrying more men, more vehicles, and more supplies, grounding squarely onto the beaches. However, the steep beach gradient coupled with the onshore swells and an inshore current running parallel to the beach, unimpeded by offshore reefs, created a fierce plunging surf that broached, then swamped many of the flat-bottomed craft before they could be completely unloaded. Each succeeding wave picked up and bodily threw sinking landing craft onto the beach. Wreckage accumulated, piling higher, creating further obstacles and damaging more craft.[17]

"Two Coast Guard-manned LST's open their great jaws in the surf that washes on Leyte Island beach, as soldiers strip down and build sandbag piers out to the ramps to speed up unloading operations." This is an excellent illustration of how the Beach Party and Shore Party (including blacks of the Depot and Ammunition Companies) unloaded supplies. 1944. Still Picture Branch (NNSP), National Archives, Washington, DC.

Wheeled vehicles off-loaded from the landing craft bogged down hub deep in the sand, adding to the clutter of swamped craft on the beaches. Japanese fire was light until after about H+30, when heavy mortar fire struck the beaches and grew in intensity to include heavy small arms fire and artillery fire.

Black Marines Ashore on Dog-Day

Arriving soon after the assault waves, Cpl. Gene Doughty led his 1st Squad of the 36th Marine Depot Company's 1st platoon ashore. Here was the place he would celebrate his 21st birthday. Lying in the black sand, Doughty looked around taking a quick head count. The men of his squad were "all flat as rugs with the salt air above them singing with shell splinters," Doughty said. Pvt. Vardell Donald-

"Carrying a Jap[anese] prisoner from stockade to be evacuated and treated for malnutrition. Iwo Jima." In the middle distance LST's are beached for unloading while others lie just off shore. The black Marines are armed with M1 carbines. February 23, 1945. Don Fox. Still Picture Branch (NNSP), National Archives, Washington DC.

son had a narrow escape — a bullet drilled a hole through his helmet. Some of the squad lay half in the surf until the Japanese fire shifted enough to allow them to move further up onto the beach. Looking around, Doughty saw "enormous swells" pick up landing craft and crash them ashore scattering ammunition, water tanks, rations all along the shore. Mortar and artillery shells exploded all around them, filling the air with fragments. Water spouts leapt high in the air when shells struck offshore.[18]

Sgt. Thomas Haywood McPhatter, a section chief in the 1st platoon, 8th Marine Ammunition Company, came in on one of the LSTs that nosed up onto the beach on Dog-Day.

The ship "forced a keel-grip on the sand, but swung to the drumming of the heavy surf. Ammo Marines were soon into her gaping bow to wrestle out the munitions. Japanese big-gun rounds and machine-gun splatters took umbrage."[19] By the evening of Dog-Day, 30,000 Marines were ashore. Japanese defenders had killed 566 and wounded 1,755 Marines.

Weather Deteriorates

On Dog + 1 the winds grew stronger in the morning, gusting to 20 knots from the west. Around noon, they shifted to become easterly again bringing rain, steep

seas, and heavy surf, halting LCVP and LCM traffic. The surf churned and added to the wreckage along the beaches. By Dog + 3 the weather was even worse. "The surf had a lateral action" that pushed even loaded LCTs and LCMs seventy-five yards laterally along the beach in ten minutes," this despite bow lines anchored on the beach and with engines full ahead.[20] Under heavy Japanese fire, struggling through deep sand, cold wind and rain amid the dangerously pounding, wreckage-cluttered surf, Shore Party Marines moved supplies and equipment off the beaches to dumps a short distance inland, and then forward again. Cpl. Gilman Brooks, 8th Marine Ammunition Company, fell wounded on the beach.[21]

On February 23, D+4, PFC Sylvester J. Cobb, another 8th Marine Ammunition Company man, was wounded, the same day the American flag was raised on Suribachi.[22] The following day the 8th Field Depot took over responsibility for moving VAC's supplies ashore. The 33d and 34th Marine Depot Companies completed their ships' platoon duties and splashed ashore into the unmitigated hell that raged on Iwo. The beaches were still under fire, causing temporary work stoppages, but the Japanese were never able to completely stop the unloading. On February 25, two men of the 34th were killed: Cpl. Hubert E. Daverny died of wounds received on the shell-raked beach and PFC James M. Wilkins was killed in action.[23]

Incoming!

Japanese artillery and mortar fire blew up several ammunition dumps, one of which the 8th Marine Ammunition Company was building the morning of March 2. "Like a lightning stroke, a mortar round or two dropped into the ammunition dump," Sgt. McPhatter recalled. "We were in foxholes right beside the dump." After the rounds struck, the stored ammunition began exploding, and, "We raced away and down to the beach for safety and to assemble what we could," he explained. "It was a disaster. So much ammo was destroyed. We needed instant supply from Guam and Saipan."[24]

A call made its way to the 7th Field Depot on Saipan, and on March 4, "the planes were ... overhead and [the] munitions [floated down] under brightly colored parachutes [that] the Japanese could see very well. The Japanese potshot at the

Opposite Top: "Two Negro duck [DUKW] drivers turn riflemen after their vehicle is destroyed." Photo taken on D-Day at Iwo Jima, February 19, 1945. Christian. Still Picture Branch (NNSP), National Archives, Washington DC. *Bottom:* "Smashed by Jap mortar and shellfire, trapped by Iwo's treacherous black-ash sands, amtracs and other vehicles of war lay knocked out on the black sands of the volcanic fortress." In the foreground clockwise from the right are two crawler cranes for unloading cargo from landing craft, an LVT (A) with short-barreled 75mm howitzer, the stern of a wrecked LCI, and three LVT's. Across the beach clutter and foxholes dug into the black sand, LST's crowd the beach for unloading in the middle distance, while Mt. Suribachi looms in the distance. PhoM3c. Robert M. Warren, ca February/March 1945. Still Picture Branch (NNSP), National Archives, Washington, DC.

Marines running helter-skelter anywhere the wind blew the chutes." McPhatter continued with something of an understatement. "Things got really intense." He took shelter in a ruined bunker, where he found a dead Marine "who, no doubt, died only moments before as he held the photographs of his family to his bloodied chest. With my helmet I scooped a shelter for my head and promised the Almighty that if he spared me at this moment, I'd dedicate the rest of my life to Him." He kept his word, graduating after the war from Johnson C. Smith University to become a minister. He joined the Navy Chaplain Corps, served in Vietnam, and retired as a captain. He went on the get his doctorate, eventually taking a second retirement as a Presbyterian minister.[25]

Pvt. Roland B. Durden of the 34th Marine Depot Company was attached to the Graves Registration Section, grim duty. "We were day on, day on, day on burying them in long, bulldozed trenches, first wrapped in ponchos, then sheets, and finally nothing at all," Durden said, "and those were the casualties of only the first days."[26] The 34th continued to take casualties, with Sgt. William L. Bowman, PFC Raymond Glenn, and Pvt. James Hawthorne, Sr., hit on February 25, as was PFC William T. Bowen, newly assigned to the 34th from the 24th Replacement Draft.[27]

On March 1 the 8th Marine Ammunition Company saw PFC Melvin L. Thomas killed in action while Pvt. William L. Jackson was wounded and evacuated.[28] The fighting shifted to the northern end of the island, and it seemed as if the black Marines of the 8th Field Depot were finally out from under Japanese guns. The island was declared secured on March 16, and withdrawal of some Marine forces began. Elements of the 8th Field Depot, including the 8th Marine Ammunition Company and the 36th Marine Depot Company, now garrison troops, moved north into a camp near the northern airfield.

Final Attack at Iwo

In the predawn darkness of March 26, a force numbering between 200 and 300 Japanese silently approached the Marines and soldiers camped near the airfield. When ready, they launched a well-organized attack beginning about 0515. "We were security forces for the sleeping airmen, and we were more relaxed now that the island had been secured ... but our perimeters were as tight as ever," explained Gene Doughty. Sgt. McPhatter recalled that one of his Marines, PFC Burnett, first became aware of the Japanese and "began firing to alert everybody."

"Oh, it was well planned," Doughty continued, the Japanese "came at us from three directions. They wanted maximum confusion and destruction, but because we were in foxholes, combat situated and ready, we were fast to respond. I recall James Whitlock and James Davis [36th Marine Depot Company] rapidly cranking off rounds, flashes on flashes in the dark. They [the Japanese] were bloody with their bayonets and swords. With a little later backlighting, our people could see faint wispy sword-swinging, grenade-sowing figures as they charged us."[29] Many of the attackers carried American weapons, but a large part of the Japanese force carried swords, a good indication that they were officers and senior NCOs. After three hours of intense and confused fighting, over 250 Japanese died and 18 were captured. Marines gathered up 40 samurai swords from the dead.[30]

PFC Davis and Pvt. Whitlock were each awarded the Bronze Star medal for their part in the fighting. Earning Purple Hearts were PFC Charles Davis, Pvt. Miles Worth and Pvt. Vardell Donaldson of the 36th Marine Depot Company. Donaldson later died of his wounds. Purple Hearts also went to the 8th Marine Ammunition Company's PFC Melvin L. Thomas who was killed that morning, and to Corporals Richard M. Bowen and Warren J. McDaugherty who were wounded.[31]

Recognition

The performance of the black Marines on Iwo Jima earned high praise from the commander of the 8th Field Depot, Col. Leland S. Swindler:

The Corps Shore Party Commander is highly gratified with the performance of these colored troops, whose normal function is that of labor troops, while in direct action against the enemy for the first time. Proper security prevented their being taken unawares, and they conducted themselves with marked coolness and courage. Careful investigation shows they displayed modesty in reporting their own part in the action.[32]

All the black Marines of the 8th Field Depot earned the right to wear the ribbon of the Navy Unit Commendation:

The Secretary of the Navy takes pleasure in commending the

SUPPORT UNITS OF THE FIFTH AMPHIBIOUS CORPS
UNITED STATES FLEET MARINE FORCE

for service as follows:

For outstanding heroism in support of Military Operations during the seizure of enemy Japanese-held Iwo Jima, Volcano Islands, February 19 to 28, 1945. Landing against resistance which rapidly increased in fury as the Japanese pounded the beaches with artillery, rocket and mortar fire, the Support Units of the FIFTH Amphibious Corps surmounted the obstacles of chaotic disorganization, loss of equipment, supplies and key personnel to develop and maintain a continuous link between thousands of assault troops and supply ships. Resourceful and daring whether fighting in the front line of combat, or serving in rear areas or on the wreck-obstructed beaches, they were responsible for the administration of operations and personnel; they rendered effective fire support where Japanese pressure was greatest; they constructed roads and facilities and maintained communications under the most difficult and discouraging conditions of weather and rugged terrain; they salvaged vital supplies from craft lying crippled in the surf or broached on the beaches; and they ministered to the wounded under fire and provided prompt evacuation to hospital ships. By their individual initiative and heroism and their ingenious teamwork, they provided the unfailing support vital to the conquest of Iwo Jima, a powerful defense of the Japanese Empire.

All personnel attached to and serving with the following Support Units of FIFTH Amphibious Corps, United States Fleet Marine Force, during the Iwo Jima Operation from February 19 to 28, 1945, are authorized to wear the NAVY UNIT COMMENDATION Ribbon.

Included in the list of units are the 8th Field Depot (plus Headquarters Shore Party); 33d Marine Depot Company; 34th Marine Depot Company; 36th Marine Depot Company; 8th Marine Ammunition Company.

/s/
John L. Sullivan
Secretary of the Navy[33]

The men distinguished themselves in their first test under fire on the beaches and once again a few weeks later in close combat with the Japanese, up close, at hand grenade range. They stood among the more than 10,000 men working as laborers moving supplies, equipment, and ammunition at Iwo Jima, men drawn mainly from battle replacement drafts, division bands, naval construction personnel, and army port troops. As has been said before, "the success of any sustained assault depended in great part on these men."[34] Fleet Admiral Chester Nimitz spoke eloquently of the Marines, all Marines, at Iwo Jima when he said, "Uncommon valor was a common virtue."[35]

The black Marines had no time to rest on their laurels. There was more to prove, and the prospect of more fighting loomed. The men returned to Hawaii, resuming their training at Hilo; their next objective: the invasion of Japan itself.

26

Hounded by the Press

Black Officer Candidates

The black press continued to write about the absence of black officers in the Corps, with a January 27, 1945, article in a Houston, Texas, newspaper trumpeting "Navy Now Has 34 Officers; Marines None."[1] Four black enlisted Marines, V-12 students — Branch, Brewer, Davis and Johnson — were in the pipeline for commissioning, but received little attention. Nevertheless, in March 1945, three highly qualified black enlisted Marines were selected to attend the 9th Platoon Commanders Class at Marine Corps Schools, Quantico, Virginia. Two years earlier the acting commandant in a letter to all major Marine Corps commands had acknowledged the power of the "Negro Press." He wrote, "Every possible step should be taken to prevent the publication of inflammatory articles by the Negro press."[2]

Sergeant Major Charles F. Anderson of Birmingham, Alabama, was a graduate of Morehouse College of Atlanta University and sergeant major of the Montford Point Camp. First Sergeant George F. Ellis, Jr., of Brooklyn, New York, was a graduate of Virginia Union University, Richmond, Virginia, and a Marine who had served overseas with the 26th Marine Depot Company. The last of the three, First Sergeant Charles W. Simmons of Centralia, Illinois, had a Master of Science degree in Secondary Education from Alcorn A&M College, Mississippi, and was the former sergeant major of the 51st Defense Battalion.

The three reported to Quantico in April 1945, and OWI clippings from the black press at the time show many articles were written about the men, most accompanied by photographs. It was a proud moment. HQMC had deflected the black public's ire aroused by some of the "inflammatory articles." However, all three black candidates were among the 13 percent of the class that failed to earn a commission; one was given a medical discharge and the other two failed to maintain the required scholastic grades.[3]

"There were a number of questions asked and quite a bit of consternation," when the three men failed to complete the course, said Sergeant Major Gilbert Johnson at Montford Point Camp. There was reason for the questions, because each was successful in the Corps and would do well later in civilian life. Anderson became a lawyer, Ellis a physician, and Simmons a college professor and author. Three black officer candidates who came after them also failed to complete the course.[4] Sergeant Major Johnson was ordered to the Pacific where he would join the 52d Defense Battalion to become the new battalion sergeant major.

Branch Stirs Things Up

Recalling his experiences as a V-12 student at Purdue, Herbert Brewer speaks of the early days of his lifelong friendship with Fred Branch, who had come back with Brewer from the 51st Defense Battalion in the Ellice Islands. Branch, he says, "left a couple of semesters earlier than we did, and we were told that because he had been to college before he came to Purdue he didn't need to stay two years. That was our understanding of what happened." According to Brewer, Branch's comments made in later years suggested that, "maybe they might have been glad to get rid of him there because [he laughs] of some of his [Branch's] actions in the community in trying to speed up the removal of segregation. In one instance, he was asked to sit upstairs in a movie and he said that he wasn't going to sit there. As I understand it from the [newspaper] article about him, the theatre manager called our commander at Purdue and said, 'Will you get him back on base?' The captain said, 'Branch, come on back. I'm ordering you to come back.' Anyway, soon after that he left and went to basic school, and we were told that because he had already had a year of college when he came there, he didn't have to stay the two years. He left and was enrolled in a basic class."[5]

The 52d Shifts Again

All across the Pacific, as the war advanced, units were constantly in motion, moving forward from the rear areas to be near the front, and the black defense battalions were no exception. In January, Lt. Col. David W. Silvey had taken over as the new commanding officer of the battalion. Then, while the fighting raged on Iwo Jima, movement orders came to the 52d once again, this time to move by echelons to Guam.

Detachment A embarked aboard the USS *DeGrasse* (AP-164) on March 9 and sailed for Guam, arriving on March 23. The detachment set up camp on the eastern side of the island and began actively patrolling for Japanese holdouts. A month later, the rest of the battalion boarded the SS *George W. Julian* at Roi-Namur for the six-day voyage to Guam, arriving on May 4, 1945.[6]

Several of the patrols the 52d sent out during April encountered Japanese soldiers, killing three and wounding four. PFC Ernest J. Calland of the 52d was wounded in one of the firefights. Detachment A was disbanded, and Lt. Col. T. C. Moore, Jr., became the battalion commander.[7] The intense training regimen continued; however, as John Griffin recalls, there were opportunities for sightseeing. "The Red Cross Recreation Center had eight Negro women as hostesses (these were the only Negro females in the Pacific)." Griffin also visited "the Northeast Airfield where I used to get a plane ride each and every Sunday when I wasn't on guard duty." Griffin went on to compare Guam to a city in the southern United States because of the discrimination he found there.[8] It seems the racial climate on Guam had improved little, if any, since the troubles of the previous December.

27

Okinawa — Operation ICEBERG

Japan's Doorstep

The Ryukyu Archipelago, in Japanese the Nansei Shoto, is a chain of islands extending about 800 miles southwest of the Japanese Home Island of Kyushu (the Japanese Home Islands are the principal islands of Hokkaido, Honshu, Shikoku, and Kyushu, and the hundreds of smaller adjacent islands). In the middle of the Archipelago is Okinawa, the largest of the Ryukyu Islands. Over sixty miles long, its width varies from eighteen miles to two miles at the Ishikawa Isthmus.

The Ishikawa Isthmus divides the ruggedly hilly and heavily wooded northern part of the island with its 1,650 high central spine skirted by steep ravines dropping down to the sea, from the southern one-third. Below Ishikawa, the terrain ranges from generally rolling and lightly wooded, extensively cultivated, to extremely hilly with steep limestone scarps trending east to west, with ravines cutting away from the heights in the southern area. In 1945, three quarters of the island's population lived south of Ishikawa.[1]

Strategic Objectives

Location was the key: Okinawa lies only 350 miles from Kyushu. Once captured, the island would provide numerous sites for airfields from which American warplanes could easily reach major industrial areas in southern Japan. Deep bays offered some of the best fleet anchorages for advanced naval bases in the western Pacific. Finally, the island would provide an excellent staging area for men and materiel in the coming assault into the heart of the Japanese Empire.

Scheme of Maneuver

ICEBERG was to be an operation unprecedented in scope in the Pacific war. Organized as the Tenth Army, the landing force consisted of the 6th and 1st Marine

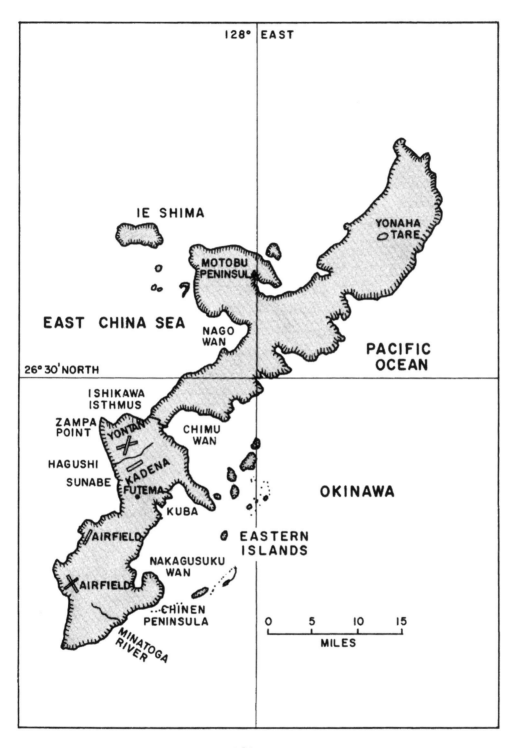

Okinawa.

Source: Dyer, *The Amphibians*, Vol II, 1076.

Divisions of the IIIAC (the 2d Marine Division was in reserve) alongside the army's XXIV Corps (landing four divisions and holding one in reserve). These units would force their way ashore on the southwestern coast of the island below Zampa Point. At the same time on the east coast, the 2d Marine Division would engage in a turn-away landing (a demonstration, or feint) to distract Japanese defenders. The boundary separating the areas of responsibility of the two corps divided the island from a point just north of the town of Hagushi on the southwestern coast (see map 12, Okinawa). Kadena airfield lay in the XXIV Corps's area, while Yontan airfield was inland from the IIIAC beaches.[2] The immensity of Iceberg and the amounts of supplies and equipment involved is revealed by the numbers of men and things the Americans brought: 458 ships, 193,852 men, and almost 825,000 measurement tons of supplies and equipment.[3] Love-Day was set for April 1, 1945 — Easter Sunday — with H-Hour at 0830. On Love-Day (L-Day), skies were mostly clear, winds light and easterly, and the temperature was a pleasant 75 degrees Fahrenheit.

High Water Mark for Black Marines

More than 2,000 Montford Point Marines from three ammunition companies and eight depot companies as well as stewards and cooks attached to ground combat unit headquarters would serve on Okinawa during Operation ICEBERG.[4] The 7th Field Depot on Saipan became part of IIIAC and brought three ammunition companies and four depot companies that were present on L-Day.

The 1st and 3d Marine Ammunition Companies and the 5th, 38th, and elements of the 37th Marine Depot Companies took part in the 2d Marine Division's turn-away landings on the east coast of Okinawa, which were repeated on L+1. The 12th Ammunition Company and the 18th Marine Depot Company with the remainder of the 37th landed with the 1st and 6th Marine Divisions on April 1, 1945. Japanese resistance to the landings was light, and there were only light casualties.

Supply Pile-up at the Waterline

While Japanese resistance was no problem on L-Day, Okinawa's skirt of coral reefs slowed the flow of supplies from the ships to the shore. As in earlier operations, troops and supplies had to be "cross decked" seaward of the reef from landing craft to DUKWs or LVTs, which could then negotiate the reef and cross inshore lagoons to the beaches. The men moved from LCVPs and LCMs quickly, but the shift of cargo did not.

The navy beachmaster started work on a causeway from the beach to the reef, but the 1st Marine Division capitalized on a lesson learned at Peleliu. The men mounted swinging cranes onto powered causeway sections, like the pontoon barges used the previous September, which were anchored at the reef edge. Landing craft loaded with supplies pulled alongside the crane. Crane operators lifted cargo nets loaded with supplies and swung them into the open bay of a DUKW or an LVT idling on the reef alongside the crane; then the supplies were shuttled to the beaches. The rapid push of supplies led to congestion on the beaches. The shore parties, organized to manage the huge volume of materiel, had many inexperienced men drawn from replacement drafts, which further slowed the flow of supplies. The problems, though expected, were nothing that could not be overcome. However, the rapid advance of the infantry units across the rugged terrain became a supply concern because of a lack of roads for trucks loaded with supplies.[5] Within three days, all of the 7th Field Depot's black Marine units were ashore.[6]

A War of Attrition

The lessons learned in the earlier battles with the Americans, beginning with Tarawa and including the recently concluded battle at Iwo Jima, were not lost on the Japanese defending Okinawa. It is an established precept of war that an amphibious assault is one of the most difficult to carry out and one of the easiest to prevent. Instead of attempting to defeat the Americans at the beaches, the Japanese commander at Okinawa took the exact opposite position. He chose to concede the landings and wage a war of attrition aided significantly by the newly organized suicide or kamikaze units. The Japanese expected to crash their aircraft into American ships, forcing them to withdraw and leave the landing force without naval gunfire support or supply support. Then, the Japanese could crush the stranded Americans in the rugged terrain at the southern end of the island. It was a fact that the kamikaze tactics caused unprecedented naval casualties during the battle, but they never achieved the hoped for level of success.[7]

In the first few days ashore, the Americans made rapid gains. However, by L+4 the Japanese, especially in the south, began to bleed the Americans and would continue to do so for the almost three months to come.

A Different Kind of War

During April, IIIAC Marines fighting their way across the northern two-thirds of the island encountered a kind of fighting much different from that faced by their army counterparts of the XXIV Corps south of the corps boundary. In past island assaults, Marines moving quickly in the attack by-passed isolated pockets of Japanese, leaving them to be attacked and killed by following units of the reserve force. The men were familiar with hunting down Japanese holdouts hiding in the jungles. Here, however, they encountered organized Japanese soldiers fighting as guerillas and saboteurs. These Japanese posed a real threat to rear area units and supply convoys.[8]

Early Casualties among Black Marines

Twenty-one casualties among the black Marines were incurred steadily in April and May, with nine men hit during each month. Two more were hit in June, but there is no day or month given for the wound received by the 37th Marine Depot Company's PFC Edgar Mitchell, only the year, 1945.

From what is known, the first black Marine casualty on Okinawa came on April 5, L+4, when Steward's Assistant 1st Class Joe N. Bryant, assigned to Headquarters, 29th Marines, 6th Marine Division, was wounded. The following day PFC Willie Hampton, 5th Marine Depot Company, was wounded. The 1st Marine Ammunition Company's PFC Thomas Early was wounded on April 10. On April 12, Steward's Assistant 1st Class Ralph Woodkins of Headquarters, 1st Marine Division was hit in the face by a shell fragment. April 15 saw three black Marines hit: PFC Joshua Nickens, 1st Marine Ammunition Company, was wounded; 3d Ammo's Clifford Bryant was hit; and Pvt. Therrance J. Mercier of the 5th Marine Depot Company was the third man hit.[9]

In order to manage the flow of supplies consumed by units of the IIIAC in the intense fighting, more men were needed. On April 26 at Guadalcanal the 9th and 10th Marine Depot Companies, now a part of the 4th Service and Supply Battalion, Supply Service, FMFPac, were called forward. The men filed aboard the USS *Alkaid* (AK-114) for the slow journey northwest.[10]

Back on Okinawa, the end of April saw the arrival of the 20th Marine Depot Company from Saipan. No other black Marines were hit until April 27, when PFC Alvin A. Fitzpatrick of the 38th Marine Depot Company was hit, and the last black casualty of April came the following day when the 5th Depot's Pvt. Eldridge O. Oliver took a wound.[11]

Marines Go South

On the last day of April the 1st Marine Division was attached to the army's XXIV Corps, which had been badly mauled by Japanese resistance in the south. Shortly thereafter, the 6th Marine Division followed the 1st Marine Division in turning south.[12]

Casualties abated among the black Marines during the transition, until on May 9, when shell fragments wounded Cpl. Willie Crenshaw and killed Steward's Assistant 2d Class Warren N. McGrew, Jr., at the 1st Marine Division headquarters. McGrew was the first black Marine killed in action on Okinawa.[13]

On May 11, Pvt. Arthur Bowman, Jr., of the 12th Ammo was hit, and then on May 13 the 6th Marine Division's Cook 3d Class Horace D. Holder and Steward's Assistant 3d Class Norman "B" Davis were struck by shell fragments. A week later Pvt. Charles L. Burton of the 3d Ammo was hit by Japanese fire.[14]

Gene Smith's Arrival

Sailing slowly to battle came the *Alkaid* with the 9th and 10th Marine Depot Companies embarked. Their first waypoint was Eniwetok in the Marshall Islands, where the ship arrived on May 1 and lay at anchor until getting under way again on May 9. *Alkaid* arrived at the fleet anchorage at Ulithi on May 14 and then joined a convoy that departed on May 15 bound for Okinawa.[15] *Alkaid* finally arrived on May 21, anchored in the transport area off Hagushi beach, and the two companies went ashore on the following day. "Our camp was between the beach and the airfield," Smith said. Their arrival six days before a full moon coincided with a time of increased Japanese air attacks on the airfield during the increasingly bright moonlit nights, and with a veteran's cool understatement Smith recalls, "May 22, 1945. Experienced our first bombing raid by the Nips."[16] Fortunately, the depot company Marines escaped unharmed. May 22 also marked the beginning of a nine-day period of rain, at times intermittent but with deluges that turned roads into mud bogs, flooded artillery gun pits to the wheel tops of the pieces, and further slowed the movement of supplies.[17]

Turner Blount arrived with the 19th Marine Depot Company at about the same time as the 9th and 10th Marine Depot Companies from Guadalcanal. "We dug in near the airfield there, Kadena airfield," Blount said. "You had to watch out for Japanese infiltrators moving through the lines, you know. A lot of people were scared of them coming in at night, out of caves. There was no real safe place."[18]

Soon after Eugene Smith arrived and moved into his camp between Kadena airfield and Hagushi Beach, the Japanese launched a suicide attack on nearby Yontan airfield. Around 2230 on May 24, several Japanese Mitsubishi bombers — between five and seven; the exact number has never been determined — loaded with soldiers attempted to land in the darkness on Yontan airfield. Most of the bombers (the Mitsubishis were code named "Betty") were shot down and crashed in flames killing all aboard. However, one Betty managed a wheels-up crash landing on a Yontan runway. Japanese soldiers, firing small arms, ran from the plane throwing grenades and explosive charges at nearby American planes. Airfield defense personnel, pilots and ground crews returned fire in a wildly confused shootout. Morning light revealed 69 Japanese bodies. Two Marines were dead and 18 wounded. Eight planes were destroyed, 24 damaged, and 70,000 gallons of aviation fuel burned when the Japanese set fire to a fuel dump.

The Golden Gate in '48

Amid the brutal yard-by-yard fighting on Okinawa, during the deadly and effective kamikaze attacks against the ships supporting the operation, no one dared talk of an end to the war any time soon. Rather, a common saying among the men was, "The Golden Gate in '48," an expectation that there were years of hard fighting to come before the Japanese were defeated and the men could go home. It was not that the men were pessimistic, but based on their first hand experiences with

Japanese soldiers, the saying voiced a realistic assessment of what lay ahead. The fact that Germany surrendered on May 8, and the war in Europe was over, meant little to the troops in the Pacific.

Half a world away, the Joint Chiefs of Staff (JCS) in Washington DC understood that much bloody fighting remained before Japan capitulated. On May 25, the JCS issued the order setting in motion Operation OLYMPIC, the amphibious assault on Japan. The target date for invasion was November 1, 1945.[19]

Bryant's Second Purple Heart

There was no let up in the intensity of the fighting on Okinawa. At Headquarters, 29th Marines, during this period Steward's Assistant 1st Class Joe N. Bryant was hit by shell fragments on May 26th, earning the unenviable distinction of becoming the first black Marine on Okinawa to receive his second Purple Heart. Hit by shell fragments at the same instant as Bryant were Steward's Assistant 3d Class Jerome Caffey and Pvt. Morris E. Clark, the last black casualties to occur in May. As the battle for Okinawa ground on to its inevitable conclusion, PFC Richard E. Hines of the 10th Marine Depot Company, recently arrived from Guadalcanal, had his thigh torn open by bomb fragments during a Japanese air raid on June 9.[20] Also wounded in June was PFC Clarence H. Jackson, 3d Ammo, but no day is given for his injury.

In the fighting south of the city of Naha, a reporter for the Associated Negro Press (ANP) found the veteran 3d Marine Ammunition Company camped some 500 yards behind the front lines. The men were under "a roaring inferno" of Japanese artillery and mortar fire, but they continued to move tons of ammunition forward to the Marines in the lines. Some of the men from the 3d Ammo were detailed to guard a bridge on the supply route against a possible Japanese attack. However, the reporter wrote, the attack "never came off." We are left to wonder whether the bridge guards were as disappointed as the reporter.[21]

The 52d's Near Miss

Okinawa was declared secure on June 22, 1945.[22] The 52d Defense Battalion was called to move forward to Okinawa, preparations were made and the men packed their gear. On July 9 they began loading aboard LSTs. Then, the night before they were to sail, the word came down canceling the move. The 52d was to remain on Guam where it would relieve the 9th Antiaircraft Artillery Battalion. They would not take part in the fighting. It was a crushing blow to the men.

"This ... is when our morale dropped 99%," John Griffin said. "For the next week or ten days the men stayed around their tents writing letters and whatnot, mad at the world and everyone in it. Instead of being a Defense Unit, we turned out to be nothing more than a working battalion." There followed several months of daily working parties at the docks unloading ammunition or at the 5th Field Depot stacking lumber, and standing guard. Worse, chow was terrible. "Breakfast: dehydrated eggs, bread and coffee. Dinner: lamb stew, dehydrated potatoes and onions, warm water. Supper: beans, C or K rations, bread and water." By August, there was no need for most of the working parties, so the men kept busy taking the guns apart and cleaning them.[23]

Okinawa's Cost

Total American battle casualties exceeded 49,000, of which about 12,500 were killed or missing. Thirty-six American ships went to the bottom, 368 were damaged, and 768 airplanes were lost. Japanese losses were an estimated 110,000 killed and over 7,000 taken prisoner. Almost eight thousand Japanese planes were shot down. But most importantly, the Japanese lost to the Americans a land base from which to launch Operation OLYMPIC, the final assault on the Home Islands.[24]

28

"...A very lovely day..."

Atomic Bomb

The attack on Pearl Harbor by Japan in 1941 had sown seeds of shock and anger among the American people, uniting them as no nation had ever done before. Unprepared, America responded with what at first were weak, tentative counter blows. But, by exponential leaps, those blows had grown in devastating intensity and in a surprisingly short time became an almost irresistible whirlwind of death and destruction blowing across the Pacific to reach the Home Islands, culminating in the release of the unimaginable power of nuclear war on the Japanese people.

"August 8, 1945, and a very lovely day it was!" John Griffin wrote. "The word came over the radio of the invention of the 'Atomic Bomb' and later, that it had been dropped on one of the Japanese cities named Hiroshima. This day brought about a week of dramatic developments."[1]

On August 14, a message went out to U.S. forces in the Pacific: "OFFENSIVE OPERATIONS AGAINST JAPANESE FORCES WILL CEASE AT ONCE X CONTINUE SEARCHES AND PATROLS X MAINTAIN DEFENSIVE AND INTERNAL SECURITY MEASURES AT HIGHEST LEVEL AND BEWARE OF TREACHERY."[2] Later that day President Truman announced that a cease-fire was in effect. Negotiations involving the details of the surrender began, but the war was over. September 2, 1945, the day the Japanese formally signed the surrender documents on board the battleship USS *Missouri* in Tokyo Bay, is called VJ Day — Victory over Japan.

Demobilization Point System

The Marine Corps's strength at VJ Day stood at 485,833, with 242,043 serving overseas.[3] With the war over, the men felt it was time to go home. But it was not to be as easy as that. One of the major problems HQMC had anticipated was how to demobilize yet still carry out duties related to the surrender of Japanese armed forces and to the occupation. A plan had been staffed, received the commandant's okay, and was presented to the Secretary of the Navy, who approved it.

On August 15, the Point System, the general plan governing the discharge and separation of enlisted Marines, went into effect. In an attempt to make the process equal, service credit points for each enlisted Marine were computed on the following basis: one point for each month of service from September 16, 1940; one point for each month overseas from September 16, 1940; five points for each decoration and for each campaign or engagement for which a battle star was awarded; and 12 points for each child under 18 months of age (but not more than 36 points for children). Initially the critical score to get a veteran back to the States and out of the Corps was determined to be 85 points, but that number would be adjusted downward as the mission required and as time passed. Within a few months most of the old timers had gone stateside and the critical score was down to 45.[4]

The flow of men remained a two-way thing, for the units in the Pacific had to be kept up to strength. Glenn White, a member of the 4th Colored Replacement Draft, boarded a troop train at Camp Lejeune, bound for Oceanside, California, and Camp Pendleton, and then boarded ship to sail from San Diego. After a brief stop in Hawaii, the men left the ship at Saipan in the Marianas early in 1946.[5]

Slim Options

On Okinawa, the 18th and 19th Marine Depot Companies and the 3d Marine Ammunition Company were reassigned to the 12th Service Battalion, Service Command, FMFPac, as the supply service continued to evolve. The battalion was soon to take part in the occupation of North China, but before that happened, the black units were ordered home.

All Marines of the 9th and 10th Marine Depot Companies remained on Okinawa until November 19, 1945, when the men with less than 50 points left the companies to remain behind.[6] Then the old-timers of both companies sailed for the States on an escort aircraft carrier, the USS *Roi* (CVE-103). Eugene Smith recalls that the ship stopped at Pearl Harbor in Hawaii with generous liberty for all hands. Arriving at San Diego on December 8, Smith spent a week at Camp Pendleton. It was the routine for returning black units. Smith found himself in San Diego on liberty, in uniform, proud of the overseas ribbons on his chest. He walked into a bar to get a drink only to hear, "Sorry, you'll have to leave." Segregation was still the rule, and in "white" bars, blacks were not served. It made no difference if a man was a returning war veteran. The memory lingers.[7] Returning to Montford Point Camp, "The Barracuda Leathernecks" were disbanded on December 22, 1945.

With the 19th Marine Depot Company, Turner Blount said, "We stopped off in California, and were interviewed there." When asked if he wanted to stay in,

Blount asked what options he had. "The only option was to stay in as a cook, a messman. I can't cook, so I elected to take a discharge." He traveled to Montford Point where the 19th Marine Depot Company was deactivated on February 25, 1946. Turner Blount's Marine Corps journey then took an odd turn. "After being out for a while, I said, I want to be back in the Marine Corps. They wouldn't let me reenlist." After a short while, Blount received a recruiting flyer in the mail. *If you want to join the Marine Corps Reserves, just fill out this form*, it read. He did. Soon after, "Knocking on my door ... was an officer and an enlisted man from the Marine Corps and they enlisted me in the service in my living room at the house. So I was in the Reserves."[8]

The 18th Marine Depot Company was proudly singled out in the black press for its accomplishments in an articled datelined, "Okinawa." The men of the 18th were authorized "two combat stars on their Asiatic-Pacific Campaign Ribbon, which they earned at Saipan and Okinawa; one star on their Presidential Unit Citation which was awarded for action in the Marianas."[9] The company, waiting orders back to the States, was due to pass out of existence on January 29, 1946.

The 52d in Transition

Most of the men of the 52d Defense Battalion had been with the unit when it sailed from San Diego in late September 1944, but some — like Sgt. Maj. Gilbert Johnson — came even later. The men understood that as latecomers to the war, they were low on the rotation totem pole. John Griffin commented on the daily working parties sent out from the battalion in July, but in addition large numbers of men stood guard duty with the military police. The unit was treated as if it were a large depot company. At the end of September, the battalion, no longer tactically deployed, was reassigned to the 5th Service Depot, joining two ammunition and nine depot companies already there.[10]

The Black Press Discovers the 51st

Shortly after VJ-Day, Lester Granger, executive secretary of the National Urban League, traveled on a far-reaching inspection tour of black units in the Pacific at the request of the Secretary of the Navy. A reporter from the *Baltimore Afro-American* traveled with the inspectors. In October the *Afro-American* and its regional papers ran a scathing indictment of the treatment of the men of the 51st Defense Battalion in an article entitled, "Plight of Marines, Ignored 21 Months in Pacific, Told," and datelined "Eniwetok." The article painted a grim picture of the hardships the black Marines faced, but failed to mention the 5,000 whites who shared the same island.[11]

In an extensive press conference on November 1, 1945, Granger, in a more

The original caption reads, "Surrounded by a veteran crew of Marines who have spent 15 months in the Southwest and Central Pacific, this gun, named the 'Lena Horne' by its crew, points majestically skyward. The gun is manned by members of [the 51st] Defense Battalion, one of two such Negro units in the Corps." 1945. Nicholson. The gun, emplaced in a sandbagged pit on Eniwetok or Kwajalein Atoll (the 51st defended both atolls) in the Marshall Islands, is an M1 90mm antiaircraft gun. Note the tampion (muzzle cover) lying on the sandbags in the foreground. Still Picture Branch (NNSP), National Archives, Washington, DC.

objective assessment of the situation, spoke of some of the black Marine units in the Pacific. "We found one on the island of Eniwetok, a little island a mile and a half long and a quarter of a mile to a half mile wide, full of sand with exactly seventy-three palm trees on it — I counted them — and with the highest point above sea-level less than 10 feet. On that island were six thousand men of whom about twelve or fourteen hundred were Negroes. We found race relations as such on an island in pretty good shape and an intelligent commanding officer doing all he could to make up for the physical and geographic inadequacy in the men's environment. We found the marine outfit there unhappy because they [sic] were stranded on a distant tiny island base, having been trained for combat and never had a chance to see it, and they felt they were among the war's neglected."[12] Granger found the 52d on Guam in much the same straits.

Lieutenant Branch

November 10, 1945, on the 170th birthday of the United States Marine Corps, Frederick C. Branch took the oath as a Second Lieutenant in the Marine Corps Reserve. His wife pinned single gold bars on the shoulder straps of his uniform as Branch beamed his happiness. He was the first of his race to earn the distinction.

The 52d to the Rescue

Six days after joining the 5th Field Depot, the 52d was directed to turn in all its equipment to the depot. On October 18, two days before publication of the *Baltimore Afro-American* article, the 52d's battalion commander was notified that his unit would be relieving the 51st. The orders for relieving the 51st may have been coincidence. However, given the sensitivity of HQMC to any negative comments from the black press, one must wonder today whether HQMC somehow got advance notice from the *Afro-American* and was stung into quick action to head off any controversy.

Regardless of the cause, as the operating checks, cleaning, inventory and turn-in of gear neared completion, the unit once again divided into detachments. H&S Battery and the Light Antiaircraft Group remained on Guam. John Griffin, a clerk with H&S Battery, said, "I was promoted again, to corporal, and put in charge of a searchlight battery acting as Battery First Sergeant." Most of the equipment was gone, so "there wasn't too much work to be done."[13]

On November 16, Battery A (Reinforced) with 4 searchlight sections was slated to relieve elements of the 51st Defense Battalion on Kwajalein; the Heavy Antiaircraft Group (less two firing batteries) along with the rest of the Searchlight Battery would relieve units on Eniwetok. High-point men would sail with the detachments and continue to the States with the 51st Defense Battalion.

The men embarked on transports, and on November 16 the Kwajalein detachment sailed on the USS *Sibik* (AK-121) while the Eniwetok detachment sailed on the USS *Wyandot* (AKA-92). After relieving the 51st, the men settled into a non-tactical routine of general duties and soon fell into a mind-numbing tedium that lasted until they were reunited with the rest of their battalion on Guam on January 29, 1946.[14]

"The first Negro to be commissioned in the Marine Corps has his second lieutenant's bars pinned on by his wife. He is Frederick C. Branch of Charlotte, NC." November 10, 1945. Still Picture Branch (NNSP), National Archives, Washington, DC.

The End for the 51st

After 19 months overseas, the Marine Corps's first black combat unit was going home. On November 22 — it really was Thanksgiving Day — the USS *Sibik* sailed for San Diego with the 51st Defense Battalion embarked.[15] From San Diego the battalion went up to Camp Pendleton where in the coming week high-point men from west of the Mississippi were discharged. The remaining men boarded a troop train for the east, arriving at Camp Lejeune on Christmas Day, 1945. High-point men from the east began processing out. The few low-point men were reassigned to other units at Montford Point, and the battalion formally deactivated on January 31, 1946.

Occupation of Japan

VAC, which would have made the amphibious assault on Kyushu, took on the new mission of occupation of that island. The 5th Marine Division arrived at Sasebo, Japan, on September 22, and the 2d Marine Division came ashore at Nagasaki on September 26, 1945.[16] The 8th Service Regiment (8th Field Depot had been redesignated on June 1, another step in the on-going evolution of supporting units), as part of VAC Corps Troops, also landed at Sasebo Naval Base on the northwest coast of Kyushu. Sasebo was about 50 miles north of Nagasaki, the city destroyed by an atomic bomb dropped from a Tinian-based B-29 bomber on August 9. With the 8th Service Regiment were the following black units: [17]

> 6th Marine Ammunition Company
> 8th Marine Ammunition Company
> 10th Marine Ammunition Company
> 24th Marine Depot Company
> 33d Marine Depot Company
> 34th Marine Depot Company
> 42d Marine Depot Company
> 43d Marine Depot Company

The 36th Marine Depot Company landed at Sasebo near the end of October.[18] The men helped to move the supplies and equipment needed by the VAC, but without the accustomed pressures and danger of an amphibious assault.

Their stay in Japan was to be a short one, for the point system was thinning VAC's ranks of the high-point veterans, white as well as black. By the end of December the 24th Marine Depot Company and the 6th Marine Ammunition Company had been deactivated and the men reassigned to other units. In January 1946 the 8th Marine Ammunition Company, 33d, 34th and 36th Marine Depot Companies sailed for Guam, where they would become part of the 5th Service Depot (the redesignated 5th Field Depot). The 33d and 34th deactivated by end of the month;

the 36th sailed for San Francisco, eventually arriving back in North Carolina, where it deactivated on June 17, 1946, after less than two years in existence.

The end was in sight as well for the remaining black units in Japan, the 10th Marine Ammunition Company and the 42d and 43d Marine Depot Companies. High-point men eligible for discharge were reassigned to the 10th Marine Ammunition Company while all those with time yet to serve were transferred to the 6th Service Depot, Service Command, FMFPac, at Oahu, Territory of Hawaii. The 10th Marine Ammunition Company, the last black unit in the VAC's occupation of Japan, filed aboard the SS *Dashing Wave* at Sasebo on April 5 and sailed for San Diego. It had to be a whirlwind of emotions and experiences, this much-anticipated yet sudden change. The men traveled half way around the world by ship — no zig-zagging this time — and by train in a few short weeks, crossing eleven time zones and the International Date Line, and back again at Montford Point Camp hustled through their final days as Marines. On May 6, 1946, one month after sailing from Sasebo, the 10th Marine Ammunition Company ceased to exist, the men scattered, going home.[19]

Occupation of North China

On September 26 the VAC (less the 6th Marine Division) sailed from Okinawa for the Gulf of Chihli where units landed and the IIIAC Shore Brigade began unloading on September 30 at the low-lying delta that marked the mouth of the Hai River at Tangku. They would move inland 36 miles to Tientsin, a city about 80 miles southeast of Peiping (Beijing). The 7th Service Regiment (the 7th Field Depot had also been redesignated on June 1), as part of IIIAC Corps Troops, included the following black units:[20]

1st Marine Ammunition Company
12th Marine Ammunition Company
5th Marine Depot Company
20th Marine Depot Company
37th Marine Depot Company
38th Marine Depot Company

The 1st Marine Ammunition Company and the 38th Marine Depot Company landed on September 30 and moved to Tientsin, while the other black units came ashore and joined them a few days later.[21]

On October 6, IIIAC's commanding general accepted the surrender of over 50,000 Japanese soldiers from the surrounding area. The Japanese were cooperative and followed all agreed upon procedures. However, the same day Chinese communist forces ambushed a Marine convoy on the Tientsin-Peiping road, wounding three Marines.[22] These may well have been the opening shots in a skirmish that marked the overture for a new war. However, that war would not officially begin until June 1950, far to the east on the Korean peninsula.

While IIIAC went about the business of repatriating Japanese soldiers, photos contributed to the Montford Point Marine Museum by an anonymous donor show the ceremony marking the Japanese surrender, black Marines on liberty, the usual kind of photos a young Marine might want for keepsakes. However, included are other photos showing the Chinese conducting a series of gruesome public mass executions — beheadings — of other Chinese, and the photographer appears to have been allowed to go about with impunity. There are no annotations to show whether Communist or Nationalist forces did the bloody work.

The 6th Marine Division landed at Tsingtao on the Yellow Sea on October 11, and the 12th Marine Ammunition and the 20th Marine Depot Companies shifted there to support operations. The workload for the black units increased on October 15 when the IIIAC Shore Brigade disbanded and the 7th Service Regiment shouldered its duties.[23] The black Marines discovered that the Chinese could handle most of the heavy labor work, so the Marines were used for guard duty. Liberty was good, but China was a dangerous place and a man had to be careful. Within a week the first ships loaded with Japanese repatriates sailed from Tientsin.[24]

By January 1946, as was happening to VAC in Japan, low-point men were reassigned to units slated to remain in China while the high-point veterans shifted to the 1st Marine Ammunition Company and the 5th Marine Depot Company. On January 7, both companies boarded the USS *Bolivar* (APA-34) at Tangku, sailed around the Shantung Peninsula to Tsingtao and embarked the 20th Marine Depot Company en route to San Diego. At Camp Pendleton, just north of San Diego, west coast Marines took their discharges and the remaining Marines were sent to Montford Point where the companies deactivated on February 21, 1946.[25]

The End of the 52d

While the last men were preparing to case the colors of the first black Marine combat unit back at Montford Point, the men of the second such unit were moving toward the same end. The USS *Hyde* (APA-173) brought the men of the 52d from the Marshalls back to Guam at the end of January. Yet another reorganization awaited them, but first the high-point men were ordered home. The Heavy Antiaircraft Group, 52d Defense Battalion, took the low-point men, and took the name Heavy Antiaircraft Group (Provisional), Saipan, leaving the 52d as little more than a shell. The new Group prepared for a move to Saipan.

Glenn J. White arrived during this time as a member of the 4th Colored Replacement Draft. He joined the Heavy Antiaircraft Group (Provisional), where he was assigned to a searchlight battery. He was the junior man. The Group's training program was very active, and White recalls that the NCOs in the battery were patient with the new men. "They took the time to show us what to do and what not to do."[26]

The much-reduced 52d Defense Battalion, down to fewer than 400 officers and men, came back to the States on the USS *Wakefield* (AP-21), arriving at San Diego on March 26. Once again following in the footsteps of the 51st, the men went first to Camp Pendleton to discharge West Coast men. The few men left returned the colors to Montford Point in early April, and the unit was deactivated on May 15, 1946.

Occupation Ends for Black Units

On March 2, the last of the black units to land in China with IIIAC, the 37th and 38th Marine Depot Companies, sailed from Tangku the same day the 12th Marine Ammunition Company sailed from Tsingtao for the States. In another whirlwind of travel the depot companies reached Montford Point to be deactivated on April 2, while the ammo company came to the same fate on April 5.[27]

It was the same all across the Pacific. Black units were being sent home, the men demobilized and the units deactivated. Montford Point Marines were no longer part of the occupation forces. As of December 31, 1945, one ammunition and 13 depot companies had been deactivated. The end of 1946 would see the deactivation of all but two of the remaining black units. Of the World War II depot and ammunition companies and the two black defense battalions, only the 8th Marine Ammunition Company and the 49th Marine Depot Company would exist a few months more, deactivating on September 30, 1947.

However, that ending marked a new beginning, at least of sorts. Black Marines continued to serve as part of the Heavy Antiaircraft Group (Provisional) on Saipan, while the 3d Antiaircraft Artillery Battalion (Composite) activated from the elements of the 52d Defense Battalion at Montford Point.

29

Future for Black Marines

After the War, What?

In the summer of 1945, on Okinawa, in the midst of preparations for the invasion of Japan that was sure to come next, a white Marine said to Eugene Smith,

Sgt. Eugene Smith, USMCR, 10th Marine Depot Company, "The Barracuda Leathernecks." Photograph used by permission from Eugene Smith.

"What are they going to do with you niggers after the war?" Smith, who had never met the man, said of the incident, "If he is still living I'm sure that he still remembers me, 'cause I beat the hell out of him."[1]

What *were* the Marine Corps's postwar plans for blacks? Staff officers at HQMC were trying to come up with an answer as 1945 came to an end.

The Ten Percent Solution

Demobilization gained momentum while at Montford Point Camp the flow of black recruits dwindled to a trickle. In October 1945, the commandant approved a plan to reduce the number of black Marines from a war strength of approximately 17,135 to a proposed peace strength of 2,800.[2] The number of blacks in the Corps dropped to 15,808 in December 1945, and that number continued to fall in order to meet the commandant's goal.[3] "By the time the Corps stopped drafting men early in 1946 it had received over 16,000 Negroes through the Selective Service. Including the 3,129 black volunteers, the number of Negroes in the Marine Corps during World War II totaled 19,168, approximately 4 percent of the Corps's strength."[4] The Recruit Training Battalion at Montford Point Camp graduated the 575th Platoon, the last of the World War II era, in January 1946 and then the battalion disbanded in May 1946. In June, a Training Company, commanded by a lieutenant colonel, activated to continue the function of training black recruits but at a greatly reduced rate.

At the end of February 1946, the navy published Circular Letter 48–46 lifting "all restrictions governing types of assignments" for blacks, and furthermore, it specified, that "in housing, messing and other facilities" there would be no special accommodations for blacks. The navy's move garnered the usual skepticism from the black press. Lester Granger of the National Urban League, on behalf of the Secretary of the Navy, invited 23 leading black editors and publishers on an inspection tour to see the changes made by the navy. None accepted, preferring their business as usual approach to the military services, that is, "givin' 'em hell."[5]

Near the end of February, the Marine Corps was still smarting after another attack by the black press in the *Chicago Defender*, dated February 16, 1946. In "Bare Secret Marine Order on Race,"[6] a reporter asked Brigadier General Franklin A. Harte, Director, Division of Public Information at HQMC, to confirm the long rumored existence of a CONFIDENTIAL letter about handling blacks in the Corps [Letter of Instruction (Number 421) from the Commandant of the Marine Corps to all commanding officers issued in May 1943]. Harte confirmed that such a letter had been issued. The article was more of the "givin' 'em hell" genre.

At about the same time a memorandum from the Director, Division of Plans and Policies to the Commandant of the Marine Corps declared the foundation for the Corps's preferred postwar race policy. The memo first identified two problems:

(a) Should separate Negro units be maintained in the postwar Marine Corps, or should Negroes be assimilated into white units and all marines, irrespective of race or color, be assigned alike?

(b) What is the total number of Negro marines that the Marine Corps can absorb and utilize in the postwar organization?

Next, the memo summarized army and navy racial policies — note that the Corps was not bound to follow either of those services but was responsible for establishing its own policy — and then took the moral high ground with a declaration that "the Negro question is a national issue which grows more controversial yet is more evaded as time goes by." The memo next pointed an accusing finger at politicians for appeasing the black press at the expense of [military] service needs, and declared that until someone at a "higher level" resolved the issue, the services were not required to go any further in solving the problem. In other words, the Marine Corps's stance became one of, *We're busy. It's your problem, you fix it.* At the bottom line, the memo proposed that the commandant continue to maintain separate black units and limit the number of black Marines to no more than 10 percent of the total authorized strength of the Corps. The recommendations were approved.[7]

Rebirth of Black Boot Camp

Sgt. Maj. Gilbert "Hashmark" Johnson became sergeant major of the new Training Company that activated on June 10, 1946, with First Sergeant Edgar R. Huff assigned as the field sergeant major. The pre-war "little green huts" no longer existed and the company occupied what had been the Steward's Branch camp. The training cycle for black recruits resumed with four platoons in the camp by the summer of 1946.[8]

In the fall of 1946, a black Marine wearing his dress blue uniform visited Caribou, Georgia. Eighteen-year-old Paul Hagan saw the Marine and made up his mind on the spot. "I'm going into the Marine Corps. That's why I came in. Because of that uniform."[9] He enlisted.

Paul Hagan arrived at Montford Point in November 1946. At Recruit Receiving a DI asked his name. "Paul Hagan."

"Get out of my office," roared the DI.

Hagan left. Outside, a Marine told Hagan how to report. He tried again. "Private Paul Hagan, sir. Reporting as instructed, sir." His receiving process began.

Adner Batts, Jr., an outgoing nineteen-year-old from Hampstead, North Carolina, came through the gate at Montford Point and immediately decided, "They're gonna kill me!" Small wonder. The truck bringing the new black recruits from the Jacksonville bus station to Montford Point halted at a cemetery beside Highway 24 where the road forks to the camp. "These are the men that didn't make it" through boot camp, he was told.[10]

Paul Hagan joined the 17th Platoon, 32 recruits billeted in a spacious, open squadbay. That squadbay became Hagan's refuge after a day of rough treatment at the hands of his DIs. "When we secured in the afternoon was the thing I liked best. We worked so hard and drilled and trained and ran all day long. They even ran us in the water," Hagan said, "and ran you until you were dry." The hardest part of the training for Hagan was the hand-to-hand combat, but "it made you strong."[11]

For Batts, the obstacle course was the worst. The training program burned a great amount of energy, and "chow" was an important part of the day. "They served family style, and I'd never seen anything like that before," Batts said. "I got a-plenty to eat. And quite frankly, plenty of the fellows hadn't been getting too much before."[12]

Gone were the days when black recruits boarded landing boats at Montford Point to go to the rifle range at Stone Bay. "I went in what they called a cattle car," Hagan said. These were closed cargo trailers modified with windows and bench seats along both sides and down the center. Gone as well were the days when blacks were not allowed to stay overnight at the range — they were assigned a barracks for the week of snapping in (learning how to adjust their rifle sights, practice in each firing position without ammunition) and a week of live firing culminating in firing for record. "If you didn't qualify, they made you stay out there until you did," Hagan said. After graduation, the men were given liberty and could go to Jacksonville, still segregated, still divided by the railroad tracks and enforced by military police. Now a PFC, Hagan was ordered overseas to Guam, where he joined the 8th Air Mobile Depot. His work consisted of loading and unloading trucks and stacking ammunition. There were still Japanese holdouts on the island, he recalls. "Every once in a while we'd hear shots or see fire up in the mountains."[13] Hagan eventually became an ammunition technician.

Graduation from boot camp was a great day for Adner Batts, but then came a letdown; he got the assignment he did not want, that of a Steward/Cook, with orders to Cooks and Bakers School. It would take time, but Batts persisted and enjoyed a long Marine Corps career as an engineer.[14]

Even as the boot camp was being reborn, some of the old hands were still being separated. John R. Griffin had been one of 4,000 soldiers, sailors, and airmen who departed Guam back on March 18 on the USS *Manhattan*. His arrival at San Diego was memorable, for "the docks were filled with bands and beautiful women." The men were given fresh "sweet milk and donuts." After a brief home leave came a stint of duty at the separation center at Montford Point until his turn came. On June 22, 1946, "I packed my bags and said farewell to Camp Lejeune. I changed my forest greens for a gray civilian suit. All I wanted to do was to return to school and finish my education." And so he did.[15]

Black V-12s Commissioned

The commandant's goal of 2,800 black Marines touched the V-12 students as well, but with a difference. Herbert Brewer recalls, "The Marine Corps decided that because we had completed most of the program we had a choice: we could go back to our previous status in the Marine Corps (in my case I was a sergeant) or we could accept our commissions in the reserves and be assigned to inactive duty. The war was over anyway, so I elected to accept a commission and take the inactive reserve status because I did want to go back to Purdue and finish my senior year. As for the others, Judd B. Davis and Master Sergeant Charles C. Johnson also elected to receive commissions. We were commissioned together as second lieutenants at the Naval Base, Great Lakes in Illinois (I guess it was because that base was near Purdue) and assigned to the inactive reserve." Brewer is a tall man, so for that reason alone he would have been on the left — the "big end" of a file of men — as the three men formed one rank in front of the officer who administered the oath of office. Alphabetically, his name comes up first, so, by a matter of seconds, Herbert Lawrence Brewer was more than likely the second black man to be commissioned a lieutenant of Marines. His good friend Fred Branch was the first. "Johnson, later on he transferred to the Public Health Service. Davis, Judd Davis, had some sort of physical problem so he resigned. So Branch and I were the only ones left out of that Purdue group."[16]

The Last of the First

Near the end of 1946, Glenn J. White expected to be sent to North China for occupation duty but was disappointed to learn that, as one of the World War II draftees, he was going home to be demobilized. He came back to the States at San Diego, went up to Camp Pendleton, and from there to the Naval Station, Great Lakes, Illinois, for separation.[17]

On December 1, 1946, the Marine Corps simplified its old rank structure. It assigned one rank title to each of the seven pay grades: In the first pay grade was Master Sergeant, followed by Technical Sergeant, Staff Sergeant, Sergeant, Corporal, Private First Class, ending at the seventh pay grade, Private.[18] "Sergeant Major" became a billet title rather than a rank.

By January 1947, the number of blacks that could serve in the Corps — 2,800 — was further reduced to 1,500.[19] Blacks still had a long and difficult road ahead. Presidential Order 9981, "Integration of the Armed Forces," would not be signed until July 1948.

The Montford Point Marines took their race where it had never been before. Whether taking one painful step at a time or brashly kicking down doors, they set high standards for members of *all* races who dare enter behind them.

Let no one forget.

30

A Few of the Men, Continued

Blount, Turner

Mr. Blunt is today a city councilman in Jacksonville, North Carolina, a town where once he was not allowed to walk on certain streets. Speaking to young blacks today, he says they "can be whatever they want to be. The door is open, wide, and they have a choice." There is a recurring theme among the men interviewed, spoken with obvious pride by each in his own way. "Men like us paved the way.... I'm proud I was able to make it."[1]

Borden, Melvin

Mr. Borden reminds young blacks today that, "We paved the way," and offers this reminder: "Don't let us down. We proved what we could do and were willing to do, so don't

Finney Greggs, the retired Marine who is today the Director, Montford Point Marines Museum, Camp Lejeune, NC. Photograph used by permission from Finney Greggs.

let us down. If you're gonna be a man, be a man. If you're going to be a military man, be a military man or don't come here. You have to be willing to die." After a short pause, he softens his comments. "If it's not your time [to die] you can't rush it. You can have plans and all but until God's ready for you, you're not going to die."[2]

Smith, Eugene

Talking about racism, Eugene Smith says the country has come a long way in the last fifty years. But there is still a lot of work to be done. After the Marine Corps, Smith went on to a long and successful career, becoming the Executive Chef at the Sears Tower in Chicago. He retired to a similar position with a professional sports organization — not full time, but enough to keep his hand in. "With all the abuse I have experienced as a black man in this country, I still love it and would defend it without hesitation. I also love the Marines."[3]

White, Glenn

Glenn J. White, discharged in 1946, had found a home. He soon reenlisted and remained in the Marine Corps until 1973, when he retired as a Gunnery Sergeant. White remembers a most enjoyable time when he served as an instructor at Montford Point, a time when his men called him "Pops" behind his back. "But," he smiles, "that was okay."[4]

Batts, Adner

"The Marine Corps did a magnificent job in making me a man. I would never have been the man I am. I'm a seventh-grade drop-out. I didn't finish high school until I got a GED in the Marine Corps. I got a chance to take some college courses, and I would not have got to do that if I hadn't have come into the Marine Corps. The Corps gave me discipline.... it gave me travel." Talking of the men he served with, white and black, he says they "knew you were there and you had made a point." Referring to his wife, he simply says, "I couldn't have done it without her."[5]

Now he is The Reverend Adner Batts, becoming a minister after retiring from the Corps.

Hagan, Paul

Paul Hagan's career in the Marine Corps spanned 20 years. "The thing I got was discipline. Being in the Marine Corps was like being with your parents."[6]

Cottman, Orvia O.

Orvia Cottman tells us that "the Montford Point Marines from 1942 to 1949 were a good and close group. There were good men and bad." He visits Camp Johnson and volunteers at the Montford Point Marines Museum nearly every day. He says, "Montford Point is really what I consider my second home. It was the first place I came when I left my childhood home."[7]

Brewer, Herbert L.

Herbert Brewer completed his studies and took a B.S. degree in Civil Engineering at Purdue University. Transferring to the University of Pennsylvania, he earned a Master's Degree.

"When we finished the V-12 program we really hadn't gone through basic school; they just gave us commissions because we had enough time in under that program. So, for Korea, we went to the basic school at Quantico. I was in Basic Class Number Seven (7), I believe. Branch, the first African American officer, had already been through basic school and I believe he was at San Diego. During basic school, as far as Marine Corps treatment went, we had no complaints there, except for little things; when you look back on them they just sort of amuse you. I remember one time when we were marching down the street while we were in the basic school, and when we passed by the mess hall the crew sitting out back said 'Look here, they are going to have some nigger officers.'

"Anyway, we were in ranks and I couldn't do anything about it. But as for the Marine Corps officially, they treated us very well. There were three hundred and fourteen [314] of us, I believe, in our graduating class, and 300 of them were in the infantry and went right over to Korea within a week or two. Those of us that were not infantry were sent to Army schools for additional training."

At the time of his retirement in 1973, Colonel Herbert Brewer was the senior black officer in the Marine Corps Reserve. He retired to several full careers since the Marine Corps and today continues work as an engineering consultant.[8]

Appendices

Appendix A: Monthly Inductions into the Marine Corps, 1941–1945

Month	1941 Volunteers	1942 Volunteers	1943 Volunteers	Sel. Serv.	% Sel.Serv.
January		22,686	3,463	6,111	63.8
February	963	12,037	3,485	9,349	72.8
March	1,883	7,913	2,575	10,639	80.5
April	1,360	7,405	1,215	10,911	90.0
May	1,297	9,357	1,866	8,518	82.0
June	2,704	10,721	3,777	8,711	69.8
July	2,449	14,029	1,909	8,614	81.9
August	2,649	15,569	2,949	11,153	79.1
September	2,416	18,592	2,809	9,957	78.0
October	2,116	16,240	2,273	12,084	84.2
November	1,978	15,107	2,998	12,759	81.0
December	10,224	18,083	2,191	11,253	83.7
Aggregate by year	30,039	167,039	31,520	120,059	79.2

Month	1944 Volunteers	Sel. Serv.	% Sel. Serv.	1945 Volunteers	Sel. Serv.	% Sel.Serv.
January	2,584	7,855	75.2	1,429	3,333	70.0
February	1,446	5,678	79.7	1,223	2,156	63.8
March	3,584	14,305	80.0	1,749	1,768	50.3
April	3,725	13,126	77.9	2,134	3,624	62.9
May	1,136	11,056	90.7	1,822	3,417	65.2
June	728	11,756	94.2	3,739	1,871	33.4
July	1,191	5,003	80.8	4,214	5,506	56.6
August	1,010	2,117	67.7			
September	1,123	1,138	50.3			
October	1,055	922	46.6			
November	1,476	799	35.1			
December	1,623	1,569	49.1			
Aggregate by year	20,681	75,324	78.4	16,310	21,675	57.0

Appendix B: USMC Rank and Pay Structure—1942

Grade	Line	Insignia	Staff	Insignia	Monthly Pay
First	Sergeant Major Master Gunnery Sergeant	3 chevrons and 3 arcs	Master Technical Sergeant Master Technical Sergeant (Mess) Quartermaster Sergeant Paymaster Sergeant	3 chevrons and 3 bars	$126
Second	First Sergeant Gunnery Sergeant	3 chevrons and 2 arcs	Technical Sergeant Technical Sergeant (Paymaster Department) Technical Sergeant (Mess) Drum Major Supply Sergeant	3 chevrons and 2 bars	$84
Third	Platoon Sergeant	3 chevrons and 1 arc	Staff Sergeant (Clerical) Staff Sergeant (Mechanical) Staff Sergeant (Mess)	3 chevrons and 1 bar	$72
Fourth	Sergeant Mess Sergeant Chief Cook Drum Sergeant Trumpet Sergeant	3 chevrons			$60
Fifth	Corporal Mess Corporal Field Cook Drum Corporal Trumpet Corporal	2 chevrons			$54
Sixth	Private First Class Assistant Cook Drummer First Class Trumeter First Class	1 chevron			$36
Seventh	Private	No chevron			$21

Appendix C: Supply Service Base and Field Depots— August 31, 1944

Theatre	Location	Unit	USMC T/O	USN T/O
Hawaiian Area	Oahu	6th Base Depot, Supply Service, FMFPac 7th, 8th Marine Depot Companies, Supply Service, FMFPac	169/4211	8/41

Theatre	Location	Unit	USMC T/O	USN T/O
		8th Field Depot, Supply Service, FMFPac 24th Marine Depot Co, Supply Service, FMFPac 8th Marine Ammunition Co, Supply Service, FMFPac	24/424	1/13
	Hawaii	1st Service and Suppy Bn, Supply Service, FMFPac	22/477	0/4
	Kaui	3d Service and Supply Bn, Supply Service, FMFPac	11/278	0/2
	Maui	2d Service and Supply Bn, Supply Service, FMFPac	6/268	0/0
Southwest	Auckland, NZ	3d Field Depot, Supply Service, FMFPac	15/106	2/8
	Russell Islands	4th Base Depot, Supply Service, FMFPac 1st, 4th, 30th, 31st, 32d Marine Depot Companies, Supply Service FMFPac	94/2613	7/26
	Guadalcanal	16th Field Depot, Supply Service, FMFPac	43/1204	3/16
	Nooumea, New	1st Field Depot, Supply Service, FMFPac 2d, 3d, 9th, 10th Marine Depot Companies, Supply Service, FMFPac	38/664	3/13
Central Pacific	Guam	5th Field Depot, Supply Service, FMFPac	64/1447	4/16
	Roi-Namur	15th Marine Depot Company, Supply Service, FMFPac	5/197	0/0
	Saipan	7th Field Depot, Supply Service, FMFPac 3d Marine Ammunition Co, 17th, 18th, 19th, 20th Marine Depot Companies, Supply Service, FMFPac	90/1780	5/36

Appendix D: Marine Division Service and Supply Units—World War II

Tables of Organization, Marine Divisions, World War II

Unit	D Series IN EFFECT AT START OF WAR	E Series 5 APR 1943	F Series 5 MAY 1944	G Series 4 SEP 1945
SERVICE TROOPS	1,946	2,200	1,889	2,247
Service Bn				
HqCo				
Serv&Sup Co	(352)	(455)	(502)	
Service Co	(276)			
Supply Co	(157)			
Ordnance Co	(109)	(144)	(178)	(242)

Tables of Organization, Marine Divisions, World War II

Unit	D Series IN EFFECT AT START OF WAR	E Series 5 APR 1943	F Series 5 MAY 1944	G Series 4 SEP 1945
Div TransCo				
3 RegtlTransCos				
MT Bn				
Med Bn				
EngrRegt				
Pioneer Bn	743	744	745	740
HqCo				
3 PionCos	(208)	(208)	(206)	(202)

Note: Strengths shown are for those units that performed tasks similar to the black Depot and Ammunition Companies.

Appendix E: Depot and Ammunition Companies 1943–1946

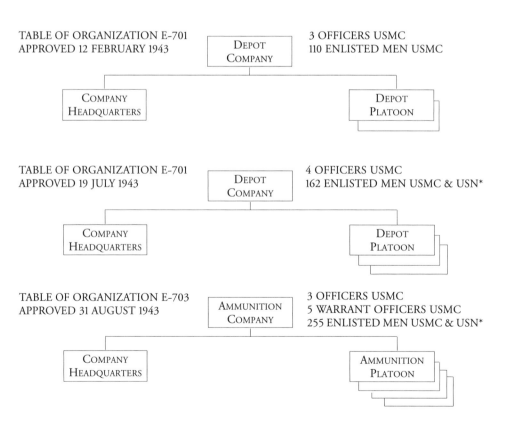

*USN Medical Personnel (3 per depot and 4 per ammunition company) were added after T/O's E-701 and 703 were approved.

Appendix F: Target Location by Radio Set SCR-268

G – SEARCHLIGHT
F – SEARCHLIGHT CONTROL STATION
E – SEARCHLIGHT POWER UNIT
D – GUN BATTERY
C – DIRECTOR - M 4
B – ANTENNA MOUNT - K 28A
A – POWER TRAILER - K 34B

TARGET LOCATION BY RADIO SET SCR-268

Appendix G: Pacific Ocean Area Units of Fire for Ground Weapons

Weapon	Total Rounds Per Unit of Fire
.30-caliber carbine	45
.30-caliber rifle	100
.30-caliber BAR	500
.30-caliber machine gun	1,500
.12-gauge shotgun	25
.45-caliber automatic revolver	14
.45-caliber submachine gun	200
.50-caliber machine gun	600
20-mm. antiaircraft machine gun	540
27-mm. antitank or tank gun	100
37-mm. antiaircraft gun	270
40-mm. antiaircraft gun	270
57-mm. antitank gun	90
60-mm. mortar	100
81-mm. mortar	100
4.2-inch chemical mortar	100
75-mm. howitzer field or pack	300

Weapon	*Total Rounds Per Unit of Fire*
75-mm. self-propelled tank gun or LVT howitzer	150
75-mm. gun	100
3-inch self-propelled or antitank gun	50
90-mm. self-propelled or antitank gun	125
105-mm. M3 (short barrel) howitzer	150
105-mm. field howitzer	200
105-mm. self-propelled or tank gun howitzer	100
4.7-inch antiaircraft gun	75
155-mm. M1 howitzer	150
155-mm. M1 gun	100
8-inch howitzer	100
240-mm. howitzer	60
75-mm. gun	300
3-inch antiaircraft mobile	150
Hand grenade	1 per Enlisted Man
Rifle antitank grenade launcher	2M9AT grenade
2.36-inch antitank rocket launcher (bazooka)	6 rockets

Chapter Notes

Preface

1. Morris J. MacGregor, Jr., *Integration of the Armed Forces 1940–1965* (Washington, DC: Government Printing Office, Center of Military History, United States Army, 1985), 100.

2. Ray A. Robinson, General USMC (Ret.), personal interview dated 18–19 Mar 1968 (Oral History Collection, Marine Corps History Division, USMC).

3. Tony Hillerman, ed., *Best of the West: An Anthology of Classic Writing from the American West* (New York: HarperCollins, 1991), xv.

Chapter 1

1. Henry I. Shaw, Jr., and Ralph W. Donnelly, *Blacks in the Marine Corps* (Washington, DC: GPO, History and Museums Division, HQMC, 1975), ix (hereafter cited as Shaw and Donnelly, *Blacks*).

2. Herbert L. Brewer, Col. USMCR, personal interview dated November 12, 2002 (Oral History Collection, Marine Corps History Division, USMC) (hereafter cited as Brewer interview).

Chapter 2

1. Frank O. Hough, Lieutenant Colonel, USMCR, Major Verle E. Ludwig, USMC, and Henry I. Shaw, Jr., *History of U.S. Marine Corps Operations in World War II*, vol. I (Washington, DC: GPO, Historical Branch, G-3 Division, Headquarters, U.S. Marine Corps, Washington, 1958), 3 (hereafter cited as Hough, Ludwig, and Shaw, *Marine Corps Operations*, vol. I).

2. Michael A. Palmer, "The Navy: The Continental Period, 1775–1890," A History of the U.S. Navy (Washington, DC: Navy Historical Center, Washington Navy Yard) *http://www.history.navy.mil/history/history2.htm* (accessed January 26, 2006).

3. Shaw and Donnelly, *Blacks*, ix.

4. Historical Overview of the Federalist Navy, 1787–1801, The Reestablishment of the Navy, 1787–1801, Historical Overview and Select Bibliography, *Naval History Bibliographies, No. 4,* (Washington, DC: Department of the Navy, Naval Historical Center) *http://www.history.navy.mil/biblio/biblio4/biblio4a.htm* (accessed February 28, 2006).

5. Rudyard Kipling, "The White Man's Burden," The Internet Modern History Sourcebook, http://www.fordham.edu/halsall/mod/Kipling.html (accessed January 28, 2006).

6. War in the Pacific, Part 2a, History, First American Period 1898–1941, *http://www.cr.nps.gov/history/online_books/wapa/cli/part2a.htm* (accessed January 31, 2006).

7. Hough, Ludwig, and Shaw, vol. 1, *Marine Corps Operations*, 11.

8. Ibid., 14.

9. Bemis M. Frank and Henry I. Shaw, Jr., *Victory and Occupation*, vol. 5 of *History of U.S. Marine Corps Operations in World War II* (Washington, DC: GPO, Historical Branch, G-3 Division, Headquarters, U.S. Marine Corps, 1968), 688 (hereafter cited as Bemis and Shaw, *Marine Corps Operations*, vol. 5).

10. BBC News, Special Report "President Roosevelt Proclaims Neutrality," *http://news.bbc.co.uk/1/hi/special_report/1999/08/99/world_war_ii/430187.stm* (accessed February 8, 2006).

11. Charles D. Melson, Major, USMC (Ret), *Condition Red: Marine Defense Battalions in World War II* (Washington, DC: History and Museums Division, Headquarters, U.S. Marine Corps, 1996), 5. Also available online at *http://www.ibiblio.org/hyperwar/USMC/USMC-C-Defense/index.html* (accessed February 2, 2004) (hereafter cited as Melson, *Condition Red*).

12. Bemis and Shaw, *Marine Corps Operations*, vol. 5, 688.

13. Gerald C. Thomas, General, U.S. Marine Corps (Retired), Colonel Robert D. Heinl, U.S. Marine Corps (Retired), and Rear Admiral Arthur

A. Ageton, U.S. Navy (Retired), *The Marine Officer's Guide,* 3rd ed. (Annapolis, MD: United States Naval Institute, 1967), 5.

Chapter 3

1. James L. Jones, General, USMC, Commandant of the Marine Corps, testimony, House Armed Services Committee, Washington DC, July 12, 2001. Available online at: *http://www.house.gov/ hasc/openingstatementsandpressreleases/107thcongress/ 01–07–12jones.html* (accessed May 18, 2006).
2. Stephen Crane, *The Red Badge of Courage, http://www.pagebypagebooks.com/Stephen_Crane/ The_Red_Badge_of_Courage/CHAPTER_V_p2.html* (accessed December 1, 2005).
3. MacGregor, *Integration,* 100.
4. Hough, Ludwig, and Shaw, *Marine Corps Operations,* vol. 1, 47.
5. MacGregor, *Integration,* 100.
6. Henry I. Shaw, Jr., *Opening Moves: Marines Gear Up for War* (Washington, DC: Marine Corps Historical Center, 1991), http://www.ibiblio.org/hy perwar/USMC/USMC-C-Opening.html (accessed April 17, 2004) (hereafter cited as Shaw, *Opening Moves*).
7. Ibid.
8. MacGregor, *Integration,* 58.
9. Shaw and Donnelly, *Blacks,* 1.
10. Bernard C. Nalty, *The Right to Fight: African American Marines in World War II.* (Washington, DC: History and Museums Division, Headquarters, U.S. Marine Corps, 1995), 8. Also available online at: *http://www.nps.gov/wapa/indepth/extContent/usmc/pcn-190–003132–00/index.htm* (accessed October 31, 2005) (hereafter cited as Nalty, *African American Marines).*
11. Who's Who in Marine Corps History (United States Marine Corps History Division), *http://hqinet001.hqmc.usmc.mil/HD/Historical/Whos _Who/Holcomb_T.htm* (accessed March 7, 2006).
12. Shaw and Donnelly, *Blacks,* 1.
13. Memorandum from President Franklin Delano Roosevelt for the Secretary of the Navy (no subject) dated February 22, 1943 (Historical Reference Branch, History Division, USMC).

Chapter 4

1. Marine Corps Administrative History, typed manuscript dated 1946 (Historical Reference Branch, History Division, USMC), 15–17.
2. Kenneth W. Condit, Gerald Diamond and Edwin T. Turnbladh. *Marine Corps Ground Training in World War II,* typed manuscript, 1956, 158 (Historical Reference Branch, History Division, USMC).
3. Memorandum from the Director, Division of Plans and Policies, to the Commandant, U.S. Marine Corps, dated February 25, 1942. Subject: Enlistment of the colored race other than in the messman branch (Historical Reference Branch, History Division, USMC) (hereafter cited as DP&P Feb 25 memo).
4. Memorandum for the Executive Officer, Division of Plans and Policies, dated February 19, 1942 (Historical Reference Branch, History Division, USMC).
5. DP&P Feb 25 memo.
6. Craig M. Cameron, *American Samurai* (Cambridge, UK: Cambridge University Press, 1994), 60 (hereafter cited as Cameron, *American Samurai).*
7. Shaw, *Opening Moves.*
8. DP&P Feb 25 memo.

Chapter 5

1. "Navy to Accept Negroes for General Service," news release dated April 7, 1942 (Historical Reference Branch, History Division, USMC).
2. DP&P Feb 25 memo.
3. Ibid.
4. MacGregor, *Integration* , 101.
5. 20May42 News Release (Historical Division, Headquarters, U.S. Marine Corps, Washington DC), *http://hqinet001.hqmc.usmc.mil/HD/Histori cal/Docs_Speeches/Plansrecruitingblacks.htm* (accessed April 19, 2004).
6. Turner G. Blount, personal interview, October 3, 2005 (hereafter cited as Blount interview).
7. Ray A. Robinson, General USMC (Ret.), interview dated March 18–19, 1968 (Oral History Collection, Marine Corps History Division, USMC).
8. Ibid.
9. F.W. Hopkins, Lt. Col., USMC, letter to the editor, *Marine Corps Gazette,* July 1944. Used with permission of copyright owner.
10. Shaw, *Opening Moves.*
11. Edward J. Evans, Sgt., USMC, "Men from Montford Point," *Leatherneck Magazine,* November 1947, 32. Used with permission of copyright owner (hereafter cited as Evans, "Men from Montford Point").

Chapter 6

1. Letter from the Commandant, U.S. Marine Corps, to District Commanders, All Reserve Districts except 10th, 14th, 15th, and 16th, dated May 25, 1942, Subject: Enlistment of colored personnel in the Marine Corps (Historical Reference Branch, History Division, USMC).
2. Memorandum for the Secretary of the Navy from the Commandant of the Marine Corps, dated June 23, 1942, Subject: Enlistment of Negroes (Historical Reference Branch, History Division, USMC).
3. Cameron, *American Samurai,* 52.
4. Shaw and Donnelly, *Blacks* 3.
5. Fred DeCloue, *First Black Marines — Van-*

guard of a Legacy (Nashville, TN: James C. Winston Publishing Company, 1995), 26.

6. Ibid., 45.

7. Index to *San Antonio Register* "first [sic] San Antonio Race Man to Join Marines" (photo), 1942/07/17: 1, *http://www.lib.utsa.edu/Databases/Sar/sars.html* (accessed August 15, 2005).

8. Brewer interview.

9. Ibid.

10. Shaw and Donnelly, *Blacks,* 7.

11. Evans, "Men from Montford Point."

12. Gilbert H. Johnson, Sgt. Maj., interview with Hist. Div, dated June 27–28, 72 (Oral History Collection, Marine Corps History Division, USMC) (hereafter cited as Johnson interview).

13. Nalty, *African American Marines,* 6.

14. Ibid., 7.

Chapter 7

1. John Miller, Jr., *Guadalcanal, the First Offensive, U.S. Army in World War II, The War in the Pacific* (Washington, DC: GPO, Center of Military History, U.S. Army, 1995), 1. Also available online at: *http://www.ibiblio.org/hyperwar/USA-/USA-P-Guadalcanal/index.html* (accessed March 11, 2006).

2. *"D-Day and H-Hour" Combat Orders.* (Fort Leavenworth, Kansas: The General Service Schools Press, The General Service Schools, 1922) U.S. Army Center of Military History Online, *http://www.army.mil/cmh/* (accessed March 27, 2006).

3. Hough, Ludwig, and Shaw, *Marine Corps Operations,* vol. 1, 249.

4. Ibid.

5. George Carroll Dyer, Vice Admiral, USN (Ret.), *The Amphibians Came to Conquer,* vol. 1 (Washington, DC: GPO, U.S. Department of the Navy, 1972), 351. Also available online at *http://www.ibiblio.org/hyperwar/USN/ACTC/index.html* (accessed February 18, 2006) (hereafter cited as Dyer, *The Amphibians,* vol. 1).

6. Ibid., 352.

7. Jeter A. Isley and Philip A. Crowl, *The U.S. Marines and Amphibious War* (Princeton NJ: Princeton University Press, 1951), 132 (hereafter cited as Isley and Crowl, *U.S. Marines and Amphibious War*).

8. Hough, Ludwig, and Shaw, *Marine Corps Operations,* vol. I, 257.

Chapter 8

1. Bemis and Shaw, *Marine Corps Operations,* vol. 5, 679.

2. Ibid., 688–689.

3. Shaw and Donnelly, *Blacks,* 17.

4. Ibid., 5.

5. Evans, "Men from Montford Point."

6. "Negro Recruit Training Now In Progress," *Philadelphia Tribune,* date stamped September 19, 1942 (Historical Reference Branch, History Division, USMC).

7. Col. S.A. Woods, Jr., letter to Commanding General, Camp Lejeune, NC, dated January 25, 1944, Subj.: Lt. Col. Floyd A. Stephenson—Departure of the 51st Defense Battalion from Montford Point Camp, N.C. with statements (Historical Reference Branch, History Division, USMC).

8. Shaw and Donnelley, *Blacks,* 5.

9. Brewer interview.

10. Memorandum for the Director (Division of Plans and Policies) dated December 26, 1942, Subject: Colored Personnel (Historical Reference Branch, History Division, USMC).

11. Frequently Requested, Headquarters, United States Marine Corps, History and Museums Division, *http://hqinet001.hqmc.usmc.mil/HD/Historical/Customes_Traditions/Brief_History_USMC.htm* (accessed March 18, 2006).

12. Bernard C. Nalty, Truman R. Strobridge and Edwin T. Turnbladh, *United States Marine Corps Ranks and Grades, 1775–1969,* rev. ed. Roland P. Gill (Historical Reference Branch, History Division, USMC, 1970).

13. Vince Patton, Master Chief Petty Officer of the Coast Guard, *Old Military Pay Tables, http://www.uscg.mil/hq/mcpocg/1pay/ompt.html* (accessed March 6, 2006).

14. Shaw and Donnelly, *Blacks,* 6.

15. Johnson interview.

Chapter 9

1. Brewer interview.

2. "Articles for the Government of the United States Navy, 1930," Department of the Navy—Bureau of Navigation (Washington, DC: GPO, U.S. Department of the Navy, 1932), *http://www.history.navy.mil/faqs/faq59–7.htm* (accessed December 28, 2005).

3. Brewer interview.

4. Ibid.

5. Ibid.

6. Ibid.

7. Memorandum from the Director, Division of Plans and Policies, to the Commandant, U.S. Marine Corps, dated October 29, 1942, Subject: Enlistment of colored personnel in the Marine Corps Reserve (Historical Reference Branch, History Division, USMC).

8. Nalty, *African American Marines,* 10.

9. J.S. Adams, Col. USMC (Ret), personal interview, August 11, 2006 (hereafter cited as Adams interview).

10. Anonymous, "New Rifle Marksmanship Course," *Leatherneck Magazine,* September 1940, 22. Used with permission of copyright owner.

11. H.K. Jackson, "Camp Matthews ... Producer of Riflemen," *Marine Corps Gazette,* October 1943, 49. Used with permission of copyright owner.

12. Adams interview.

13. Eugene Smith, personal interview, January–August 2006 (hereafter cited as Smith interview).

14. Brewer interview.

15. Anonymous, "New Rifle Marksmanship Course," *Leatherneck Magazine*, September 1940, 22. Used with permission of copyright owner.

16. Brewer interview.

17. Shaw and Donnelley, *Blacks*, 5.

18. "Marines in World War II," fact sheet (Historical Reference Branch, History Division, USMC), 5.

19. Brewer interview.

20. Ibid.

21. Ibid.

22. Blount interview.

23. Glenn J. White, personal interview, October 4, 2005 (hereafter cited as White interview).

Chapter 10

1. Memorandum for the Chief of Naval Personnel from the Commandant of the Marine Corps, dated April 1, 1943, Subject: Negro Registrants to be Inducted into the Marine Corps (Historical Reference Branch, History Division, USMC).

2. *Selected World War II Marine Corps Chronology 1941–1946, Campaign Chronologies of the United States Marine Corps*, United States Marine Corps History Division, Headquarters Marine Corps, Washington DC, *http://hqinet001.hqmc.usmc.mil/hd/Historical/Chronologies/Campaign/WWII_1941–1946.htm* (accessed February 13, 2006).

3. Memorandum for the Director (Division of Plans and Policies) dated December 26, 1942, Subject: Colored Personnel (Historical Reference Branch, History Division, USMC).

4. Letter of Instruction No. 310, from the Commandant of the Marine Corps to All Commanding Officers, dated January 6, 1943, Subject: Change of Present Mess Branch to Commissary Branch and Establishment of a Messman Branch (Historical Reference Branch, History Division, USMC).

5. Melvin Borden, personal interview, October 3, 2005 (hereafter cited as Borden interview).

6. Letter from the Commandant, U.S. Marine Corps, to Distribution List, dated March 20, 1943, Subject: Colored Personnel (formerly classified CONFIDENTIAL) (Historical Reference Branch, History Division, USMC).

7. Ibid.

8. "Marines in World War II," undated fact sheet (Historical Reference Branch, History Division, USMC). Also, MacGregor, *Integration*, 103.

9. Letter from the Commandant of the U.S. Marine Corps to Distribution List, dated March 20, 1943, Subject: Colored Personnel (formerly classified CONFIDENTIAL) (Historical Reference Branch, History Division, USMC).

10. *Philadelphia Tribune*, "Negro Recruit Training Now in Progress," OWI date stamped September 19, 1942; *Civilians Made into Marines at LeJeune* [sic], *Baltimore Afro-American*, date stamped November 27, 1943 (Historical Reference Branch, History Division, USMC).

11. Dyer, *The Amphibians*, vol. 1, 592.

Chapter 11

1. Hough, Ludwig, and Shaw, *Marine Corps Operations*, vol. 1, 372.

2. Jon T. Hoffman, Major, USMCR, *From Makin to Bougainville: Marine Raiders in the Pacific War*, Marines in World War II Commemorative Series (Washington, DC: Marine Corps Historical Center, Building 58, Washington Navy Yard), 1995, http://www.nps.gov/wapa/indepth/extContent/usmc/pcn-190–003130–00/index.htm (accessed March 7, 2006).

3. Isley and Crowl, *U.S. Marines and Amphibious War*, 173–174.

4. Hough, Ludwig, and Shaw, *Marine Corps Operations*, vol. 1, 32.

5. George W. Garand and Truman R. Strobridge, *Western Pacific Operations*, vol. IV of *History of U.S. Marine Corps Operations in World War II* (Washington, DC: GPO, Historical Division, Headquarters, U.S. Marine Corps, 1971), 22–29 (hereafter cited as Garand and Strobridge, *Marine Corps Operations*, vol. 4).

6. Shaw and Donnelly, *Blacks*, 30.

Chapter 12

1. Brewer interview.

2. Robert L. Sherrod, *History of Marine Corps Aviation in World War II* (Baltimore, MD: The Nautical & Aviation Publishing Co., 1980), 47 (hereafter cited as Sherrod, *Aviation*).

3. Extract from Operational Diary, 7 Dec 41–31 Aug 45, G-1 (M-1) Section, Division of Plans and Policies, HQMC, title: Colored Personnel (Historical Reference Branch, History Division, USMC) (hereafter cited as Operational Diary, 7 Dec 41–31 Aug 45).

4. Shaw and Donnelly, *Blacks*, 32.

5. "Ships of the U.S. Navy, 1940–1945, DD–Destroyers," *http://www.ibiblio.org/hyperwar/USN/ships/ships-dd.html#dd674* (accessed March 2, 2006).

6. Henry I. Shaw, Jr., and Major Douglas T. Kane, USMC, *Isolation of Rabaul*, vol. 2 of *History of U.S. Marine Corps Operations in World War II* (Washington, DC: Historical Branch, G-3 Division, Headquarters, U.S. Marine Corps, 1963), 32 (hereafter cited as Shaw and Kane, *Marine Corps Operations*, vol. 2).

7. Dyer, *The Amphibians*, vol. 1, 588.

8. Bernard C. Nalty, *The Right to Fight: African American Marines in World War II* (Washington, DC: History and Museums Division, Headquarters, U.S. Marine Corps, 1995), 11. Also available

online at http://www.nps.gov/wapa/indepth/ext
Content/usmc/pcn-190–003132-00/index.htm
(accessed October 31, 2005) (hereafter cited as
Nalty, *Right to Fight*).
9. Operational Diary, 7 Dec 41–31 Aug 45, 97.
10. Shaw and Donnelly, *Blacks*, 30.
11. Ibid., 16.
12. Shaw and Donnelley, *Blacks*, 17.
13. Matt Schudel, Obituary, "Frederick C.
Branch; Was 1st Black Officer in U.S. Marine
Corps," *Washington Post*, April 13, 2005, B06,
*http://www.washingtonpost.com/wp-dyn/articles/A
48243–2005Apr12.html* (accessed March 22, 2006).
14. Elizabeth Dole, U.S. Senator for North Carolina, "North Carolina Native the First African
American to Be Commissioned as a U.S. Marine
Officer," press releases, "Senators Dole, Burr Sponsor Resolution Honoring Frederick C. Branch,"
http://dole.senate.gov/ (accessed March 22, 2006).
15. Mark Davis, "How a Phila. [sic] man
reshaped the Marines," *Philadelphia Inquirer*,
August 1, 1997, B1, B10.
16. Smith interview.
17. Letter of Instruction No. 421, from the
Commandant of the Marine Corps to All Commanding Officers, dated May 14, 1943, Subject:
Colored Personnel (formerly classified CONFI-
DENTIAL) (Historical Reference Branch, History
Division, USMC).
18. "Bare Secret Marine Order on Race,"
Chicago (IL) Defender, February 16, 1946, (Historical Reference Branch, History Division, USMC).
19. Curtis W. LeGette, Lt. Col., USMC (Ret.),
interview dated February 8, 1972 (Historical Reference Branch, History Division, USMC), 7 (hereafter cited as LeGette interview).
20. Shaw and Donnelly, *Blacks*, 17.
21. Brewer interview.
22. Ibid.
23. Ibid.
24. Shaw and Donnelly, *Blacks*, 12.
25. Gerald Astor, *The Right to Fight* (Novato:
Presidio Press, 1998), 229, 262 (hereafter cited as
Astor, *Right to Fight*).
26. Ibid., 228.

Chapter 13

1. Shaw and Donnelley, *Blacks*, 17.
2. Ibid.
3. Ibid.
4. USS *Slater*, Weapons Systems, 20mm Oerlikon gun, *http://www.ussslater.org/weapons/20mm.
html* (accessed February 27, 2006).
5. Ibid.
6. Ibid.
7. Paul E. Semmons, Col. USA, *The Hammer
of Hell: The Coming of Age of Antiaircraft Artillery
in WW II*, *http://airdefense.bliss.army.mil/adamag/
Hammer/Chapter1.htm* (accessed February 27,
2006).
8. Melson, *Condition Red*, 14.

9. "A Beginner's Guide to the *Skylighters*, WW
II Antiaircraft Artillery, Searchlights, and Radar,"
*http://www.skylighters.org/introduction/index.html#to
p* (accessed February 28, 2006).
10. Brewer interview.
11. *Standing Operating Procedure for Radar Air
and Surface Warning and Radar Fire Control in the
Marine Corps*, dated May 15, 1943 (Historical Reference Branch, History Division, USMC).
12. "Historical Electronics Museum, Inc, Baltimore, MD," letter dated February 16, 1993 (Historical Reference Branch, History Division,
USMC).
13. Melson, *Condition Red*, 26.
14. Ibid., 14.

Chapter 14

1. Nalty, *Right to Fight*, 11–12.
2. Shaw and Donnelly, *Blacks*, 32.
3. Ibid.
4. *Somewhere in the South Pacific (Russell
Islands)*, Nov. 19 [delayed] (Historical Reference
Branch, History Division, USMC).
5. Shaw and Donnelly, *Blacks*, 32.
6. MacGregor, *Integration*, 111.
7. Shaw and Donnelly, *Blacks*, 16.
8. "Historical Chronology of Atlantic Coastal
Waterways," U.S. Army Corps of Engineers,
*www.usace.army.mil/inet/usace-docs/misc/nws83–
10/chron.pdf* (accessed April 27, 2006).
9. Shaw and Donnelly, *Blacks*, 17.

Chapter 15

1. *Not One Officer in Marines*, editorial, *Richmond Afro-American*, clip forwarded by U.S.
Marine Corps Recruiting Service to OWI, date
stamped August 19, 1944 (Historical Reference
Branch, History Division, USMC).
2. Blount interview.
3. Ibid.
4. Jesse J. Johnson, Lt. Col., AUS (Ret), *Roots
of Two Black Marine Sergeants Major*, (Hampton,
VA: Ebony Publishing, 1978), 105.
5. Ibid., 48.
6. Blount interview.
7. Ibid.
8. Cameron, *American Samurai*, 57.
9. *Nightfighters*, unpublished manuscript,
authorship credited to Capt Elmer Wilde (Historical Reference Branch, History Division, USMC),
3.
10. Ibid., 4.
11. Shaw and Donnelley, *Blacks*, 30.
12. Astor, *Right to Fight*, 229.
13. MacGregor, *Integration*, 103.
14. Smith interview.
15. LSTs of the United States Navy, Navy His-
tory.com, *http://www.multied.com/NAVY/patrol/10.
html* (accessed February 27, 2006).

16. Smith interview.
17. "Ships of the U.S. Navy, 1940–1945: Transports," http://www.ibiblio.org/hyperwar/USN/USN-ships.html#ap (accessed February 27, 2006).
18. Smith interview.
19. Isely and Crowl, *Amphibious War*, 179.

Chapter 16

1. George Carroll Dyer, Vice Admiral, USN (Ret.), *The Amphibians Came to Conquer*, vol. 2 (Washington, DC: U.S. Department of the Navy), 725. Also available online at *http://www.ibiblio.org/hyperwar/USN/ACTC/index.html* (accessed February 18, 2006) (hereafter cited as Dyer, *The Amphibians*, vol. 2).
2. Henry I. Shaw, Jr., Bernard C. Nalty and Edwin T. Turnbladh, *Central Pacific Drive*. vol. III of *History of U.S. Marine Corps Operations in World War II* (Washington, DC: GPO, Historical Branch, G-3 Division, Headquarters, U.S. Marine Corps,1968), 112 (hereafter cited as Shaw, Nalty, and Turnbladh, *Marine Corps Operations*, vol. 3).
3. Ibid.
4. Marine Corps Administrative History, typed manuscript dated 1946 (Historical Reference Branch, History Division, USMC), 15.
5. John R. Griffin, "My Life in the Marine Corps," unpublished manuscript (Archives Branch, Alfred M. Gray Research Center, Marine Corps University), 3 (hereafter cited as Griffin MS).
6. Ibid., 2.
7. Ibid., 4.
8. Alvin J. Banker, M. Sgt., USMCR, interviewed by Steve Heffner, December 20, 2000, WW II through the Eyes of the Cape Fear, UNCW and Cape Fear Museum, Wilmington, NC, *http://capefearww2.uncwil.edu/voices/banker046.html* (accessed February 13, 2006).
9. Griffin MS, 4.
10. Ibid.
11. Ibid., 6.
12. Ibid.
13. Ibid., 7.
14. Brewer interview.
15. LeGette interview, 7.
16. Shaw and Donnelley, *Blacks*, 23.
17. Memorandum to the Commanding Officer [Montford Point Camp] from Provost Marshal dated January 20, 1944, Subject: Report of disturbance around the theater at Montford Point, January 19, 1944 (Historical Reference Branch, History Division, USMC).
18. From Col. S. A. Woods, Jr., to Commanding General, Camp Lejeune, NC, dated January 25, 1944, Subj.: Lt. Col. Floyd A. Stephenson—Departure of the 51st Defense Battalion from Montford Point Camp, N.C. with statements (Historical Reference Branch, History Division, USMC).
19. Ibid.
20. Brewer interview.
21. "Marines in World War II," undated fact sheet (Historical Reference Branch, History Division, USMC).
22. MacGregor, *Integration*, 109.
23. LeGette interview, 4.
24. Shaw and Donnelley, *Blacks*, 17.

Chapter 17

1. Nalty, *Right to Fight*, 17.
2. Griffin MS, 8.
3. Ibid., 9.
4. Dyer, *The Amphibians*, vol. 2, 846.
5. *Staff Officers' Field Manual for Amphibious Operations, Organization, Technical and Logistical Data* (Fleet Marine Force, Pacific, September 10, 1944), 40 (SECRET—Declassified August 10, 1969). Also available online at *http://www.ibiblio.org/hyperwar/USMC/* (accessed March 16, 2006).
6. Shaw, Nalty, and Turnbladh, *Marine Corps Operations*, vol. 3, 134.
7. Dyer, *The Amphibians*, vol. 2, 745.
8. Griffin MS, 8.
9. Melson, *Condition Red*, 10.
10. Shaw and Donnelly, *Blacks*, 23.
11. *7th Separate Pack Howitzer Battery*, working papers (Historical Reference Branch, History Division, USMC).

Chapter 18

1. Smith interview.
2. Ibid.
3. Melson, *Condition Red*, 10.
4. LeGette, interview, 6.
5. *Staff Officers' Field Manual for Amphibious Operations, Organization, Technical and Logistical Data* (Fleet Marine Force, Pacific, September 10, 1944), 67 (SECRET—Declassified August 10, 1969). Also available online at *http://www.ibiblio.org/hyperwar/USMC/* (accessed March 16, 2006).
6. Shaw and Donnelly, *Blacks*, 19.
7. American Merchant Marine at War, World War II, *http://www.usmm.org/index.html#anchor 252856* (accessed March 16, 2006).

Chapter 19

1. J. Leon Holley, Cpl., *20th Marine Depot Company, 7th Field Depot*, dated April 13, 1945 (Historical Reference Branch, History Division, USMC), 1 (hereafter cited as Holley, *20th Marine Depot Company*).
2. Blount interview.
3. Holley, *20th Marine Depot Company*, 1.
4. Ibid.
5. Dyer, *The Amphibians*, vol. 2, 623.
6. LeGette interview, 4.
7. Dyer, *The Amphibians*, vol. 2, 728
8. Tuvalu (Ellice Islands), *http://www.pacificwrecks.com/provinces/tuvalu.html* (accessed March 20, 2006).

9. Sherrod, *Aviation*, 223.
10. American Merchant Marine at War, *http://www.usmm.org/index.html#anchor252856* (accessed March 16, 2006).
11. Shaw and Donnelly, *Blacks,* 19.
12. Brewer interview.
13. Mark Davis, "How a Phila. [sic] man reshaped the Marines," *Philadelphia Inquirer*, August 1, 1997, B1, B10.
14. MacGregor, *Integration*, 109.
15. LeGette interview, 5.
16. Ibid., 7.
17. Shaw and Donnelly, *Blacks,* 20.
18. LeGette interview, 9.
19. Nalty, *African American Marines*, 16.
20. Melson, *Condition Red,* 19.
21. Garand and Strobridge, *Marine Corps Operations,* vol. 4, 23–24.
22. Ibid., 27–28.

Chapter 20

1. Dyer, *The Amphibians*, vol. 2, 728.
2. Shaw, Nalty, and Turnbladh, *Marine Corps Operations,* vol. 3, 439.
3. Carl W. Hoffman, Major, USMC, *Saipan: The Beginning of the End*. USMC Historical Monograph (Washington, DC: GPO, Historical Branch, G-3 Division, Headquarters, U.S. Marine Corps, 1950), 2. Also available online at *http://www.ibiblio.org/hyperwar/USMC/USMC-M-Saipan/USMC-M-Saipan-7.html* (hereafter cited as Hoffman, *Saipan*).
4. Shaw, Nalty, and Turnbladh, *Marine Corps Operations,* vol. 3, 44.
5. Phillip A. Crowl, *Pacific Ocean Area Unit of Fire for Ground Weapons (TF 56 Rpt FORAGER, Incl E, G-4 Rpt, Incl A), Appendix B, Campaign in the Marianas, The War in the Pacific, U.S. Army in World War II* (Washington, DC: GPO, U.S. Army Center of Military History, 1959), 452.
6. Hoffman, *Saipan:* 23.
7. Blount interview.
8. Hoffman, *Saipan,* 279.
9. Dyer, *The Amphibians*, vol. 2, 903.
10. Blount interview.
11. Dyer, *The Amphibians*, vol. 2, 902.
12. Ibid.
13. Ibid., 903.
14. Shaw and Donnelley, *Blacks*, 34.
15. "Ships of the U.S. Navy, 1940–1945, Small Landing Craft," *http://www.ibiblio.org/hyperwar/USN/ships/ships-dd.html#dd674* (accessed March 2, 2006).
16. Hoffman, *Saipan,* 56.
17. Holley, *20th Marine Depot Company,* 2.
18. Ibid.
19. Shaw and Donnelley, *Blacks*, 34.
20. Charles R. Vandergrift, Sgt., Marine Corps Combat Correspondent, *Saipan, Marianas Islands* #831 [delayed] (Historical Reference Branch, History Division, USMC), 3 (hereafter cited as Vandergrift, *Saipan.*).

21. Ibid., 1.
22. Ibid., 3.
23. David M. Davies, First Sgt., *Officers Pleased with Performance of Race Fighters*, distributed by the Associated Negro Press (Historical Reference Branch, History Division, USMC) (hereafter cited as Davies, *Officers Pleased with Performance*).
24. Isley and Crowl, *U.S. Marines and Amphibious War*, 328.
25. Davies, *Officers Pleased With Performance.*
26. Vandergrift, *Saipan*, 1.
27. Vandergrift, *Saipan*, 4.
28. Shaw and Donnelley, *Blacks*, 33.
29. Shaw, Nalty, and Turnbladh, *Marine Corps Operations,* vol. 3, 278.
30. Shaw and Donnelley, *Blacks*, 34.
31. Isley and Crowl, *U.S. Marines and Amphibious War*, 328.
32. Vandergrift, *Saipan*, 3.
33. *Nightfighters,* unpublished manuscript, authorship credited to Capt Elmer Wilde (Historical Reference Branch, History Division, USMC), 2 (hereafter cited as Wilde, *Nightfighters*).
34. Wilde, *Nightfighters,* 2.
35. Vandergrift, *Saipan*, 2.
36. Davies, *Officers Pleased with Performance.*
37. Holley, *20th Marine Depot Company,* 2.
38. Blount interview.
39. Ibid.
40. *Negro Marine Battle Casualties*, HQMC Casualty Card Printout 9 April 1948 (Historical Reference Branch, History Division, USMC) (hereafter cited as *Negro Marine Battle Casualties*).
41. Shaw and Donnelley, *Blacks*, 35.
42. Holley, *20th Marine Depot Company*, 3.
43. Gilbert B. Bailey, Sgt., Marine Corps Combat Correspondent, *Saipan, Marianas Islands* #165 [delayed] (Historical Reference Branch, History Division, USMC).
44. Isley and Crowl, *U.S. Marines and Amphibious War*, 310.
45. Dyer, *The Amphibians*, vol. 2, *968.*
46. Shaw and Donnelley, *Blacks*, 35.
47. Shaw, Nalty, and Turnbladh, *Marine Corps Operations,* vol. 3, 639.

Chapter 21

1. Shaw and Donnelly, *Blacks*, 35.
2. Isley and Crowl. *U.S. Marines and Amphibious War*, 368.
3. O. R. Lodge, Major, USMC, *The Recapture of Guam*, USMC Historical Monograph (Washington, DC: GPO, Historical Branch, G-3 Division, Headquarters, U.S. Marine Corps, 1950), 55 (hereafter cited as Lodge, *Guam*).
4. Dyer, *The Amphibians*, vol. 2, *937.*
5. Ibid., 968.
6. Shaw, Nalty, and Turnbladh, *Marine Corps Operations,* vol. 3, 474.
7. Lodge, *Guam,* 55.
8. Ibid., 56.

9. Shaw and Donnelly, *Blacks*, 35.
10. Ibid., 36.
11. Shaw, Nalty, and Turnbladh, *Marine Corps Operations,* vol. 3, 641.
12. Wilde, *Nightfighters*, 8.
13. Shaw and Donnelly, *Blacks*, 37.
14. The Guam Web site, *http://ns.gov.gu/index.html* (accessed April 8, 2006).

Chapter 22

1. Melson, *Condition Red*, 22.
2. Griffin MS, 10.
3. Shaw and Donnelley, *Blacks*, 21.
4. Griffin MS, 10.
5. Shaw and Donnelley, *Blacks*, 21.
6. Ibid.
7. Griffin MS, 12.
8. Ibid., 13.
9. *Philadelphia Afro-American,* "Not One Officer in Marines," August 19, 1944, clip forwarded by U.S. Marine Corps Recruiting Service to OWI, date stamped August 19, 1944 (Historical Reference Branch, History Division, USMC).
10. Operational Diary, 7 Dec 41–31 Aug 45, 103.
11. Robert Sherrod, "Army & Navy, Marines," *Time*, July 24, 1944, 59. (Also, Historical Reference Branch, History Division, USMC).
12. *Philadelphia Afro-American,* "Not One Officer in Marines," August 19, 1944, clip forwarded by U.S. Marine Corps Recruiting Service to OWI, date stamped August 19, 1944 (Historical Reference Branch, History Division, USMC).
13. *Baltimore Afro-American*, "Mr. President, What of the Marines?" and "Suggestion for the Next Broadcast," August 19, 1944, OWI date stamped August 19, 1944 (Historical Reference Branch, History Division, USMC).
14. Mark J. Campbell, "Enlisted Naval Aviation Pilots: A Legacy of Service," *Naval Aviation News* 86, no. 1, November–December 2003, 34–37. Also available online at *http://www.history.navy.mil/nan/backissues/2000s/2003/nd03.htm* (accessed March 22, 2006).
15. Bemis M. Frank and Henry I. Shaw, Jr., *Victory and Occupation*, vol. 5 of *History of U.S. Marine Corps Operations in World War II* (Washington, DC: GPO, Historical Branch, G-3 Division, Headquarters, U.S. Marine Corps, 1968), 445 (hereafter cited as Frank and Shaw, *Marine Corps Operations,* vol. 5).
16. Operational Diary, 7 Dec 41–31 Aug 45, 103.
17. Brewer interview.
18. Ibid.
19. Ibid.
20. Ibid.
21. Shaw and Donnelley, *Blacks*, 25.
22. *52d Defense Battalion*, dated November 8, 1949 (Historical Reference Branch, History Division, USMC), 2.
23. Shaw and Donnelley, *Blacks*, 21.

Chapter 23

1. Miles Q. Romney, *A Brief Account of the Twenty-third Marine Depot Company,* unpublished manuscript (Historical Reference Branch, History Division, USMC), 1 (hereafter cited as Romney, *Twenty-third Marine Depot Company*).
2. Ibid., 2.
3. Ibid., 3.
4. "Marines in World War II," fact sheet (Historical Reference Branch, History Division, USMC).
5. Memorandum to Asst. Comdt. from Dir, Plans & Policies, dated July 5, 1944, Subject: Stewards' Branch Personnel (Historical Reference Branch, History Division, USMC).
6. MacGregor, *Integration,* 108.
7. Garand and Strobridge, *Marine Corps Operations,* vol. 4, 52.
8. Wilde, *Nightfighters*, 6.
9. Garand and Strobridge, *Marine Corps Operations,* vol. 4, 83.
10. Wilde, *Nightfighters*, 8.
11. Garand and Strobridge, *Marine Corps Operations,* vol. 4, 87.
12. Ibid., 109.
13. Bill D. Ross, *Peleliu: Tragic Triumph* (New York: Random House, 1991), 194.
14. Gordon D. Gayle, B. Gen., USMC (Ret.), *Bloody Beaches: The Marines at Peleliu*, USMC Historical Monograph (Washington, DC: Marine Corps Historical Center, Bldg. 58, Washington Navy Yard, 1996). Also available online at *http://www.nps.gov/wapa/indepth/extContent/usmc/pcn-190-003137-00/sec12.htm* (accessed April 14, 2006) (hereafter cited as Gayle, *Bloody Beaches*).
15. Garand and Strobridge, *Marine Corps Operations,* vol. 4, 85.
16. Gayle, *Bloody Beaches* (accessed April 14, 2006).
17. Ross, *Peleliu,* 196.
18. Gayle, *Bloody Beaches* (accessed April 14, 2006).
19. *Negro Marine Battle Casualties.*
20. Ibid.
21. Shaw and Donnelley, *Blacks*, 37.
22. *Unit Citations*, working papers (Historical Reference Branch, History Division, USMC).
23. Gayle, *Bloody Beaches* (accessed April 14, 2006).
24. Isley and Crowl, U.S. Marines and Amphibious War, 575.
25. *10th Marine Depot Company "The Barracuda Leathernecks,"* working papers (Historical Reference Branch, History Division, USMC) (hereafter cited as *10th Marine Depot Company*).
26. Smith interview.
27. Hough, Ludwig, and Shaw, *Marine Corps Operations,* vol. 1, 243, 245.
28. Smith interview.
29. Ibid.
30. *10th Marine Depot Company.*

Chapter 24

1. John R. Griffin, "My Life in the Marine Corps," unpublished manuscript (Archives Branch, Alfred M. Gray Research Center, Marine Corps University), 13.
2. Henry I. Shaw, Jr., Bernard C. Nalty and Edwin T. Turnbladh, *Central Pacific Drive*, vol. 3 of *History of U.S. Marine Corps Operations in World War II* (Washington, DC: GPO, Historical Branch, G-3 Division, Headquarters, U.S. Marine Corps, 1968), 568.
3. Romney, *Twenty-third Marine Depot Company*.
4. Lodge, *Guam*, 164.
5. MacGregor, *Integration*, 92.
6. Shaw and Donnelley, *Blacks*, 45.
7. Nalty, *Right to Fight*, 23.
8. Shaw and Donnelley, *Blacks*, 45.
9. Romney, *Twenty-third Marine Depot Company*.
10. Borden interview.
11. Orvia O. Cottman, personal interview, October 4, 2005.

Chapter 25

1. "Marines in World War II," undated fact sheet (Historical Reference Branch, History Division, USMC).
2. Frank and Shaw, *Marine Corps Operations*, vol. 5, 23.
3. Ibid., 24.
4. White interview.
5. Ibid.
6. Ibid.
7. Dyer, *The Amphibians*, vol. 2, 980.
9. Garand and Strobridge, *Marine Corps Operations*, vol. 4, 443.
10. Isely and Crowl, *U.S. Marines and Amphibious War*, 432.
11. Garand and Strobridge, *Marine Corps Operations*, vol. 4, 478.
12. Shaw and Donnelley, *Blacks*, 39.
13. Isely and Crowl, *U.S. Marines and Amphibious War*, 438.
14. Dyer, *The Amphibians*, vol. 2, 1023.
15. Ibid.
16. Isely and Crowl, *U.S. Marines and Amphibious War*, 478.
17. Dyer, *The Amphibians*, vol. 2, 1024, 25.
18. Cyril J. O'Brien, "Montford Point to Iwo Jima: Combat Bridged the Racial Divide," *Leatherneck*, April 2005. Used with permission of copyright owner (hereafter cited as O'Brien, *Montford Point to Iwo Jima*).
19. Ibid.
20. Dyer, *The Amphibians*, vol. 2, 1027.
21. *Negro Marine Battle Casualties*.
22. Ibid.
23. Shaw and Donnelley, *Blacks*, 39.
24. O'Brien, *Montford Point to Iwo Jima*.

25. Ibid.
26. Ibid.
27. *Negro Marine Battle Casualties*.
28. Ibid.
29. O'Brien, *Montford Point to Iwo Jima*.
30. Garand and Strobridge, vol. 4, *U.S. Marine Corps Operations*, 708.
31. O'Brien, *Montford Point to Iwo Jima*.
32. Garand and Strobridge, vol. 4, *U.S. Marine Corps Operations*, 710.
33. Whitman S. Bartley, Lt. Col., USMC, *Iwo Jima: Amphibious Epic*, Marines in World War II Historical Monograph (Washington, DC: Historical Section, Division of Public Information, Headquarters, U.S. Marine Corps, 1954) 242.
34. Isely and Crowl, *U.S. Marines and Amphibious War*, 520.
35. Garand and Strobridge, *Marine Corps Operations*, vol. 4, 712.

Chapter 26

1. *Houston Informer*, "Navy Now Has 34 Officers; Marines None," January 27, 1945, OWI date stamped January 27, 1945 (Historical Reference Branch, History Division, USMC).
2. Letter from the Commandant of the U.S. Marine Corps to Distribution List, dated March 20, 1943, Subject: Colored Personnel (formerly classified CONFIDENTIAL) (Historical Reference Branch, History Division, USMC).
3. *A Brief History of the Negro Officer in the Marine Corps* (Historical Reference Branch, History Division, USMC), 1.
4. Shaw and Donnelley, *Blacks*, 47, 48.
5. Brewer interview.
6. *52d Defense Battalion*, dated November 8, 1949 (Historical Reference Branch, History Division, USMC), 3.
7. Shaw and Donnelley, *Blacks*, 27.
8. Griffin MS, 14.

Chapter 27

1. Dyer, *The Amphibians*, vol. 2, 1066.
2. Frank and Shaw, *Marine Corps Operations*, vol. 5, 59.
3. Ibid., 240.
4. Shaw and Donnelley, *Blacks*, 41.
5. Joseph H. Alexander, Col., USMC (Ret), *The Final Campaign: Marines in the Victory on Okinawa*, Commemorative Series (Washington, DC: Marine Corps Historical Center, Building 58, Washington Navy Yard, 1996).
6. Nalty, *Right to Fight*, 24.
7. Isely and Crowl, *U.S. Marines and Amphibious War*, 539.
8. Frank and Shaw, *Marine Corps Operations*, vol. 5, 169.
9. *Negro Marine Battle Casualties*.
10. *10th Marine Depot Company*.
11. Shaw and Donnelley, *Blacks*, 41.

12. Frank and Shaw, *Marine Corps Operations,* vol. 5, 197.
13. *Negro Marine Battle Casualties.*
14. Ibid.
15. *10th Marine Depot Company.*
16. Smith interview.
17. Frank and Shaw, *Marine Corps Operations,* vol. 5, 256, 272.
18. Blount interview.
19. Frank and Shaw, *Marine Corps Operations,* vol. 5, 402.
20. *10th Marine Depot Company.*
21. *Cleveland Herald,* "Negro Marines Show Mettle in 'Passing the Ammunition,'" July 13, 1945 (Historical Reference Branch, History Division, USMC).
22. Shaw and Donnelley, *Blacks*, 41.
23. Griffin MS, 14, 15.
24. Isely and Crowl, *U.S. Marines and Amphibious War,* 579.

Chapter 28

1. Griffin MS, 16.
2. Frank and Shaw, *Marine Corps Operations,* vol. 5, 436.
3. Ibid., 441.
4. Ibid., 442.
5. White interview.
6. *Kansas City (MO) Call,* "Depot Companies and High Point Men Home," December 14, 1945, OWI date stamped December 14, 1945 (Historical Reference Branch, History Division, USMC).
7. Smith interview.
8. Blount interview.
9. *Kansas City (MO) Call,* "Leathernecks to Return Home Soon," November 23, 1945, OWI date stamped November 23, 1945 (Historical Reference Branch, History Division, USMC).
10. Shaw and Donnelley, *Blacks*, 27.
11. *Baltimore Afro-American,* "Plight of Marines, Ignored 21 Months in Pacific, Told," October 20, 1945, OWI date stamped October 20, 1945 (Historical Reference Branch, History Division, USMC).
12. Bernard C. Nalty and Morris J. MacGregor, eds., *Blacks in the Military: Essential Documents* (Wilmington, DE: Scholarly Resources, 1981), 185.
13. Griffin MS, 19.
14. *52d Defense Battalion,* dated November 8, 1949, working papers (Historical Reference Branch, History Division, USMC).
15. Shaw and Donnelley, *Blacks*, 22.
16. Frank and Shaw, *Marine Corps Operations,* vol. 5, 815.
17. *Locations* (black Marine units) 1/1/46, working papers (Historical Reference Branch, History Division, USMC).
18. Shaw and Donnelley, *Blacks*, 42.
19. Ibid.
20. *Locations* (black Marine units) 1/1/46, working papers (Historical Reference Branch, History Division, USMC).

21. Shaw and Donnelley, *Blacks*, 43.
22. Frank and Shaw, *Marine Corps Operations,* vol. 5, 558.
23. Ibid., 816.
24. Shaw and Donnelley, *Blacks*, 43.
25. Ibid., 22.
26. White interview.
27. Shaw and Donnelley, *Blacks*, 43.

Chapter 29

1. Smith interview.
2. Memorandum from Director, Division of Plans and Policies, for Commandant of the Marine Corps, May 13, 1946, Subject: Negro personnel in the postwar Marine Corps (Historical Reference Branch, History Division, USMC).
3. "Marines in World War II," fact sheet (Historical Reference Branch, History Division, USMC), 6.
4. MacGregor, *Integration*, 103.
5. Ibid., 169.
6. *Chicago (IL) Defender,* "Bare Secret Marine Order on Race," February 16, 1946 (Historical Reference Branch, History Division, USMC).
7. Shaw and Donnelley, *Blacks*, 49.
8. Ibid., 50.
9. Paul Hagan, personal interview, October 4, 2005 (hereafter cited as Hagan interview).
10. Adner Batts, Jr., personal interview, October 3, 2005 (hereafter cited as Batts interview).
11. Hagan interview.
12. Batts interview.
13. Hagan interview.
14. Batts interview.
15. Griffin MS.
16. Brewer interview.
17. White interview.
18. Shaw and Donnelley, *Blacks*, 54.
19. Ibid., 51.

Chapter 30

1. Blount interview.
2. Borden interview.
3. Smith interview.
4. White interview.
5. Batts interview.
6. Hagan interview.
7. Cottman interview.
8. Brewer interview.

Appendix A

Marine Corps Administrative History, typed manuscript dated 1946 (Historical Reference Branch, History Division, USMC).

Appendix B

Bernard C. Nalty, Truman R. Strobridge and Edwin T. Turnbladh, *United States Marine Corps*

Ranks and Grades, 1775–1969, 1970 rev. ed. Roland P. Gill (Historical Reference Branch, History Division, USMC).

Vince Patton, Master Chief Petty Officer of the Coast Guard, *Old Military Pay Tables, http://www. uscg.mil/hq/mcpocg/1pay/ompt.html* (accessed March 6, 2006).

Appendix C

Garand and Strobridge, *Marine Corps Operations,* vol. 4, 765–773; Shaw and Donnelly, *Blacks,* 31–46.

Appendix D

Frank and Shaw, *Marine Corps Operations,* vol. 5, 843.

Appendix E

Shaw and Donnelley, *Blacks,* 30.

Appendix F

Historical Reference Branch, History Division, USMC.

Appendix G

Phillip A. Crowl, Pacific Ocean Area Unit of Fire for Ground Weapons (TF 56 Rpt FORAGER, Incl E, G-4 Rpt, Incl A), Appendix B, Campaign in the Marianas, The War in the Pacific, U.S. Army in World War II (Washington, DC: GPO, U.S. Army Center of Military History, 1959), 452.

Map Sources

1. Montford Point 1943–1945: Shaw and Donnelley, *Blacks,* 6.

2. Solomon Islands, Santa Cruz Islands and New Caledonia: Dyer, *The Amphibians,* vol. 1, 236.

3. Central and South Pacific: Dyer, *The Amphibians,* vol. 1, 231.

4. Guadalcanal Supply Lines: Dyer, *The Amphibians,* vol. 1, 418.

5. Japan to the Gilberts: Dyer, *The Amphibians,* vol. 2, 735.

6. Lower Marianas: Dyer, *The Amphibians,* vol. 1, 231.

7. Saipan: Dyer, *The Amphibians,* vol. 2, 871.

8. Guam: Dyer, *The Amphibians,* vol. 2, 926.

9. The Marshall Islands: Dyer, *The Amphibians,* vol. 1, 231.

10. Peleliu: Historical Reference Branch, History Division, USMC.

11. Iwo Jima: Dyer, *The Amphibians,* vol. 2, 990.

12. Okinawa: Dyer, *The Amphibians,* vol. 2, 1076.

Bibliography

Print

Anderson, Charles R. *Western Pacific: The United States Army Campaigns of World War II*. Washington, D.C.: U.S. Government Printing Office, Defense Department, Army, Center of Military History, 1994.

Bartley, Whitman S., Lt. Col., USMC. *Iwo Jima: Amphibious Epic*. Marines in World War II Historical Monograph. Washington, D.C.: Historical Section, Division of Public Information, Headquarters, U.S. Marine Corps, 1954.

Breard, Harold A., Cpl., USMC. "New River." *Marine Corps Gazette*, April 1944. Used with permission of copyright owner.

A Brief History of the Negro Officer in the Marine Corps. Quantico, VA: Historical Reference Branch, History Division, USMC.

Cameron, Craig M. *American Samurai*. Cambridge, UK: Cambridge University Press, 1994.

Condit, Kenneth W., Gerald Diamond, and Edwin T. Turnbladh. *Marine Corps Ground Training in World War II*. Typed manuscript, 1956. Quantico, VA: Historical Reference Branch, History Division, USMC.

Daily Digest, (Restricted), Analysis Section, Office of Public Relations, Navy Department. Dated September 2, 1944. Quantico, VA: Historical Reference Branch, History Division, USMC.

Davis, Mark. "How a Phila. [sic] man reshaped the Marines." *Philadelphia Inquirer*, August 1, 1997, B1, B10.

DeClouet, Fred. *First Black Marines: Vanguard of a Legacy*. Nashville, TN: James C. Winston, 1995.

Dyer, George Carroll, Vice Admiral, USN (Ret.). *The Amphibians Came to Conquer*. Vols. 1 and 2. Washington, D.C.: U.S. Government Printing Office, 1972.

Evans, Edward J., Sgt., USMC. "Men from Montford Point." *Leatherneck Magazine*, November 1947. Used with permission of copyright owner.

Extract from Operational Diary, 7 Dec 41–31 Aug 45, G-1 (M-1) Section, Division of Plans and Policies, HQMC. Title: Colored Personnel. Quantico, VA: Historical Reference Branch, History Division, USMC.

52d Defense Battalion. Working papers dated November 8, 1949. Quantico, VA: Historical Reference Branch, History Division, USMC.

Frank, Benis M., and Henry I. Shaw, Jr. *Victory and Occupation: History of U.S. Marine Corps Operations in World War II*. Vol. 5. Washington, D.C.: U.S. Government Printing Office, Historical Branch, G-3 Division, Headquarters, U.S. Marine Corps, 1968.

Garand, George W., and Truman R. Strobridge. *Western Pacific Operations*. Vol. 4 of *History of U.S. Marine Corps Operations in World War II*. Washington, D.C.: U.S. Government Printing Office, Historical Branch, G-3 Division, Headquarters, U.S. Marine Corps, 1971.

Griffin, John R. "My Life in the Marine Corps." Unpublished manuscript. Quantico, VA: Archives Branch, Alfred M. Gray Research Center, Marine Corps University.

Hillerman Tony, ed. *Best of the West: An Anthology of Classic Writing from the American West.* New York: HarperCollins, 1991, xv.

"Historical Electronics Museum, Inc., Baltimore, MD." Letter dated February 16, 1993. Quantico, VA: Historical Reference Branch, History Division, USMC.

History Division Comment. June 7, 1976. Quantico, VA: Historical Reference Branch, History Division, USMC.

Holley, J. Leon, Cpl. "20th Marine Depot Company, 7th Field Depot." Dated April 13, 1945. Working papers. Quantico, VA: Historical Reference Branch, History Division, USMC.

Hopkins, F. W., Lt. Col., USMC. Letter to the editor. *Marine Corps Gazette*, July 1944. Used with permission of copyright owner.

Hough, Frank O., Lieutenant Colonel, USMCR, Major Verle E. Ludwig, USMC, and Henry I. Shaw, Jr. *History of U.S. Marine Corps Operations in World War II.* Vol. 1. Washington, D.C.: U.S. Government Printing Office, Historical Branch, G-3 Division, Headquarters, U.S. Marine Corps, 1958.

Isley, Jeter A., and Philip A. Crowl. *The U.S. Marines and Amphibious War.* Princeton, NJ: Princeton University Press, 1951.

Johnson, Jesse J., Lt. Col., AUS (Ret). *Roots of Two Black Marine Sergeants Major.* Hampton, VA: Ebony, 1978.

Letter from Col. S.A. Woods, Jr., to Commanding General, Camp Lejeune, NC. Subj: Lt. Col. Floyd A. Stephenson — Departure of the 51st Defense Battalion from Montford Point Camp, N.C. with statements. Dated January 25, 1944. Quantico, VA: Historical Reference Branch, History Division, USMC.

Letter from Maj. Gen. Charles F.B. Price to Keller [E. Rockey, Maj. Gen., USMC, Director, Division of Plans and Policies, HQMC] (no subject). Dated April 24, 1943. Quantico, VA: Historical Reference Branch, History Division, USMC.

Letter from the Chief of Naval Personnel to Director of Selective Service (no subject). Dated February 6, 1943. Quantico, VA: Historical Reference Branch, History Division, USMC.

Letter from the Commandant of the U.S. Marine Corps to Distribution List. Subject: Colored Personnel (formerly classified CONFIDENTIAL). Dated March 20, 1943. Quantico, VA: Historical Reference Branch, History Division, USMC.

Letter from the Commandant, U.S. Marine Corps to District Commanders, All Reserve Districts except 10th, 14th, 15th, and 16th. Subject: Enlistment of Colored Personnel in the Marine Corps. Dated May 25, 1942. Quantico, VA: Historical Reference Branch, History Division, USMC.

Letter from the Commanding Officer, Fourth Marine Ammunition Company, Fifth Field Depot, Supply Service, Fleet Marine Force, Pacific, to the Commandant of the Marine Corps. Subj: Colored Personnel, Report of. Dated November 8, 1944. Quantico, VA: Historical Reference Branch, History Division, USMC.

Letter of Instruction No. 310. From the Commandant of the Marine Corps to All Commanding Officers. Subject: Change of Present Mess Branch to Commissary Branch and Establishment of a Messman Branch. Dated January 6, 1943. Quantico, VA: Historical Reference Branch, History Division, USMC.

Letter of Instruction No. 421. From the Commandant of the Marine Corps to All Commanding Officers. Subject: Colored Personnel (formerly classified CONFIDENTIAL). Dated May 14, 1943. Quantico, VA: Historical Reference Branch, History Division, USMC.

Locations (black Marine units) 1/1/46. Working papers. Quantico, VA: Historical Reference Branch, History Division, USMC.

Lodge, O. R., Major, USMC. *The Recapture of Guam.* USMC Historical Monograph. Washington, D.C.: U.S. Government Printing Office, Historical Branch, G-3 Division, Headquarters, U.S. Marine Corps, 1950.

MacGregor, Morris J., Jr. *Integration and the Armed Forces 1940–1965.* Washington, D.C.: U.S. Government Printing Office, Center of Military History, United States Army, 1985.

Marine Corps Administrative History. Typed manuscript dated 1946. Quantico, VA: Historical Reference Branch, History Division, USMC.

"Marines in World War II." Undated fact sheet. Quantico, VA: Historical Reference Branch, History Division, USMC.

Melson, Charles D., Major, USMC (Ret.). *Condition Red: Marine Defense Battalions in World War II.* Washington, D.C.: Marine Corps Historical Center, 1996.

Memorandum for the Chief of Naval Personnel from the Commandant of the Marine Corps. Subject: Negro Registrants to be Inducted into the Marine Corps. Dated April 1, 1943. Quantico, VA: Historical Reference Branch, History Division, USMC.

Memorandum for the Director (Division of Plans and Policies). Subject: Colored Personnel. Dated December 26, 1942. Quantico, VA: Historical Reference Branch, History Division, USMC.

Memorandum for the Executive Officer, Division of Plans and Policies, dated February 19, 1942 (black Raider Battalion). Quantico, VA: Historical Reference Branch, History Division, USMC.

Memorandum for the Secretary of the Navy from the Commandant of the Marine Corps. Subject: Enlistment of Negroes. Dated June 23, 1942. Quantico, VA: Historical Reference Branch, History Division, USMC.

Memorandum from Director, Division of Plans and Policies, for Commandant of the Marine Corps, May 13, 1946. Subject: Negro Personnel in the Postwar Marine Corps. Quantico, VA: Historical Reference Branch, History Division, USMC.

Memorandum from President Franklin Delano Roosevelt for the Secretary of the Navy (no subject). Dated February 22, 1943. Quantico, VA: Historical Reference Branch, History Division, USMC.

Memorandum from the Director, Division of Plans and Policies, to the Commandant, U.S. Marine Corps. Subject: Enlistment of Colored Personnel in the Marine Corps Reserve. Dated October 29, 1942. Quantico, VA: Historical Reference Branch, History Division, USMC.

Memorandum from the Director, Division of Plans and Policies, to the Commandant, U.S. Marine Corps. Subject: Enlistment of the Colored Race Other Than in the Messman Branch. Dated February 25, 1942. Quantico, VA: Historical Reference Branch, History Division, USMC.

Memorandum from the Secretary of the Navy for Rear Admiral Randall Jacobs (no subject). Dated February 5, 1943. Quantico, VA: Historical Reference Branch, History Division, USMC.

Memorandum to Asst. Comdt. from Dir, Plans & Policies. Subject: Stewards' Branch Personnel. Dated July 5, 1944. Quantico, VA: Historical Reference Branch, History Division, USMC.

Memorandum to the Commanding Officer [Montford Point Camp] from Provost Marshal. Subject: Report of disturbance around the theater at Montford Point, January 19, 1944. Dated January 20, 1944. Quantico, VA: Historical Reference Branch, History Division, USMC.

Nalty, Bernard C. *The Right to Fight: African American Marines in World War II*. Washington, D.C.: Marine Corps Historical Center, 1995.

Nalty, Bernard C., and Morris J. MacGregor, eds. *Blacks in the Military: Essential Documents*. Wilmington, DE: Scholarly Resources, 1981.

Nalty, Bernard C., Truman R. Strobridge, and Edwin T. Turnbladh. *United States Marine Corps Ranks and Grades, 1775–1969*. Rev. ed. Edited by Roland P. Gill. Quantico, VA: Historical Reference Branch, History Division, USMC, 1970.

Navy to Accept Negroes for General Service. News release dated April 7, 1942. Quantico, VA: Historical Reference Branch, History Division, USMC.

Negro Marine Battle Casualties. HQMC Casualty Card Printout April 9, 1948. Quantico, VA: Historical Reference Branch, History Division, USMC.

O'Brien, Cyril J. "Montford Point to Iwo Jima: Combat Bridged the Racial Divide." *Leatherneck*, April 2005. Used with permission of copyright owner.

Romney, Miles Q. "A Brief Account of the Twenty-third Marine Depot Company." Unpublished manuscript. Quantico, VA: Historical Reference Branch, History Division, USMC.

Ross, Bill D. *Peleliu: Tragic Triumph*. New York: Random House, 1991.

7th Separate Pack Howitzer Battery. Working papers. Quantico, VA: Historical Reference Branch, History Division, USMC.

Shaw, Henry I., Jr., and Ralph W. Donnelly. *Blacks in the Marine Corps*. Washington, D.C.: History and Museums Division, Headquarters, U.S. Marine Corps, 1975.

Shaw, Henry I., Jr., and Major Douglas T. Kane, USMC. *Isolation of Rabaul*. Vol. 2 of *History of U.S. Marine Corps Operations in World War II*. Washington, D.C.: U.S. Government Printing Office, Historical Branch, G-3 Division, Headquarters, U.S. Marine Corps, 1963.

Shaw, Henry I., Jr., Bernard C. Nalty, and Edwin T. Turnbladh. *Central Pacific Drive*. Vol. 3 of *History of U.S. Marine Corps Operations in World War II*. Washington, D.C.: U.S. Government Printing Office, Historical Branch, G-3 Division, Headquarters, U.S. Marine Corps, 1968.

Sherrod, Robert. "Army & Navy, Marines." *Time*, July 24, 1944, 59. (Also, Quantico, VA: Historical Reference Branch, History Division, USMC).

Standing Operating Procedure for Radar Air and Surface Warning and Radar Fire Control in the Marine Corps. Dated May 15, 1943. Quantico, VA: Historical Reference Branch, History Division, USMC.

10th Marine Depot Company "The Barracuda Leathernecks." Working papers. Quantico, VA: Historical Reference Branch, History Division, USMC.

Thomas, Gerald C., General, USMC (Ret.), Colonel Robert D. Heinl, Jr., USMC (Ret.), and Rear Admiral Arthur A. Ageton, USN (Ret.). *The Marine Officer's Guide.* 3rd ed. Annapolis, MD: United States Naval Institute Press, 1967.

20th Marine Depot Company, 7th Field Depot. Working papers dated April 13, 1945. Quantico, VA: Historical Reference Branch, History Division, USMC.

Unit Citations. Working papers. Quantico, VA: Historical Reference Branch, History Division, USMC.

[Wilde, Elmer, Capt.?]. "Nightfighters." Unpublished manuscript. Quantico, VA: Historical Reference Branch, History Division, USMC.

Combat Correspondent News Releases

Bailey, Gilbert B., Sgt., Marine Corps Combat Correspondent. "Saipan, Marianas Islands" #165 [delayed]. Quantico, VA: Historical Reference Branch, History Division, USMC.

Davies, David M., First Sgt. "Officers Pleased with Performance of Race Fighters." Distributed by the Associated Negro Press. Quantico, VA: Historical Reference Branch, History Division, USMC.

"Somewhere in the South Pacific (Russell Islands)." Nov. 19 [delayed]. Quantico, VA: Historical Reference Branch, History Division, USMC.

Vandergrift, Charles R., Sgt., Marine Corps Combat Correspondent. "Saipan, Marianas Islands" #831 [delayed]. Quantico, VA: Historical Reference Branch, History Division, USMC.

Newspaper Articles Tagged by U.S. Marine Corps Recruiting Service

Brower, W.A., ed., Richmond editor for AFRO. "Not One Officer in Marines," *Philadelphia Afro-American*, August 19, 1944. Quantico, VA: Historical Reference Branch, History Division, USMC.

Newspaper Articles Tagged by Division of Press Intelligence, Office of War Information (OWI)

Baltimore Afro-American, "Civilians Made into Marines at LeJeune" [sic], date stamped November 27, 1943. Quantico, VA: Historical Reference Branch, History Division, USMC.

Baltimore Afro-American, "Mr. President, What of the Marines?" and "Suggestion for the Next Broadcast," August 19, 1944. OWI date stamped August 19, 1944. Quantico, VA: Historical Reference Branch, History Division, USMC.

Baltimore Afro-American, "Plight of Marines, Ignored 21 Months in Pacific, Told," October 20, 1945. OWI date stamped October 20, 1945. Quantico, VA: Historical Reference Branch, History Division, USMC.

Chicago (IL) Defender, "Bare Secret Marine Order on Race," February 16, 1946. Quantico, VA: Historical Reference Branch, History Division, USMC.

Cleveland Herald, "Negro Marines Show Mettle in 'Passing the Ammunition,'" July 13, 1945. Quantico, VA: Historical Reference Branch, History Division, USMC.

Houston Informer, "Navy Now Has 34 Officers; Marines None," January 27, 1945. OWI date stamped January 27, 1945. Quantico, VA: Historical Reference Branch, History Division, USMC.

Houston Informer, "No Negro Fighter in Navy Parade," November 11, 1944. OWI date stamped November 11, 1944. Quantico, VA: Historical Reference Branch, History Division, USMC.

Kansas City (MO) Call, "Depot Companies and High Point Men Home," December 14, 1945. OWI date stamped December 14, 1945. Quantico, VA: Historical Reference Branch, History Division, USMC.

Kansas City (MO) Call, "Leathernecks to Return Home Soon," November 23, 1945. OWI date stamped November 23, 1945. Quantico, VA: Historical Reference Branch, History Division, USMC.

Philadelphia Afro-American, "Not One Officer in Marines," August 19, 1944. Clip forwarded by U.S. Marine Corps Recruiting Service to OWI, date stamped August 19, 1944. Quantico, VA: Historical Reference Branch, History Division, USMC.

Philadelphia Tribune, "Negro Recruit Training Now in Progress," OWI date stamped September 19, 1942. Quantico, VA: Historical Reference Branch, History Division, USMC.

Washington, D.C., Evening Star, "Attitude on Negro Question Distorted, Says Mrs. Roosevelt," September 6, 1944. Quantico, VA: Historical Reference Branch, History Division, USMC.

Internet

Alexander, Joseph H., Col., USMC (Ret). *The Final Campaign: Marines in the Victory on Okinawa.* Washington, D.C.: Commemorative Series, Marine Corps Historical Center, Building 58, Washington Navy Yard, 1996. *http://www.nps.gov/wapa/indepth/extContent/usmc/pcn-190–003135–00/ sec8.htm#Top* (accessed June 7, 2006).

"American Merchant Marine at War, World War II." *http://www.usmm.org/index.html#anchor252856* (accessed March 16, 2006).

"Articles for the Government of the United States Navy, 1930." Department of the Navy — Bureau of Navigation. Washington, D.C.: U.S. Government Printing Office, 1932. *http://www.history. navy.mil/faqs/faq59–7.htm* (accessed December 28, 2005).

Banker, Alvin J., M.Sgt, USMCR. Interviewed by Steve Heffner December 20, 2000. WW II through the Eyes of the Cape Fear. UNCW and Cape Fear Museum. Wilmington, NC. *http://cape-fearww2.uncwil.edu/voices/banker046.html* (accessed February 13, 2006).

BBC News. Special Report "President Roosevelt Proclaims Neutrality." *http://news.bbc.co.uk/1/hi/special_report/1999/08/99/world_war_ii/430187.stm* (accessed February 8, 2006).

"A Beginner's Guide to the *Skylighters,*" WW II Antiaircraft Artillery, Searchlights, and Radar." *http://www.skylighters.org/introduction/index.html#top* (accessed February 28, 2006).

Campbell, Mark J. "Enlisted Naval Aviation Pilots: A Legacy of Service." *Naval Aviation News* 86, no. 1, November–December 2003, 34–37. *http://www.history.navy.mil/nan/backissues/2000s/2003/ nd03.htm* (accessed March 22, 2006).

Crane, Stephen. *The Red Badge of Courage. http://www.pagebypagebooks.com/Stephen_Crane/The_ Red_Badge_of_Courage/CHAPTER_V_p2.html* (accessed December 1, 2005).

Crowl, Phillip A. *Pacific Ocean Area Unit of Fire for Ground Weapons (TF 56 Rpt FORAGER, Incl E, G-4 Rpt, Incl A). Appendix B, Campaign in the Marianas, the War in the Pacific, U.S. Army in World War II.* (Washington, D.C.: U.S. Government Printing Office, U.S. Army Center of Military History. 1959). *http://www.ibiblio.org/hyperwar/USA/USA-P-Marianas/USA-P-Marianas-B.html* (accessed March 29, 2006).

"D-Day and H-Hour." Combat Orders. The General Service Schools, Fort Leavenworth, Kansas. Fort Leavenworth, KS: The General Service Schools Press, 1922. U.S. Army Center of Military History Online. *http://www.army.mil/cmh/* (accessed March 27, 2006).

Dole, Elizabeth, U.S. Senator for North Carolina. "North Carolina Native the First African American to Be Commissioned as a U.S. Marine Officer." Press releases, "Senators Dole, Burr Sponsor Resolution Honoring Frederick C. Branch." *http://dole.senate.gov/* (accessed March 22, 2006).

Gayle, Gordon D., Brig. Gen., USMC (Ret.). *Bloody Beaches: The Marines at Peleliu.* USMC Historical Monograph. Washington, D.C.: Marine Corps Historical Center, Bldg. 58, Washington Navy Yard, 1996. *http://www.nps.gov/wapa/indepth/extContent/usmc/pcn-190–003137–00/sec12.htm* (accessed April 14, 2006).

The Guam Web site. *http://ns.gov.gu/index.html* (accessed April 8, 2006).

Hoffman, Carl W., Major, USMC. *Saipan: The Beginning of the End.* USMC Historical Monograph. Washington, D.C.: Historical Branch, G-3 Division, Headquarters, U.S. Marine Corps, 1950. *http://www.ibiblio.org/hyperwar/USMC/USMC-M-Saipan/USMC-M-Saipan-7.html*

Hoffman, Jon T., Major, USMCR. *From Makin to Bougainville: Marine Raiders in the Pacific War.* Marines in World War II Commemorative Series. Washington, D.C.: Marine Corps Historical Center, Building 58, Washington Navy Yard, 1995. *http://www.nps.gov/wapa/indepth/extContent/usmc/pcn-190–003130–00/index.htm* (accessed March 7, 2006).

Jones, James L., General, USMC, Commandant of the Marine Corps. Testimony, House Armed Services Committee, Washington, D.C., July 12, 2001. *http://www.house.gov/hasc/openingstatementsandpressreleases/107thcongress/01–07–12jones.html* (accessed May 18, 2006).

Kipling, Rudyard. "The White Man's Burden." The Internet Modern History Sourcebook. http://www.fordham.edu/halsall/mod/Kipling.html (accessed January 28, 2006).

"Marines Announce Plans For Recruiting Negroes in USMC." News release dated May 20, 1942. Washington, D.C.: Historical Division, Headquarters, U.S. Marine Corps. *http://hqinet001.hqmc.usmc.mil/HD/Historical/Docs_Speeches/Plansrecruitingblacks.htm* (accessed April 19, 2004).

Miller, John, Jr. *Guadalcanal: The First Offensive. U.S. Army in World War II. The War in the Pacific.* Washington, D.C.: U.S. Government Printing Office, Center of Military History, U.S. Army, 1995. *http://www.ibiblio.org/hyperwar/USA/USA-P-Guadalcanal/index.html* (accessed March 11, 2006).

Palmer, Michael A. "The Navy: The Continental Period, 1775–1890." A History of the U.S. Navy. Washington, D.C.: Navy Historical Center, Washington Navy Yard. *http://www.history.navy.mil/history/history2.htm* (accessed January 26, 2006).

Patton, Vince, MCPOCG. *Old Military Pay Tables. http://www.uscg.mil/hq/mcpocg/1pay/ompt.html* (accessed March 6, 2006).

Phillips, Earl H., Colonel, USMC. Obituary. Arlington National Cemetery Web site. *http://www.arlingtoncemetery.net/ehphillips.htm* (accessed April 1, 2006).

Schudel, Matt. Obituary. "Frederick C. Branch; Was 1st Black Officer in U.S. Marine Corps." *Washington Post,* April 13, 2005, B06. *http://www.washingtonpost.com/wp-dyn/articles/A48243–2005Apr12.html* (accessed March 22, 2006).

Selected World War II Marine Corps Chronology 1941–1946, Campaign Chronologies of the United States Marine Corps. Washington DC: United States Marine Corps History Division, Headquarters Marine Corps. *http://hqinet001.hqmc.usmc.mil/hd/Historical/Chronologies/Campaign/WWII_1941–1946.htm* (accessed February 13, 2006).

Semmons, Paul E., Col., USA. *The Hammer of Hell: The Coming of Age of Antiaircraft Artillery in WW II. http://airdefense.bliss.army.mil/adamag/Hammer/Chapter1.htm* (accessed February 27, 2006).

Shaw, Henry I., Jr. *Opening Moves: Marines Gear Up for War.* Washington, D.C.: Marine Corps Historical Center, 1991. *http://www.ibiblio.org/hyperwar/USMC/USMC-C-Opening.html* (accessed April 17, 2004).

"Ships of the U.S. Navy, 1940 1945, DD–Destroyers." *http://www.ibiblio.org/hyperwar/USN/ships-/ships-dd.html#dd674* (accessed March 2, 2006).

"Ships of the U.S. Navy, 1940–1945: Transports." http://www.ibiblio.org/hyperwar/USN/USN-ships.html#ap (accessed February 27, 2006).

"Staff Officers' Field Manual for Amphibious Operations, Organization, Technical and Logistical Data" (SECRET). Fleet Marine Force, Pacific, September 10, 1944. Declassified August 10, 1969. *http://www.ibiblio.org/hyperwar/USMC/* (accessed March 16, 2006).

Tuvalu (Ellice Islands). *http://www.pacificwrecks.com/provinces/tuvalu.html* (accessed March 20, 2006).

U.S. Army Corps of Engineers. "Historical Chronology of Atlantic Coastal Waterways." *www.usace.army.mil/inet/usace-docs/misc/nws83–10/chron.pdf* (accessed April 27, 2006).

USS *Slater,* Weapons Systems, 20mm Oerlikon gun. *http://www.ussslater.org/weapons/20mm.html* (accessed February 27, 2006).

War in the Pacific, Cultural Resources Inventory. National Park Service. Part 2a. History. First American Period 189801941. *http://www.cr.nps.gov/history/online_books/wapa/cli/part2a.htm* (accessed January 31, 2006).

"Who's Who in Marine Corps History." United States Marine Corps History Division. *http://hqinet001.hqmc.usmc.mil/HD/Historical/Whos_Who/Holcomb_T.htm* (accessed March 7, 2006).

Interviews

Adams, J.S., Col., USMC. Personal interview. August 15, 2006.

Batts, Adner, Jr. Personal interview. October 3, 2005.

Blount, Turner G. Personal interview. October 3, 2005.

Borden, Melvin. Personal interview. October 3, 2005.

Brewer, Herbert L., Col., USMCR. Interview dated November 12, 2002. Quantico, VA: Oral History Collection, Marine Corps History Division, USMC.

Cottman, Orvia O. Personal interview. October 4, 2005.

Hagan, Paul. Personal interview. October 4, 2005.

Smith, Eugene. Personal interview. January–July, 2006.

White, Glenn J. Personal interview. October 4, 2005.

Index